Deploying Voice over Wireless LANs

Jim Geier

Cisco Press

Cisco Press
800 East 96th Street
Indianapolis, Indiana 46240 USA

Deploying Voice over Wireless LANs

Jim Geier

Copyright © 2007 Cisco Systems, Inc.

Published by:
Cisco Press
800 East 96th Street
Indianapolis, IN 46240 USA

Printed in the United States of America 1 2 3 4 5 6 7 8 9 0

First Printing March 2007

Library of Congress Cataloging-in-Publication Number: 2004117087

ISBN-10: 1-58705-231-8

ISBN-13: 978-1-58705-231-6

Trademark Acknowledgments

All terms mentioned in this book that are known to be trademarks or service marks have been appropriately capitalized. Cisco Press or Cisco Systems, Inc. cannot attest to the accuracy of this information. Use of a term in this book should not be regarded as affecting the validity of any trademark or service mark.

Warning and Disclaimer

This book is designed to provide information about the technologies and implementation strategies for deploying voice over wireless LANs. Every effort has been made to make this book as complete and as accurate as possible, but no warranty or fitness is implied.

The information is provided on an "as is" basis. The author, Cisco Press, and Cisco Systems, Inc. shall have neither liability nor responsibility to any person or entity with respect to any loss or damages arising from the information contained in this book or from the use of the discs or programs that may accompany it.

The opinions expressed in this book belong to the author and are not necessarily those of Cisco Systems, Inc.

Corporate and Government Sales

Cisco Press offers excellent discounts on this book when ordered in quantity for bulk purchases or special sales.

For more information please contact: **U.S. Corporate and Government Sales**   1-800-382-3419
corpsales@pearsontechgroup.com

For sales outside the U.S. please contact: **International Sales**   international@pearsoned.com

Feedback Information

At Cisco Press, our goal is to create in-depth technical books of the highest quality and value. Each book is crafted with care and precision, undergoing rigorous development that involves the unique expertise of members from the professional technical community.

Readers' feedback is a natural continuation of this process. If you have any comments regarding how we could improve the quality of this book, or otherwise alter it to better suit your needs, you can contact us through e-mail at feedback@ciscopress.com. Please make sure to include the book title and ISBN in your message.

We greatly appreciate your assistance.

Publisher	Paul Boger
Cisco Representative	Anthony Wolfenden
Cisco Press Program Manager	Jeff Brady
Executive Editor	Karen Gettman
Acquisitions Editor	Elizabeth Peterson
Managing Editor	Patrick Kanouse
Development Editor	Dan Young
Project Editor	Tonya Simpson
Copy Editor	Paula Lowell
Technical Editors	Shawn Merdinger
	Joseph Roth
Team Coordinator	Vanessa Evans
Book and Cover Designer	Louisa Adair
Composition	Trina Wurst
Indexer	WordWise Publishing
Proofreader	Gayle Johnson

Americas Headquarters	Asia Pacific Headquarters	Europe Headquarters
Cisco Systems, Inc.	Cisco Systems, Inc.	Cisco Systems International BV
170 West Tasman Drive	168 Robinson Road	Haarlerbergpark
San Jose, CA 95134-1706	#28-01 Capital Tower	Haarlerbergweg 13-19
USA	Singapore 068912	1101 CH Amsterdam
www.cisco.com	www.cisco.com	The Netherlands
Tel: 408 526-4000	Tel: +65 6317 7777	www-europe.cisco.com
800 553-NETS (6387)	Fax: +65 6317 7799	Tel: +31 0 800 020 0791
Fax: 408 527-0883		Fax: +31 0 20 357 1100

Cisco has more than 200 offices worldwide. Addresses, phone numbers, and fax numbers are listed on the Cisco Website at **www.cisco.com/go/offices.**

About the Author

Jim Geier is the founder of Wireless-Nets, Ltd., and the company's principal consultant. His 25 years of experience includes the analysis, design, software development, installation, and support of numerous wireless network-based systems for enterprises, airports, homes, retail stores, manufacturing facilities, warehouses, hospitals, and cities worldwide.

Jim has been active within the Wi-Fi Alliance, responsible for certifying interoperability of 802.11 (Wi-Fi) wireless LANs. He has also been active with the IEEE 802.11 Working Group, responsible for developing international standards for wireless LANs. He served as Chairman of the IEEE Computer Society, Dayton Section, and Chairman of the IEEE International Conference on Wireless LAN Implementation. Jim is an advisory board member of several leading wireless LAN companies.

Jim is the author of several books, including *Wireless Networks First Step* (Cisco Press), *Wireless LANs* (Sams), *Wireless Networking Handbook* (MTP), and *Network Reengineering* (McGraw-Hill), as well as numerous articles.

Jim's education includes a bachelor's and master's degree in electrical engineering and a master's degree in business administration.

Contact Jim Geier at jimgeier@wireless-nets.com.

About the Technical Reviewers

Shawn Merdinger is an independent security researcher and consultant based in Austin, Texas. He was previously a Research Engineer with the Cisco Security Technologies Assessment Team (STAT) and TippingPoint, a division of 3Com, where he performed vulnerability assessments on a variety of devices, technologies, and implementations.

Mr. Merdinger holds a master's degree from the University of Texas at Austin, where his studies focused on computer and network security. He is currently researching VoIP and is developing tools and assessment methodologies to address VoIP security issues.

Joseph Roth is a lieutenant commander in the United States Navy. He currently is serving as the communications officer for the Nimitz Strike Group, which recently completed a six-month deployment to the 5th Fleet (Middle East) and 7th Fleet (Asia) area of operations. His previous tour was as a military professor and Network Security Group Department Head at the Naval Postgraduate School (NPS). He is currently a Ph.D. candidate in Information Systems at Nova Southeastern University. He holds four master's degrees: computer science (NPS), information system technology (NPS), public administration (University of Maryland), and national security and strategic studies (Naval War College). Joseph also holds a bachelor's degree in computer engineering from George Washington University and two certificates of higher education from the University of Cambridge. He has obtained numerous industry certifications, including CCNA, CWNA, Security +, Network +, and MCP. His articles have been published in *InfoWorld* and *Federal Computer Week*. Joseph served in Europe for five years and has been deployed to the Balkans and Bahrain.

Dedication

This book is dedicated to Madison and Kimberlyn.

Acknowledgments

I would like to give special thanks to Shawn Merdinger and Joseph Roth for offering their technical wisdom during the editing process. Their feedback was extremely useful and enabled the creation of a great book.

Also, I would like to thank the entire production team for their time and effort with this book. I had most contact with Christopher Cleveland and Dan Young; these guys are incredibly professional and fantastic editors. As with other books that I have written for Cisco Press, the production team never ceases to amaze me. Thanks for a job well done!

This Book Is Safari Enabled

The Safari® Enabled icon on the cover of your favorite technology book means the book is available through Safari Bookshelf. When you buy this book, you get free access to the online edition for 45 days.

Safari Bookshelf is an electronic reference library that lets you easily search thousands of technical books, find code samples, download chapters, and access technical information whenever and wherever you need it.

To gain 45-day Safari Enabled access to this book:

- Go to http://www.ciscopress.com/safarienabled
- Complete the brief registration form
- Enter the coupon code V5G7-IDEI-NBWF-35IT-EZJL

If you have difficulty registering on Safari Bookshelf or accessing the online edition, please e-mail customer-service@safaribooksonline.com.

Contents at a Glance

Table of Contents

Icons Used in This Book

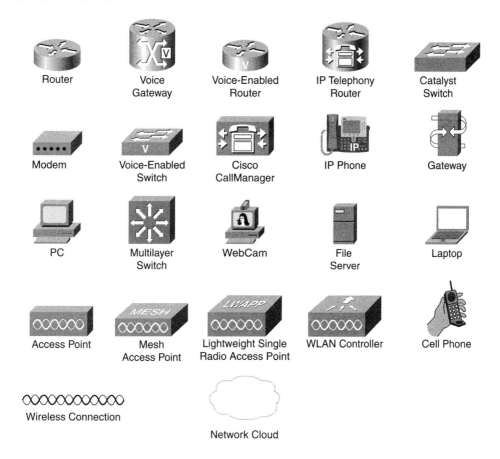

Command Syntax Conventions

The conventions used to present command syntax in this book are the same conventions used in the IOS Command Reference. The Command Reference describes these conventions as follows:

- **Boldface** indicates commands and keywords that are entered literally as shown. In actual configuration examples and output (not general command syntax), boldface indicates commands that are manually input by the user (such as a **show** command).
- *Italic* indicates arguments for which you supply actual values.
- Vertical bars (|) separate alternative, mutually exclusive elements.
- Square brackets [ ] indicate an optional element.
- Braces { } indicate a required choice.
- Braces within brackets [{ }] indicate a required choice within an optional element.

Introduction

This book focuses on technologies and implementation strategies for deploying voice over wireless LANs. Companies have been deploying wireless LANs for more than a decade, but recent advancements in data rates and quality of service mechanisms are enabling companies to effectively make integrated voice and video communications (along with common data applications) over wireless LANs a replacement for traditional, relatively costly wired telephone and video surveillance systems. The significantly lower support costs, combined with mobility, make voice and video killer applications. The deployment of a wireless voice and video system is much different from traditional wired and wireless networks. As a result, this book is necessary to educate readers on how to deploy voice and video systems. This book is based on practical experience that the author has gained through related real-world projects.

Who Should Read This Book?

This book is intended for readers having moderate knowledge of networking concepts and protocols. For example, the reader should be familiar with communications protocols, handshaking processes, and Ethernet network infrastructures. Readers should also be conversant with computer terminology, such as local-area network, client/server, and application software.

The following constitutes the book's intended audience:

- Information technology (IT) staff and system integrators involved with analyzing, designing, installing, and supporting wireless voice and video systems.

- Engineers developing voice and video products and solutions.

- Technical project managers planning and executing projects that develop or install wireless voice and video products or systems.

- University professors and students learning details of wireless voice and video systems in undergraduate or graduate-level courses.

How This Book Is Organized

Although this book could be read cover to cover, it is designed to be flexible to allow you to easily move between chapters and sections of chapters to cover just the material that you need more work with or more information on. The chapters cover the following topics:

- **Part I—Fundamental Elements**
  - **Chapter 1, "VoWLAN Applications and Benefits"**—This chapter defines all components that are part of a wireless voice and video system, such as phones, client software, and voice encoders/decoders. Examples of actual components are given, with emphasis on Cisco products. Descriptions of how multimedia integrates with existing systems found in enterprise settings are also given.

— **Chapter 2, "VoWLAN System Components"**—This chapter defines all components that are part of a wireless voice system, such as phones, client software, and voice encoders/decoders. Examples of actual components are given, with emphasis on Cisco products. Descriptions of how multimedia integrates with existing systems found in enterprise settings are also given.

— **Chapter 3, "VoWLAN Signaling Fundamentals"**—This chapter provides an overview of the primary elements of voice communications, such as voice signal characteristics, analog-to-digital conversion, compression techniques, and so on.

• **Part II—Critical Technologies**

— **Chapter 4, "Wireless LAN Technologies"**—To effectively design a wireless LAN that supports voice applications, it is important that readers fully understand the 802.11 standard. This chapter describes standard elements, such as MAC layer frames and physical layer options, and how these elements impact multimedia operation. Special attention is given to options that govern the behavior of a multimedia system.

— **Chapter 5, "VoWLAN Security Solutions"**—Wireless voice systems have unique security implications that solution providers must realize and offer applicable countermeasures. This chapter explains security issues related to voice systems and describes effective methods to provide security that meets relevant requirements.

• **Part III—Implementation Steps**

— **Chapter 6, "Analyzing VoWLAN Requirements"**—Before designing a wireless LAN that supports voice applications, you must fully understand requirements, such as number of users, existing data traffic, roaming needs, security needs, and anything else that will provide a basis for the design. A designer uses these requirements when deciding which technologies to use and how to configure the network. This chapter describes each type of requirement that needs definition to implement a quality multimedia system. The chapter offers plenty of real-world examples and methods for determining requirements.

— **Chapter 7, "Designing a VoWLAN Solution"**—This chapter discusses the technical elements that need consideration when designing a wireless LAN for voice applications. This includes determination of technology, mechanisms for providing required capacity, optimum 802.11 configuration settings, roaming, and integration with cellular systems. The chapter provides examples of which technical elements to consider, with specific requirements in mind.

— **Chapter 8, "Installing, Configuring, and Testing a VoWLAN System"**—This chapter defines all necessary installation steps and provides real-world tips that minimize risks when installing the system. The chapter describes details on the various types of tests that should be run to verify and validate that the system is meeting requirements and needs of the users.

— **Chapter 9, "Supporting a VoWLAN System"**—Wireless voice systems require unique support practices and tools. This chapter discusses these elements and provides examples of tools and methods that are effective at supporting the system.

Fundamental Elements

Objectives

Upon completing this chapter, you will be able to

- Understand the role of Voice over Wireless LANs (VoWLAN).
- Define VoWLAN applications.
- Determine ROI of a VoWLAN solution.

CHAPTER 1

VoWLAN Applications and Benefits

This chapter describes various applications of Voice over Wireless LAN (VoWLAN) systems. Real-world examples and case studies provide you with a solid understanding of how VoWLAN can benefit a company. Details are also given about tangible benefits and expected return on investment (ROI).

The Role of VoWLAN Solutions

VoWLAN systems are an extension to wired Voice over Internet Protocol systems and an alternative to traditional analog and digital voice communications. VoWLANs offer significant benefits of providing mobility and wirelessly converging voice with data applications. With VoWLANs, hospitals, enterprises, retail stores, warehouses, and home owners can reduce telephony costs and enable mobile applications.

Examples of the systems that VoWLANs can replace include the following:

- Wired telephones
- Cellular telephones
- Two-way radios

With VoWLANs, people can use VoWLAN phones to communicate by voice wirelessly with others inside and outside a facility. The experience is very similar to using a traditional wired telephone, except the user is free to move about the building. Furthermore, a VoWLAN phone can operate from many of the growing Wi-Fi hotspots, enabling a person to make use of the same mobile phone while within or away from the office or home. Some cellular phones incorporate VoWLAN capability, which enables users to make calls over traditional cellular networks when no wireless local-area network (wireless LAN) is available.

Figure 1-1 shows the basic usage models of a VoWLAN system. The optimum approach depends on user requirements and existing telephone hardware.

The local-only configuration (part A of Figure 1-1), which is similar to two-way radios, consists of a wireless LAN that merely enables a user to talk to other users directly connected to the network. This supports a mix of wireless and wired VoIP telephones. For example, a clerk looking for a part in a warehouse may use a VoWLAN handset to communicate with a manager sitting at a desk and using a wired VoIP phone.

Figure 1-1   *VoWLAN Usage Models: (A) Local Only, (B) Telephone via Internet, and (C) Telephone via PSTN*

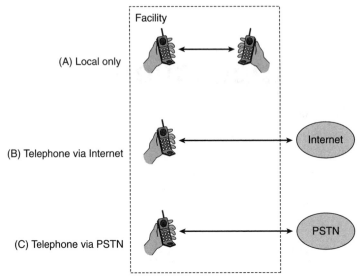

More advanced VoWLAN systems (Parts B and C of Figure 1-1), however, allow users to place actual telephone calls from their VoWLAN handsets. The telephone traffic can travel over the Internet or the Public Switched Telephone Network (PSTN). With these two models, the use of the system is virtually the same as a traditional telephone. For example, a sales agent in her home office in Ohio may dial a phone number on her VoWLAN phone to call a customer in California.

The primary benefit of VoWLAN solutions is cost savings. For instance, according to recent studies, federal, state, and local agencies could achieve savings of $4.5 billion annually by making telephone calls over the Internet. In addition, VoWLAN systems are easier to deploy and allow flexible communications. VoWLAN plays a critical role in realizing these savings by mobilizing the workforce.

History of VoWLANs

The two primary technologies of VoWLANs are wireless LANs and VoIP. Both have been evolving over the past decade and are now stable enough to support wireless voice communications.

VoIP

The earliest indication of VoIP systems was in the mid-1990s, when Vocaltec, Inc. released Internet Phone Software. This software ran on PCs and translated voice signals into digital packets that could be sent over the Internet. Both the sending and receiving callers must use the same software. Sound quality was not as good as traditional telephones, but long distance calls could be made for free.

Throughout the late 1990s, entrepreneurs began establishing gateways and switches to allow people to make free phone calls over the Internet using standard telephones. The users had to utilize a PC to set up the call, but then they were free to talk from standard wired telephones connected to a PC. With these systems, the VoIP market began evolving. Many companies, including Cisco, began selling VoIP equipment about the year 2000 to enterprises to converge voice and data and provide mobility.

Wireless LANs

In the early 1990s, the first wireless LAN products, NCR WaveLAN and Motorola Altair, appeared on the market. At this time, there were no applicable standards and prices were relatively high, at around $1,500 per wireless adapter. As a result, only companies having applications with significant benefits from wireless connectivity, such as inventory management and price marking, could afford to deploy wireless LAN solutions.

Figure 1-2 summarizes the evolution of the 802.11 standard. In 1997, the Institute of Electrical and Electronics Engineers (IEEE) ratified the first version of the 802.11 wireless LAN standard. 802.11 at this point provided up to 1Mbps and 2Mbps data rate operation in the 2.4GHz frequency band using direct sequence and frequency hopping, which are both spread spectrum technologies. The capacity of these first 802.11 solutions was not good enough to effectively support voice applications.

Figure 1-2   *Evolution of the 802.11 Standard*

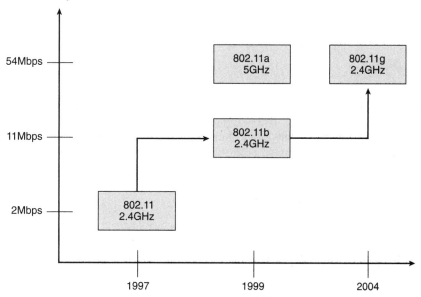

To enhance the performance of wireless LANs, the IEEE ratified the 802.11a and 802.11b standards in 1999. 802.11a provides up to 54Mbps data rates in the 5GHz band using orthogonal frequency division multiplexing (OFDM). 802.11b extends the maximum data rates of the initial 2.4GHz direct sequence 802.11 standard to 11Mbps. Later, in 2004, IEEE released 802.11g, which further extends data rates in the 2.4GHz band to 54Mbps using OFDM. The higher data rate 802.11 standards, 802.11a, 802.11b, and 802.11g, offer adequate capacity for supporting VoWLAN applications. 802.11a, however, provides the highest capacity, mainly because the Radio Frequency (RF) channels in the 5GHz band do not overlap with each other as they do in the 2.4GHz band. 802.11n, which will offer 100Mbp or more performance, is nearing ratification.

Other recent improvements to the 802.11 standard include security (802.11i), which includes much stronger encryption and authentication mechanisms than the initial standard. The use of Temporal Key Internet Protocol (TKIP) and Advanced Encryption Standard (AES), along with 802.1i protocols, makes wireless LANs very secure. Also, the ratification of the 802.11e standard in 2006 offers quality of service important for VoWLAN applications.

Within the past couple of years, the prices for wireless LAN adapters have decreased to well under $100 each. This dramatic drop in prices has fueled the proliferation of wireless LANs for a variety of applications in all markets. The Wi-Fi Alliance has also been actively promoting wireless LANs through the Wi-Fi brand and mandating interoperability testing.

Because of the proliferation of wireless LANs, VoWLAN solutions are also proliferating. Companies offering VoIP equipment, such as Cisco, have been marketing VoWLAN phones that interface with their digital telephony systems. Even service providers, such as Vonage, now offer Wi-Fi phones that interface with their Internet Protocol (IP) telephony service.

Healthcare

Hospitals were one of the first users of VoWLAN solutions, such as Vocera, mainly because of the significant need for effective communication among high-valued medical staff. The ability for doctors and nurses to respond quickly with verbal instructions is crucial for saving the lives of patients. For example, Children's Hospital in Madera, California, uses a VoWLAN system to support push-to-talk features on its VoWLAN phones to broadcast Code Blue alerts that summon emergency teams. Patients receive a higher level of care, which leads to faster recovery. VoWLAN systems allow hospital staff to not waste time looking for a phone to use.

An issue with deploying VoWLANs in hospitals, though, is the difficulty in providing adequate wireless LAN coverage. Hospitals include x-ray rooms surrounded by lead, irregular metal objects, and unpredictable traffic flows of people. These factors lead to significant signal impairments. In addition, RF interference from other wireless systems operating in the 2.4GHz band, such as frequency-hopping spread spectrum devices, can cause degradation in performance. As a result, installers must conduct thorough RF site surveys when identifying optimum placement of wireless access points.

Hospital in Northeast U.S. Benefits from VoWLAN Solution

Doctors and nurses at this hospital, as in others, are always on the move, taking care of patients. To do this effectively, the doctors and nurses must be capable of contacting each other immediately as emergencies arise, which is fairly often. For example, a nurse may find that a particular patient develops complications a few hours after surgery and needs immediate attention from a doctor. Before VoWLAN systems, the nurse would try calling the doctor on a cell phone. Cell coverage in the hospital was not very good, and the call would go immediately to the physician's voice mail. If the nurse could not make immediate contact with the doctor over the cell phone, which was about 75 percent of the time, the nurse would then call the doctor's pager. Pager coverage was very good throughout the hospital. The physician would receive the page and then find a wired phone to call the nurse. This task added significant delays because a phone could not always be found quickly, and the nurse would have to wait around a phone for the doctor to call (taking the nurse away from the patients needing assistance).

The hospital deployed a wireless LAN that supports the use of VoWLAN phones, enabling doctors and nurses to stay in immediate contact with each other. Now when a nurse needs a doctor's attention to help an ailing patient, the nurse can simply call the doctor directly using the VoWLAN phone. All calls go through because the wireless LAN was installed in a manner that provides signal coverage in all parts of the hospital. This solution significantly reduces communications delays, and patients receive immediate attention and care.

The hospital installed 120 wireless LAN access points to provide signal coverage for the VoWLAN phones. To determine optimum access point installation locations, the hospital conducted an RF site survey. Ensuring high enough signal strength and cell overlap throughout the hospital is very important to maintain effective operation of the phones and roaming.

Enterprises

Enterprises are taking advantage of VoWLAN applications to provide mobility to workers and reduce costs through a common network infrastructure for voice and data. In many cases, enterprises implementing VoWLAN are doing so as an extension to wired VoIP systems. A company, for example, can equip the majority of the employees with a wired VoIP desk phone, and VoWLAN handsets are given to the employees needing mobility. Certainly the benefit of going wireless is that users can carry their phone with them throughout the facility, which enables them to respond faster to customer needs and functions within the company. The use of VoWLAN phones also eliminates the costs associated with rewiring telephone lines when employees change offices.

Enterprise executives making the decision to spend money on the necessary hardware and services need solid numbers before committing funds. An issue with deploying VoIP, and especially VoWLAN, in enterprises, however, is accurately predicting ROI. Assessing the returns a company will achieve by enabling faster response to customer needs, for example, is difficult. A company must be capable of achieving significant productivity benefits before moving forward with a VoWLAN deployment.

Executive Management Team at Corporate Headquarters Benefits from VoWLAN Solution

A particular enterprise, as with most other companies, has an executive management team located in a centralized location of the company's headquarters facility. All of these executives are infrequently in their offices—they manage by walking around and keeping tabs on their various departments. For example, the IT manager is generally visiting with technicians distributed in various parts of the facility, making sure that projects, such as PC hardware upgrades, are going smoothly. The problem is that when issues arise, the technicians have no way of contacting the IT manager immediately. The technicians use a phone in the office where they are working to call the manager's office, and 90 percent of the time must leave a voice message. In most cases, hours would pass before the manager would receive the message.

The solution to this problem was for this company to make use of an existing wireless LAN and deploy VoWLAN phones to the managers. This solution enables just about anyone to reach an appropriate manager within seconds, without experiencing the delays of voice mail.

Universities

A university environment is highly mobile, with teaching staff and students moving among different classrooms, libraries, and offices. The use of VoWLANs at a university offers tremendous benefits by enabling university staff to stay in touch from anywhere on campus. This capability makes teachers more accessible to students, and the learning environment is much safer. A teacher, for example, can report safety issues as they occur, rather than having to wait until a class ends.

A challenge of deploying a VoWLAN system at a university is that coverage must include a wide variety of buildings and outdoor areas. An extensive RF site survey is very important to take into account the varying facility construction and obstacles blocking radio waves. Even after installing the system, reevaluating coverage from time to time is generally necessary to determine whether student traffic and campus functions offer major signal attenuation.

Retail

To satisfy the needs of customers and staff, retail store managers must be accessible from anywhere within the store. Voice communications with these managers is crucial in providing customer satisfaction. For example, a customer may need to replace a part found broken when putting together a newly purchased bicycle, or someone may need to know the status of a shipment of a particular brand of dog food. Whenever the need arises, immediate communication with the store manager is necessary, and customers cannot be kept waiting, or they will shop somewhere else. In this type of environment, VoWLAN really shines. In many cases, the retail store already has an existing wireless LAN, and the store managers and staff can benefit from low-cost telephony.

Retail stores use existing wireless LANs to support bar code applications, such as price marking and inventory management. These applications make the deployment of VoWLAN systems in retail stores more of a plug-and-play situation. The existing wireless applications, however, generally have very low capacity requirements, and the access points already in place may not be capable of supporting the much higher bandwidth demands of voice communications. For example, a store may only have a wireless LAN based on the initial 802.11 standard, such as direct sequence spread spectrum supporting up to 2Mbps data rates. This particular store would need to upgrade its access point hardware to at least 802.11b, which introduces costs for hardware and services in addition to purchasing the wireless handsets.

Retail Chain Goes with VoWLAN Solution

An electronics retailer with 230 stores throughout the United States sells PCs, software, and games. This company makes lots of calls between stores. A customer may want an item, for example, that a particular store does not have in stock. The store clerk would then begin calling other stores to check on the item's availability. This situation happens a lot throughout the day and results in extremely high telephone bills. Another issue is that the store clerk generally learns that the item is not in stock when he or she is with the customer where the item is supposed to be within the store. The time needed to walk back to the register area or office to place the calls to other stores adds enough delay that some customers decide to forego checking on the item at other stores. This delay results in losing potential sales.

To resolve these problems, the retail company decided to make use of the wireless LANs already existing in the stores and supporting bar code applications to support the VoWLAN phones. Now the store clerk can place calls immediately to other stores when performing inventory checks. This solution keeps the customer's attention and results in greater sales. The telephone bills are also much less due to being able to route the phone calls over the company's WAN infrastructure, which interconnects all the stores.

Warehouses

Warehouses involve a host of functions where VoWLAN systems can provide significant benefits. Clerks end up being scattered throughout the warehouse facility, which can be quite expansive, and communication with other clerks and managers is essential to perform various functions. In most cases, having the clerks and managers meet face-to-face to communicate is not practical. In fact, being able to even find each other is often not possible, due to the numerous rows of bins and products. For example, an order may come in for the shipment of a particular item to a customer. Rather than waiting for a clerk to return to the main office, having the shipping department call a clerk directly and have him pick the item is much faster and more productive.

As with retail environments, many warehouses already have existing wireless LANs. However, because these wireless networks primarily support relatively low-performance bar code solutions for implementing inventory management functions, the wireless LAN may not have enough capacity to support a large number of VoWLAN phones. A company must analyze the wireless LAN and ensure that adequate data rates, signal strength, and roaming exist to support wireless voice applications.

Warehouse Deploys VoWLAN Phones to Speed Up Operations

A relatively large warehouse was experiencing delays when processing orders. For example, when assembling an order for shipping, warehouse clerks would pick items from shelves based on lists prepared earlier in the day. Orders would often change, though, which would require the clerks to not pick certain items or pick others that were not on the list. To communicate this information, the warehouse manager would page the applicable clerk through an overhead loudspeaker system. The clerk would then walk all the way back to the manager's office to learn of the changes to a particular order. This process would incorporate delays, which significantly decreased the warehouse's productivity and order placement time.

The solution was to install a wireless LAN for supporting VoWLAN phones. As changes to orders take place now, the warehouse manager can call the clerk directly on the VoWLAN phone and explain the change to the order. This call avoids the need for the clerk to walk back to the manager's office, which speeds up the picking operation. In addition, the installation of the wireless LAN also makes setting up a wireless bar code system for performing inventory management functions possible. This solution will also save the company a tremendous amount of time and money when performing inventories.

Manufacturing

In manufacturing facilities, line supervisors monitor production lines, and managers must be able to contact each other and other employees immediately to check the status of various operations and solve problems that regularly arise. A division manager in charge of a particular business unit, for example, is certainly anxious to ensure that the plant is getting products ready to ship in time to make revenue numbers. If a part of the orders for that period is at risk of not being completed in time, fixes can be considered and put in place to keep manufacturing on schedule.

A VoWLAN system makes communications in manufacturing extremely beneficial because managers are constantly on the move. In many cases, a manufacturing plant will have an existing wireless LAN in place, making the deployment of a VoWLAN extremely feasible. Even if the installation of wireless access points is necessary, the VoWLAN solution is still worthwhile because of the monetary benefits associated with immediate communications. In this situation, the value of the company to shareholders depends on effective communication among stakeholders in the manufacturing process. A VoWLAN solution allows managers to communicate immediately and solve problems to keep production in line with sales.

Toy Manufacturer Benefits from a VoWLAN System

The managers at a toy manufacturer were having trouble communicating with each other. For example, the manufacturing line for a particular toy would begin having mechanical troubles, which would require the manufacturing line supervisor to shut down production until someone could perform necessary repairs. This plant is large, and a single centralized maintenance group takes care of many production lines. The line supervisor would use his office phone to call the maintenance chief, who would then need to track down the right mechanic to fix the problem. The issue was that "phone tag" would result, causing significant delays. Often an hour or more would elapse before this coordination would be done and a mechanic would be notified that he needed to work on the problem. Meanwhile, the company would be losing $500,000 each hour the production line was shut down. Something had to be done to speed up communications needed to coordinate maintenance when problems arise on one of the production lines.

To solve the problem, this company installed a wireless LAN throughout the manufacturing plant to support the use of VoWLAN phones. All managers, supervisors, and maintenance staff were equipped with VoWLAN phones. A production line supervisor can now call the maintenance chief directly via VoWLAN phones. The maintenance chief may be out of his office assisting one of the mechanics and still be able to receive the call immediately. The maintenance chief can use the VoWLAN phone to coordinate the right mechanic to fix the problem. Because everyone carries the VoWLAN phone with them at all times, telephone tag is no longer an issue, and communication is immediate. This time savings significantly reduces downtime of the production lines, which in turn improves the company's profits.

Small Offices and Homes

Many small offices and homes are installing wireless LANs to support mobile access to common Internet applications. Service providers, such as Vonage, are strongly advertising the capability of using the Internet for making phone calls to augment or replace standard

PSTN telephones. Home and small-office owners are taking advantage of Internet telephony to save money on long-distance phone calls.

The use of VoWLAN is further extending the benefits of VoIP by providing mobility and even replacing the need for a cellular phone. A consumer is likely to select a VoWLAN solution as compared to wired VoIP service to enable mobility similar to what cordless phones offer. Someone can take the phone around the house and talk while doing house chores.

A single access point can easily support most home and small-office voice applications. Range is sufficient for the entire home, and a single 802.11b or 802.11g access point can support the limited number of phones (generally only one) that will be in use simultaneously. RF interference from microwave ovens and neighboring wireless LANs set to the same channel can cause significant impacts on performance, however. Consumers may have to reconfigure the RF channel of their access point to have effective wireless voice service.

Unfamiliarity with wireless technologies may preclude some consumers from purchasing VoWLAN equipment. In addition, the inability of Internet telephony to operate during power outages and limited operation of 911 services may keep some consumers from moving forward with a wired or wireless VoIP solution. Despite these issues, though, VoWLANs in homes and small offices is expected to proliferate over the next few years.

Home Owner Finds Value in Internet Telephony

Madison Leigh of Fairborn, Ohio, found that her monthly long-distance phone bill was running more than $100 per month because she was making regular phone calls to her father, living in a rest home in Chicago. Madison was paying only 10 cents per minute, but the phone calls were running into the hours, discussing issues that her father was having living in the rest home. Madison saw an advertisement on television for Vonage Internet-based calling, so she investigated the service and found that it would save her approximately $70 per month. After hearing about Wi-Fi, she found that she could have wireless voice over Internet connectivity, which she thought was a good idea because she could talk on the phone from anywhere in the house, similar to what her cordless phone had been providing.

Jack's Foreign Auto Parts and Repair

Jack's Foreign Auto Parts and Repair, based in the eastern United States, is a small business specializing in the repair of foreign automobiles and the sale of hard-to-find automobile parts to car enthusiasts worldwide. Jack employs eight mechanics and one administrative person, who takes care of invoicing and paying the bills. Jack supervises the mechanics and provides necessary guidance on the shop floor. He is on the phone most of the day, making international calls, trying to locate rare parts worldwide for fixing the cars. His phone bill had been running nearly $1,000 per month! When purchasing a new fax machine at a local office supply store, he saw a Wi-Fi phone and router advertising the ability to slash long-distance phone call costs, especially overseas. After thinking about it a bit and doing some research on the Internet, Jack purchased the solution and installed it at his company. He now pays roughly $50 per month in phone bills.

Security Systems

The ability for people to quickly report wrongdoings and suspicious activities is vitally important for providing security in all companies and organizations. A person equipped with a wireless phone, for example, can get critical information to the appropriate organization for it to respond to an emergency situation. For example, a security person in an airport can report the findings on an unattended piece of luggage, which would trigger a reaction from the airport security team. VoWLAN systems can certainly support these types of functions to bolster security through faster response to situations.

Companies can also deploy wireless security cameras that send video over wireless LANs. This approach is much more feasible than running wires to each camera. The ease of installation allows a greater number of cameras to be put in place, which increases the viewing of the different parts of a facility or campus.

A major issue with using wireless LANs for supporting wireless voice and video is that they are vulnerable to denial of service (DoS) attacks. A person wanting to disrupt the security system can block the flow of voice and video signals by jamming the network. For example, someone can transmit either an overriding RF signal or specialized protocols (such as multiple CTS frames having long NAV values) that block phones and cameras from accessing the network. Also, wireless video cameras are vulnerable to sniffing. For example, someone could passively monitor the video stream using a tool such as driftnet. Companies must consider these threats and plan accordingly.

Airport Improves Security with VoWLAN

Security personnel at a large airport in the southern United States continually walk throughout the airport looking for potential security issues and responding to passengers needing medical assistance. In the past, the security people would use two-way radios to communicate with a central security office, which would dispatch appropriate support staff in response to situations. The radios, however, were not reliable because of range issues. In some parts of the airport, the security agents would be too far away from the office to work effectively. In some cases, the range was so great that communications were not possible. In addition, the two-way radios were limiting, because only someone else having a two-way radio was able to communicate with the roving security personnel. Having someone use a phone to contact the mobile person was not possible.

Because of the need for improved security, the airport decided to take advantage of VoWLAN technology. A wireless LAN had to be put in place, but the airport had wanted to do so anyway to offer a public wireless LAN to passengers and other airport applications. It was much more cost-effective to build a common wireless LAN infrastructure for multiple applications. The public wireless LAN users could be kept separate from the airport applications, such as the VoWLAN solution for the security personnel, through the use of different VLANs.

Now, security personnel can immediately report incidents that need attention and receive a quicker response than before.

Metro Rail Monitor Tracks with VoWLAN

A city in the midwestern United States has a passenger rail system that moves people around various parts of the city. Before implementing a wireless, video-based monitoring system, the operator of the train had to keep an eye on track conditions and report findings to maintenance staff via an unreliable two-way radio, which often fell out of range from the maintenance office, or through a cell phone. Both ways, however, took a great deal of time. The operator was finding that performing other important tasks was difficult, such as driving the train and being alert to the safety of passengers.

The city equipped the train with Wi-Fi cameras on the front of each train and mounted access points periodically along the tracks. A maintenance person can now view the entire track as the train moves—saving the time of the operator and a maintenance person riding on the train. Problems with the track can now be found and repaired much faster, saving time of staff, and making the transport system safer for passengers.

Determining ROI

Before moving forward with the installation of a VoWLAN system, companies should complete an ROI study that provides the basis for decisions on funding. A worthy ROI must indicate enough benefits before a company will put forth the money to fund the hardware and services necessary to install and support the system. In most cases, a company desires to recoup money spent within one to three years. If the benefits are not well defined or they are not sufficient, deploying the system may not be worth the expense. Not only should the ROI study indicate a positive result, but it should also be clear enough to be understood by a wide variety of decision makers.

This section describes each of the steps necessary for the ROI study and illustrates the main points through a hypothetical case study, which highlights a fictitious company, Acme Furniture. This case study defines a project that a large manufacturing and retail company undertakes to realize the benefits of VoWLAN systems in corporate offices, manufacturing plants, distribution centers, and retail stores. The case study continues throughout the remaining chapters to demonstrate the process of defining requirements, designing the solution, installing and configuring the hardware, and performing operational support.

Initial Analysis

The first step of performing an ROI study is to do some initial analysis. At least enough details must be known to define benefits and determine the costs for necessary hardware, software, and services to install and support the system. In the initial stages of the project, especially during the ROI study phase, not all details may be known; however, the details will come into full view as the project progresses with funding.

The following are tasks that a company should complete as part of the initial planning phase:

- Identify significant communications delays. Spotting problems that the company is having before justifying a VoWLAN solution is very important. If people within a company have no need to communicate with anyone while away from their desks, probably no need exists for a VoWLAN system. They can just use the existing wired telephone system. People who are often mobile and need to communicate with other employees or people outside the facility, however, will likely benefit from a VoWLAN system. Analyze these types of situations, and look for delays that employees have when responding to important events. For example, a doctor requiring even five minutes to look for an available phone is likely taking too long to respond to a page for a patient needing prompt attention.

- Identify primary goals and expected benefits. As with any project, clearly spell out what you expect to gain by deploying a VoWLAN solution. State productivity enhancement goals, such as decreasing customer response time to one minute, and costs that a company would like to eliminate by replacing existing communications mechanisms and using a converged infrastructure for data and voice.

- Define preliminary application requirements. Determine just enough requirements to assess the existing network infrastructure and adequately determine costs of the solution. In the ROI study phase, at least identify who will benefit by having VoWLAN handsets and how many you will need. Also, predict the number and frequency of calls that each person will complete on a regular basis. This information helps when determining whether upgrades are necessary for the network to support the calls. Be certain to include present and future requirements.

- Assess existing networks. Determine whether the existing wired network infrastructure has the capacity to support predicted VoWLAN traffic. If not, factor in the upgrades as a cost for deploying the VoWLAN system. Certainly, the cost of the solution depends on the presence of an existing wireless LAN. When a wireless LAN is already in place, be sure to test its ability to support voice. More access points may be necessary to achieve the coverage that is necessary for voice traffic, which introduces costs.

- Consider changes that may take place in the future. To achieve expected ROI, the VoWLAN system must continue to operate and provide benefits for several years. Company moves, growth, and mergers may introduce costs (or benefits) when moving and expanding the system. If these types of changes are known, take them into account during the life of the system.

Case Study: Acme Furniture Gets Started with a VoWLAN Solution

Acme Furniture is a fictitious company that manufactures, distributes, and sells top-quality furniture to the home market within the continental United States. The company has 750 employees, with the corporate headquarters and a single manufacturing plant in Columbus, Ohio. The company also has 80 retail stores and 10 distribution centers located throughout the United States.

Acme Furniture has been growing significantly over the past couple years as the relatively large population of baby boomers has been upgrading their furniture after their children leave home. Bob, the company president, has been happy with the company financials, but he strongly feels that improving communications is necessary based on the increasing number of issues cropping up in the warehouse and retail stores.

Line supervisors in the factory have been complaining for months about the delays in getting status on special furniture orders. The corporate executives and construction teams often play telephone tag for a day or longer before getting in touch with each other. Also, retail store managers often need to contact distribution centers to check on whether they have particular furniture in stock, which results in delays and occasionally lost sales because the customer is not willing to wait. Bob felt that mobile phone technology might be a viable solution to these problems.

In addition, long-distance phone calls between the corporate offices, stores, and distribution centers amount to approximately $3,000 per month. Bob has been eyeing this number on the financial report for several years, wondering how he can eliminate or reduce it considerably. His IT manager, Debbie, felt that the deployment of a VoWLAN system could be a feasible way of achieving the reduction in long-distance charges.

With these issues in mind, Bob contracted a consultant, Eric, to help determine whether Acme Furniture should move forward with the deployment of a VoWLAN solution. Eric's job was to define initial requirements and determine costs and savings of the resulting VoWLAN system. This information would provide Bob with the basis to approve the project.

Eric documented the communications problems and long-distance telephone costs and then took a closer look at the situation. He found that the company can significantly decrease the communications delays to a few minutes instead of hours and nearly eliminate the costs for intercompany long-distance telephone calls. Eric recommended that Acme Furniture make use of VoWLAN technology to meet these goals.

Eric's recommendation was to initially equip the following employees with VoWLAN handsets:

- Five of the clerks in each distribution center
- The store manager in each store
- Ten line supervisors in the manufacturing plant
- Seven IT personnel
- Ten corporate office executives

The total count of VoWLAN handsets is 127. Acme furniture will grow its workforce by approximately 25 percent over the next few years, and the company will revisit the benefits of adding more wireless telephones after the first year.

The retail stores, manufacturing plant, and distribution centers already have wireless LANs in place. Radio frequency signal testing was done, and they have sufficient signal strength to support voice traffic. The corporate office, a two-story building with approximately 50,000 square feet, does not have any wireless connectivity.

Costs

As part of the ROI analysis, a company must define operational and capital costs. This analysis gives a full depiction of what the company will need to pay out to realize the system and resulting benefits.

Operational Costs

For operational costs, figure all services necessary to deploy and support the solution. The following defines each of the operational cost elements for deploying a VoWLAN system:

- **Planning**—Encompasses the definition of complete requirements that address security concerns, performance needs, and project planning.
- **Network assessment**—Includes surveying existing wireless LANs and determining the capacity of the local- and wide-area networks (WANs) for supporting voice traffic requirements.
- **Installation**—Includes setting up and configuring all components, such as VoWLAN handsets, voice gateways, software that interfaces with the existing PBX, and wireless LAN access points.

- **Testing**—Ensures that the installed system operates efficiently and meets all requirements.
- **Training**—Provides necessary skills to IT staff that will be supporting the system.
- **Operational support**—Needed on a recurring basis for IT personnel to add new users, troubleshoot problems, and respond to user problems.

Some companies will perform only the planning and operational support and outsource the other elements. As a result, the costs for these operational elements generally result from bids by prospective contractors.

Capital Costs

Capital costs include hardware and software that make the system work. The following identifies the capital cost elements for deploying a VoWLAN system:

- **VoWLAN handsets**—The wireless telephone hardware needed for each user.
- **Voice gateway**—The platform that manages wireless VoIP traffic and interfaces with an existing PBX.
- **Wireless access points**—The hardware that interfaces the VoWLAN handsets to the network.

In addition, upgrading the existing routers with applicable quality of service may be necessary.

Case Study: Acme Furniture Defines Costs for a VoWLAN Solution

With the initial analysis complete, Bob, the president of Acme Furniture, directs Eric, the hired consultant, to determine the approximate costs of deploying a VoWLAN solution. The deployment costs are one part of the financial analysis that Bob needs to make a decision. After determining costs, Eric will attempt to quantify the benefits. In Table 1-1, Eric identifies the operational costs for deploying a VoWLAN solution at Acme Furniture.

Table 1-1 *Operational Costs for a VoWLAN System at Acme Furniture*

Element	Cost
Planning	$25,000
Network assessment	$20,000
Installation	$50,000
Testing	$15,000
Training	$15,000
Support	$20,000 (per year)
Total	**$145,000**

The installation costs include setting up the system, as well as the costs to install 12 access points in the corporate headquarters.

In Table 1-2, Eric identifies the capital costs for deploying a VoWLAN solution at Acme Furniture.

Table 1-2   *Capital Costs for a VoWLAN System at Acme Furniture*

Element	Cost
VoWLAN handsets (127)	$63,500
Call Manager	$50,000
Access points	$6,000
Total	**$119,500**

As a result, the total first year cost of deploying a VoWLAN solution to meet Acme Furniture's requirements is $264,500, which includes $119,500 in capital costs and $145,000 in operational costs. The company will also incur an annual cost of $20,000 for ongoing operational support.

Eric met with the IT manager, Debbie, and found that an Ethernet network resides in the corporate offices, with plenty of capacity to support voice traffic. Also, based on the call volumes as indicated by existing telephone bills, the WAN interconnecting the corporate offices, manufacturing plant, stores, and distribution centers does not need any additional capacity to support initial requirements, but it will likely need an upgrade as the company expands the system.

Savings

The calculation of savings resulting from a VoWLAN solution includes the combination of quantitative and qualitative benefits. The following sections take a look at each of these types of benefits to see how they can help justify VoWLAN costs.

Quantitative Benefits

The quantitative benefits comprise the actual dollar savings resulting from the deployment of a VoWLAN solution. This money is generally cash that a company avoids paying for particular services, but it can also include sales of hardware that the VoWLAN system is replacing. The following are the types of quantitative benefits that you can realize with a VoWLAN solution:

- **Reduced long-distance telephone charges**—The routing of intercompany VoIP telephone calls is virtually free; therefore, a VoWLAN system can eliminate the long-distance charges associated with each VoWLAN user.

- **Fewer wired telephone lines**—A company can eliminate the need for a wired telephone line for each VoWLAN user, which saves any associated fees. Because VoWLAN users are wireless, there is no need to rewire telephone lines when changes are made to the workforce.

- **Increased productivity**—This benefit is somewhat difficult to define in some cases, but it allows employees to complete work faster and better serve customers. This results in higher revenues for the company, which is certainly a benefit.

Qualitative Benefits

Qualitative benefits enhance the operation of the company, but they do not result in definable dollar savings. These types of benefits often lean management toward funding the project when quantitative benefits are marginal or not well defined. The following are the types of qualitative benefits that you should consider when performing an ROI study for a VoWLAN solution:

- **Improved safety**—This benefit is certainly very important to any company. In some cases, the regular use of VoWLAN phones can provide vital and immediate communications in times of emergency situations.

- **Better image to customers**—With the use of VoWLAN phones, customers will see company employees getting things done faster and more efficiently, which makes the customer more inclined to do business with the company.

- **Increased employee morale**—Employees equipped with VoWLAN handsets have less frustration because of the elimination of telephone tag and searching for a phone when they need one.

Case Study: Acme Furniture Defines Benefits for a VoWLAN Solution

Previously, Eric, the consultant performing an ROI study for Acme Furniture, defined the total costs of a VoWLAN solution. Eric next determined the benefits that the company will gain by spending this money. In doing so, he met with the IT manager, Debbie, and the division heads of the manufacturing plant, distribution centers, and stores, who are Brian, Denise, and Sierra, respectively.

Debbie located past telephone bills and work orders and totaled up what the costs have been for equipping potential VoWLAN users with wired telephones. The average cost of adding or changing a phone line is approximately $100, but there are only a few of the planned VoWLAN users where this applies over the past few years. As a result, Eric does not bother including this benefit in the study. If all employees were to have VoWLAN handsets, though, the savings per year would be $50,000 total per year, which would have been significant. Debbie does reiterate that the monthly long-distance telephone bill is approximately $3,000 per month, and the deployment of a VoWLAN solution will eliminate these costs.

Brian discussed lots of issues that line supervisors are having when getting status from construction teams making the furniture at the plant, but pinpointing lost revenue that could equate to quantitative benefits was not possible. However, a VoWLAN solution in this situation would result in excellent qualitative benefits. It is common for companies to not fully define productivity benefits.

In the distribution centers, Denise explains that the use of mobile telephones will improve productivity and will surely speed up the processing of orders, but no studies have been done to assess the actual impacts on revenue. As with the case with the manufacturing plant, Eric will include this as a qualitative benefit.

Sierra provides details on the sales lost due to not getting timely product availability information to customers. A study that surveyed customers as they exited the stores was conducted on this subject during the previous year, and it found that Acme Furniture was losing roughly $250,000 per year due to this problem. These people would leave the store before finding out that the particular furniture item that they wanted was in stock at a distribution center.

Eric tabulated the quantitative benefits of deploying a VoWLAN solution at Acme Furniture in Table 1-3.

Table 1-3   *Quantitative Benefits of a VoWLAN Solution at Acme Furniture*

Element	Savings
Long-distance telephone service	$36,000 per year
Increased sales at stores	$250,000 per year
Total	**$286,000 per year**

The total savings of $286,000 per year is amazing, and it is actual cash savings. Eric defines the following additional benefits:

- Better customer service due to line supervisors having more direct communications with construction teams in the manufacturing plant.

- Increased (undefined) productivity in the distribution centers because of direct communications among warehouse clerks and administrative offices.

- Improved safety because employees carrying VoWLAN phones can contact the appropriate services immediately if an emergency situation occurs.

For Acme Furniture the biggest payoff is clearly the ability to increase sales at the stores through faster inventory checks. That benefit alone is enough to invest in the project.

Payback Period

With the costs and savings of a VoWLAN deployment in mind, you should calculate the payback period to determine whether the project is worth investing in. The payback period is the amount of time that the system needs to operate to realize enough savings to pay off the initial expenses. Most companies move forward with a payback period of less than three years. The quantitative benefits, however, must exceed the support costs on a yearly basis.

For example, a company may find that a VoWLAN system will save $75,000 through lower long-distance telephone charges. If the initial cost for hardware and services amounts to $80,000 and an annual support cost of $15,000 is necessary, the payback period is just over one year. This should prompt most companies to implement the system.

Case Study: Acme Furniture Determines a Favorable Payback Period

Eric, the consultant working with Acme Furniture, utilizes the costs and benefits of deploying a VoWLAN system for the company to determine the payback period and yearly net benefits. This is something that the company president, Bob, had requested Eric find out before deciding whether it is worth installing the system. Based on a total quantitative benefit of $286,000 per year and a first-year cost of $264,500, which includes hardware, services, and first year's support costs, Eric is happy to announce that the payback period is just under one year. After this payback period occurs, the company will receive a yearly combination of cost savings and additional revenue of $266,000, which takes into account the $20,000 per year support cost.

Bob is very happy with these numbers and readily agrees to fund the project. He hands over Eric's rough financial analysis to the company's accountant, Madison, who will figure in capital depreciation, finance costs, and other details. The benefit of more than a quarter million dollars per year, though, is certainly big enough to cover any alterations that Madison might make to the analysis.

Chapter Summary

The deployment of a VoWLAN solution can provide substantial benefits to companies. In most cases, the primary benefits are increases in productivity due to improved communications and lower long-distance telephone charges. A doctor in a hospital who carries a VoIP phone is reachable immediately and can respond to patient needs quickly. Also, a company can make use of VoWLANs and route calls over the Internet or a private WAN, which makes these calls much less expensive than using the traditional PSTN. In addition, a VoWLAN solution is a lower-cost method for implementing mobile phone technology inside larger facilities as compared to cellular systems. A company should, however, complete a financial study to adequately define benefits and the costs of deploying and supporting the VoWLAN system.

Chapter Review Questions

1 What types of user devices can VoWLAN systems replace?

2 VoWLANs are an extension to a wired VoIP system. True or false?

3 Which wireless LAN technologies can adequately support voice traffic?

4 What are two quantitative benefits of VoWLAN solutions?

5 Improved safety is not a benefit of VoWLAN solutions. True or false?

6 What are examples of operational costs of a VoWLAN solution?

7 The initial financial study must include all technical details of the requirements, design, installation, and support. True or false?

8 What are the primary elements that comprise the capital costs of a VoWLAN system?

9 What is the purpose of conducting initial analysis for a VoWLAN system?

Objectives

Upon completing this chapter, you will be able to

- Identify the primary components of a VoWLAN system.

- Describe specific applications of alternative VoWLAN components.

- Differentiate the benefits of traditional "thick" access points and wireless switched solutions.

CHAPTER 2

VoWLAN System Components

This chapter defines the components that are part of a VoWLAN system, such as phones, client software, call managers, and so on. Examples of actual components are given, with emphasis on Cisco products. Descriptions of how VoWLAN integrates with existing systems found in enterprise settings are also given.

VoWLAN System Overview

A general VoWLAN system architecture consists of components that provide mobile phone usage throughout a facility or campus. Figure 2-1 illustrates the interconnection of these components.

Figure 2-1   *Primary VoWLAN System Components*

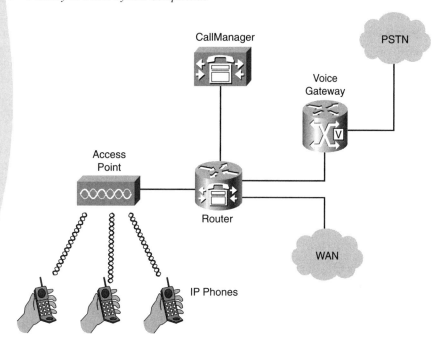

The following is a brief description of each primary component of a VoWLAN solution:

- **Wireless IP Phone**—This appliance is similar to a cell phone; however, it includes a wireless LAN adapter that interfaces with a wireless LAN for connectivity to the telephone system. The user can place calls directly to another user, similar to an office telephone system, or make calls external to the facility through the Public Switched Telephone Network (PSTN). The Cisco 7920 is an example of a wireless IP phone.

- **Call manager**—The call manager on a Voice over Internet Protocol (VoIP) network takes the place of a traditional private branch exchange (PBX). It processes calls on the network and handles functions such as registering IP phones, administering dial and route plans, and managing voice mail. The Cisco CallManager and CallManager Express are examples of a call manager.

- **Voice gateway**—This device interfaces Internet Protocol (IP) telephony to other types of networks and systems. For example, a gateway can interface a VoIP network to the traditional PSTN. This can provide a path for primary communications between internal IP phones and users of standard phones. And the gateway connection to the PSTN can act as a backup in case the wide-area network (WAN) becomes unavailable.

- **Wireless LAN infrastructure**—A wireless local-area network (LAN) handles the transport of wireless VoIP calls throughout the facility. As a result, telephone users can freely move about their workspace. The Cisco 1200 and 1300 access points are popular wireless LAN infrastructure components.

The wireless LAN adapter in the user's wireless IP phone must connect to an access point on the network before the user can make calls. When a user initiates a call, the request travels through the access point and across the wired network to the call manager, which processes the request. For example, if User A is calling User B, the call manager rings User B's phone and then makes a connection between the two users. To provide mobility, the wireless LAN adapter in the wireless IP phone of the roaming user reassociates with other access points throughout the facility as needed. The call between the two users continues uninterrupted, assuming that the transition (roaming delay) between access points is less than 100 milliseconds. If the delay is more, calls generally drop.

If a user is dialing an external phone number, the call manager forwards the call to the PBX or the Internet, which completes the external call. If the PBX is not equipped to handle IP traffic directly, an intermediate VoIP gateway is needed to translate the VoIP traffic into analog signals. The PBX directs external calls coming into the facility to the call manager, which then forwards the call using VoIP signaling to the applicable wireless IP phone.

Cisco 7920 Wireless IP Phone

The Cisco 7920 Wireless IP Phone, shown in Figure 2-2, interfaces with Cisco access points and works with Cisco CallManager. The 7920 has similar features as office phones and wireless smartphones, such as directory of incoming calls, call waiting, call transfer, conference calling, voice message indication, local phone book, and multiple ring tones. It is compatible with Cisco CallManager Version 4.1, 4.0, 3.3 and later, and CallManager Express Version 3.2, using the Skinny Client Control Protocol (SCCP).

Figure 2-2   *Cisco 7920 Wireless IP Phone*

The following is a summary of the 7920 features:

- **IP address assignment**—This is done through Dynamic Host Configuration Protocol (DHCP) or is statically configured by an administrator.

- **Firmware updates**—After it is connected to an access point, a company can perform firmware updates over the wireless LAN by using the Trivial File Transfer Protocol (TFTP) server and the Cisco web interface.

- **VLAN support**—The 7920 implements IEEE 802.1q (virtual LAN) configuration and Cisco-proprietary virtual local-area network (VLAN) technology Interswitch link protocol.

- **Site survey functions**—Using a 7920 when performing Radio Frequency (RF) site surveys is possible. This feature takes into consideration the specific wireless LAN adapter, antenna, and physical construction of the handheld device.

- **Security**—The 7920 implements a variety of security protocols, including IEEE 802.1X Cisco LEAP authentication, 40- and 128-bit static Wired Equivalent Privacy (WEP), Wi-Fi Protected Access (WPA), WPA Pre-shared Key (PSK), Cisco Centralized Key Management (CCKM), Temporal Key Integrity Protocol (TKIP), and Message Integrity Check (MIC). Users can also utilize an optional phone unlock password.

- **Wireless technology**—The wireless adapter inside the 7920 implements IEEE 802.11b, direct sequence with automatic rate or static data rates of 1, 2, 5.5, or 11 Mbps (megabytes).

- **Transmit power**—The wireless LAN adapter transmits at 1, 5, 20, 50, or 100 milliwatts, depending on configuration settings.

- **Range**—The 7920 can communicate successfully at ranges of 500–1,000 feet from the connected access point, but the actual range depends on the environment.

- **Access point support**—The 7920 interfaces with Cisco Aironet access points, including the 1300, 1200, 1130, 1100, 1000 Lightweight, 350, and 340 series. The access point must be set to support 802.11b-only or mixed 802.11b/g mode. Other configuration parameters, as discussed in detail in Chapter 8, "Installing, Configuring, and Testing a VoWLAN System," are necessary to ensure effective operation of the phone.

NOTE   Several other manufacturers offer wireless IP phones. For example, Linksys also has SIP phones, the WIP 300 and WIP 330, which integrate directly into Cisco CallManager. Also, Vonage offers a Wi-Fi phone for users to make calls from Wi-Fi hotspots.

Case Study: Acme Furniture Users Make Use of Cisco 7920 Wireless IP Phones

Brian, a division head of the Acme Furniture's manufacturing plant, is given a Cisco 7920 Wireless IP phone for making phone calls via the company's new VoWLAN system. The IT department has already configured the phone with the proper SSID, security settings, and extension number, but Brian can personalize the phone. He first sets the ring tone to sound unique to distinguish his phone from others. Brian uses the phone for the first time while on the manufacturing floor. After talking with the line supervisor, he learns that a change in the design of a new rocker requires some additional input from the design group before production can move forward. So Brian immediately uses his 7920 to locate the phone extension of the rocker's lead designer, Evan, and places the call. Evan is currently in a staff meeting, but he hears his unique ring tone and answers the call on the second ring. The problem in manufacturing has priority over the staff meeting, and he arrives on the manufacturing floor within a couple minutes. While en route, Brian and Evan continue discussing possible fixes for the issues. Brian then recalls the past, when extensive telephone tag due to fixed wired phones resulted in hours before they could mitigate a problem like this.

Cisco IP Softphone

The Cisco IP Softphone, shown in Figure 2-3, is a Microsoft Windows–based application that is an alternative to using the 7920 handset. Softphone installs on a laptop equipped with a wireless LAN card and enables a user to place calls over the VoWLAN system. You can use Softphone as a standalone phone end station or in conjunction with a Cisco IP Phone. The software allows connections to the phone system when the laptop has an online connection to the Internet. This feature makes it handy to check voice messages and place calls from anywhere within the signal coverage of the VoWLAN system or just about anywhere you are online with the Internet. Using a phone headset with this configuration can be beneficial, especially if your laptop or PC does not have a microphone and speakers. The Softphone integrates with Lightweight Directory Access Protocol 3 (LDAP3) directories, which allows placing calls by looking up people by name or e-mail address. A drag-and-drop capability makes placing calls and scheduling conference calls relatively easy.

Figure 2-3   *Cisco IP Softphone Main Screen*

Case Study: Researcher Makes Use of Cisco IP Softphone

A chemical company located in the southwestern U.S. has a Cisco VoIP system and equips each employee with a wired VoIP desk phone. Before the company implemented the system, it found that mobility requirements were limited. The company did, however, deploy wireless LANs to provide coverage in several remote locations, such as conference rooms and laboratories. To provide mobile phone coverage in these remote places, the company equipped its staff with Cisco IP Softphone on their laptops to facilitate calls. This solution was preferred over purchasing 7920 Wireless IP Phone handsets for everyone because all employees have laptops. This configuration also takes advantage of the call forwarding function. Calls made to someone's desk phone (his or her primary phone number) simultaneously ring both the desk phone and the Softphone on the laptop. If the person is sitting at his desk, he can answer the desk phone. When working somewhere else, the person can answer the Softphone. The call forwarding function makes this capability possible. To illustrate the versatility of this approach, Shanna, a researcher for the company, is working in a lab and finds that she needs to call an associate, Jared, to discuss a testing procedure that she is getting ready to commence. She does not have time to go track down Jared. Shanna uses her laptop to call Jared. Jared is working in an associate's office with his laptop. Shanna does not know this, so she calls Jared's primary phone number (his desk phone). Jared's desk phone and Softphone both ring, and he immediately answers her call from his Softphone and offers some tips on performing the test procedure.

Cisco CallManager

Cisco CallManager is a software-based call-processing component and extends traditional enterprise telephone system features and functions to packet telephony to IP phones. CallManager installs on Cisco 7800 series media convergence servers (MCS) and selected third-party servers. CallManager runs on a variety of operating systems. The older versions of CallManager run on Windows platforms, but CallManager 5 is Linux-based. CallManager Express runs on Cisco's Internetworking Operating System (IOS).

A company can deploy multiple Cisco CallManager servers and manage them as a single entity. Cisco CallManager clustering enables scalability from 1 to 30,000 IP phones per cluster. Security features verify the identity of the mobile devices and servers that they communicate with to ensure the integrity of data they are receiving. Encryption offers privacy of communications.

Case Study: Acme Furniture Chooses Cisco CallManager for Handling VoIP Calls

Acme Furniture, the hypothetical company introduced in Chapter 1, needs to select components for its voice IP telephony solution. The company has 750 employees located in corporate headquarters, a manufacturing plant, and multiple retail stores and distribution centers spread throughout the U.S. A WAN, which has plenty of capacity for the expected VoIP calls, interconnects all sites.

Debbie, the IT manager for Acme Furniture, chose Cisco's CallManager to provide call processing for users equipped with Cisco 7920 wireless IP phones. This choice enables a scalable solution that can fulfill the number of initial users and satisfy future growth. Acme will interconnect calls between its distributed sites through its existing wide-area network (WAN). Figure 2-4 illustrates the system component interconnections.

Figure 2-4   *Acme Furniture Voice Telephony System*

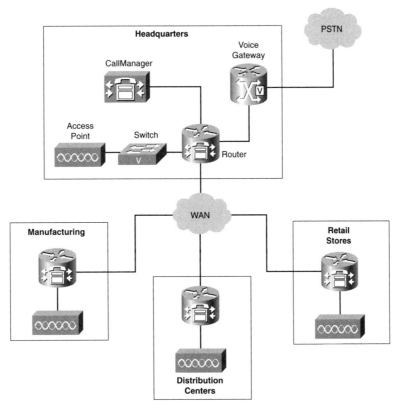

This system enables wireless VoIP communications among all of Acme Furniture's facilities. In addition, users can place and receive telephone calls from the Cisco 7920 IP Phones with standard telephone users via a gateway connection to the PSTN.

Cisco CallManager Express

To satisfy requirements for small offices, Cisco offers CallManager Express. This version of CallManager is simpler to deploy, administer, and maintain. It can handle from 24 to 240 users.

**Case Study: Chemical Company Chooses Cisco CallManager Express
for Handling VoIP Calls**

A chemical company located in the southwestern U.S. consists of 120 employees located inside a single three-floor building. The company does not expect to grow the workforce. The company has been using a relatively old PBX for handling internal and external calls from standard analog telephones. To reduce costs associated with adds/moves and long-distance phone service, the company decided to deploy a mix of wireless and wired IP telephones to replace the existing analog system.

The company chose Cisco's CallManager Express because it can easily support the total number of users. In addition, the internal IT staff can easily install, configure, and manage the solution. CallManager Express handles all internal call processing and interfaces with the external world through a connection to the PSTN.

Linksys Wi-Fi Video Cameras

The Linksys Wireless-G Internet Video Camera, shown in Figure 2-5, captures and sends live high-quality video and sound over an 802.11g wireless LAN. The unit operates independently and does not require a connection to a PC. The video signals are sent directly over the wireless LAN.

Figure 2-5   *Linksys Wireless-G Internet Video Camera*

The following is a summary of the Linksys Wireless-G Internet Video Camera specifications:

- **Integrated web server**—Makes viewing captured video from web browsers possible.

- **Motion detection**—Automatically begins capturing video and sends an e-mail notification.

- **MPEG-4 compression**—Significantly reduces load on the network.
- **640 × 480 pixels resolution**—Good quality for most applications.
- **128-bit WEP encryption**—Encrypts the video contained within 802.11 data frames.

NOTE	Keep in mind that even though the camera is wireless, it still needs to connect to electrical power. In addition, you may need to install the camera in a protective enclosure.

Case Study: Chemical Company Monitors Processes with Wireless Video

A chemical company located in the southwestern U.S. uses a Linksys Wireless-G Internet Video Camera to remotely monitor chemical mixing in one of its chemical plants. Telemetry instruments continually measure temperature and pressure of the processes, but having a human eye watch over the mixing process from time to time is also valuable. So, the company installed the wireless video camera at a good vantage point within the mixing room. This solution avoids needing to have one of the engineers personally monitor the process.

The wireless video camera connects over the wireless LAN to the nearest access point. System operators located in different buildings can occasionally view the process using a web browser on their PC. They point the web browser at the camera's IP address, and the video signals travel through the wireless LAN and over the company's wired network to the person's PC.

NOTE	In addition to Linksys, consider using Wi-Fi video cameras from Axis Communications for applications where better quality is necessary.

NOTE	Vocera Communications Systems offers a solution that includes users wearing Vocera Communications Badges and centralized Vocera System Software residing on a server that is attached to the network. This solution provides immediate communication between people wearing Vocera Communications Badges, which provide voice-controlled communication over an IEEE 802.11b wireless LAN. The badge includes a microphone, speaker, and display for showing caller ID or a text message. Vocera System Software runs on a standard Windows server and controls and manages call activity. Optional Vocera Telephony Solution Software enables users to make and receive telephone calls through their Badge.

Wireless Network Infrastructures

A wireless voice telephony system requires an effective wireless network infrastructure. You can take advantage of traditional access points or make use of the newer wireless switches. However, ensuring that enough capacity exists and that roaming delays are short enough to avoid dropped calls is very important.

Traditional Access Point Networks

The customary approach for deploying wireless LANs includes the installation of multiple intelligent ("thick") access points that interconnect via a conventional Ethernet switched network, as shown in Figure 2-6. This distribution system provides coverage throughout a facility while enabling connections with servers and the Internet residing on the wired portion of a company's network. Companies have been deploying wireless LANs having this type of architecture for more than a decade.

Figure 2-6 *Cisco Traditional Access Point Network*

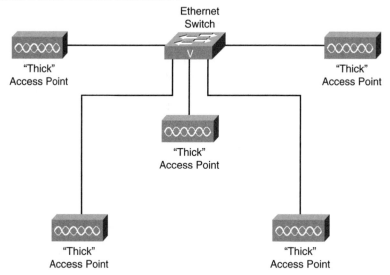

The access points implement functions of the 802.11 standard, such as medium access and association procedures. As users roam throughout the facility, their wireless client devices reassociate with an access point having the strongest beacon. Because the access points are the only wireless LAN devices on the network, the access points must contain a significant amount of intelligence to meet the essential elements of a wireless LAN that the 802.11 standards do not provide. The access points implement security and management functions in addition to basic radio connectivity.

When deploying VoWLAN solutions, a company may choose to use an existing access point network, which is usually the traditional "thick" access point architecture. This certainly reduces the initial capital expenses for hardware. This sort of access point solution, however, can be costly to scale up in terms of coverage and performance because the access points are relatively expensive. For example, a company will likely pay $500 per access point to increase coverage by 30,000 square feet. In addition, more than one access point may be necessary to increase performance in the same area. For large implementations, the cost of access points becomes a major part of the total cost of ownership (TCO). Thus, the use of an existing access point solution may not be the best long-term option, especially if the company plans to scale up the network in the future to support more users.

The "thick" access point approach may also be costly to migrate to newer technologies. For example, a company may deploy an 802.11b/g network now and find that 802.11a or something else is necessary in three years to support higher-end applications. A company may experience a lower TCO if it needs to replace expensive access points with new ones in the future.

Access points within a traditional solution generally interconnect using standard switched Ethernet, the predominant type that supports wired connections in companies worldwide. A switch connects one user, such as an access point, to another without blocking access of other users. The switch improves throughput as compared to a shared hub because of the smaller resulting collision domains. Users do not have to wait until others are finished before sending data. A switch is necessary with VoWLAN systems to maximize performance.

Handoffs from one "thick" access point to another may be too slow to support VoIP applications when users roam. The problem here is that the combination of the access points and traditional Ethernet switches in this type of solution are not fast enough. For example, someone using a wireless LAN phone will likely experience a dropped call when roaming from one access point to another. Before depending on an existing wireless LAN for supporting voice applications, you should test the roaming delays, and they should be less than 100 milliseconds to minimize dropped calls.

The "thick" access point approach requires decentralized management to support the remote functions that the access points implement. Even if the "thick" access point manufacturer provides a centralized management system, the wireless LAN must handle the additional overhead traffic necessary to communicate regularly with the access point. This traffic may reduce the capacity of the wireless LAN, which precludes the deployment of some applications that could have provided additional benefits and resulting lower TCO.

Cisco has a complete line of traditional wireless LAN hardware that supports voice applications and addresses needs for enterprises, public networks, and homes. The following identifies currently available Cisco Aironet access points:

- **Cisco Aironet 1300 Series**—The Cisco Aironet 1300 Series Outdoor Access Point/ Bridge is a multifunctional component that provides access point, bridge, and workgroup bridge functionality for network connections within an outdoor campus area. The 1300 series supports the 802.11b/g standards.

- **Cisco Aironet 1230AG Series**—The Cisco Aironet 1230AG Series has dual antenna connectors for extending range with optional antennas for enterprise solutions.

- **Cisco Aironet 1200 Series**—The Cisco Aironet 1200 Series includes a dual-slot architecture that allows flexibility when configuring radio cards for enterprise solutions. For example, a 1200 Series access point can include any combination of radio card technology, such as 802.11a and 802.11g.

- **Cisco Aironet 1130AG Series**—The Cisco Aironet 1130AG Series includes integrated antennas and dual 802.11a/g radios for enterprise solutions.

- **Cisco Aironet 1100 Series**—The Cisco Aironet 1100 Series offers an easy-to-install, single-band, 802.11b/g access point for enterprise solutions.

- **Cisco Aironet 350 Series**—The Cisco Aironet 350 Series is designed for small and medium-sized businesses. The Cisco Aironet 350 Series access point provides an ideal solution for customers who desire a nonupgradeable IEEE 802.11b solution. The 350 series supports the 802.11b standard.

All the access points can support IOS. The Cisco Aironet 350 can also support Vxworks.

Case Study: Warehouse Uses Existing Wireless LAN for VoWLAN Solution

A warehouse located in the northeastern U.S. has an existing wireless LAN that supports warehouse logistics functions. For example, warehouse clerks use wireless bar code scanners to perform inventory management. The wireless LAN consists of three Cisco Aironet 1200 access points, implementing IEEE 802.11b technology. A wireless site survey was completed a couple years ago to ensure a minimum of 15dB signal-to-noise ratio (SNR) signal coverage throughout the warehouse floor. The bar code application traffic over the network occupies only 5–10 percent of the overall capacity.

Because plenty of capacity is left to support voice traffic, the warehouse manager, Evan, decided to deploy a VoWLAN solution using the existing access points. Only five warehouse clerks will carry Cisco 7920 IP phones, which connect to the nearest access point. It is likely that only three of the clerks will be making calls at the same time, and they will probably be connected to different access points. Each access point can support up to three simultaneous callers, so there is no problem with capacity.

The minimum 15dB SNR throughout the facility is fine for supporting bar code applications, but it is not good enough for voice applications, which require a minimum of 25dB SNR. As a result, Evan scheduled a company to perform another wireless site survey and consider increasing the gain of the antennas and possibly add a fourth access point to improve the signal strength.

Wireless Switched Networks

As an effective alternative to traditional "thick" access point infrastructures, consider the use of wireless switched networks, as shown in Figure 2-7. The main idea here is to have "thin" access points focus on reliable and high-performance radio technology. The access points merely implement the 802.11 protocol, whereas the switch provides intelligence necessary to offer effective security, management, and performance. This feature results in a solution that effectively satisfies voice applications and significantly reduces TCO for most applications.

Figure 2-7   *Cisco Wireless Switched Network*

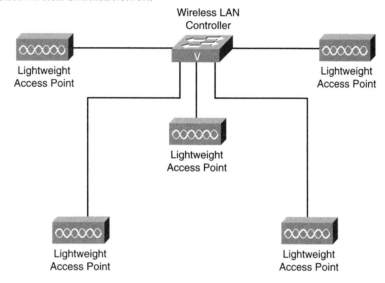

The switched wireless solution is less costly to scale up coverage and performance due to relatively inexpensive access points. The lack of intelligence in the access points makes offering access points at relatively low prices possible. The overall system is still intelligent, however, because the central switch shares the intelligence in a cost-effective and efficient manner with the access points. The smarts of the system only need to reside on one central hardware device, which reduces costs of the access points. Also, less overhead is sent over the wireless LAN when managing access control.

An intelligent wireless switch, such as that offered by Cisco, provides roaming handoffs much faster than conventional wireless LAN solutions. This enables effective support of VoIP applications. Wireless phone users are able to roam smoothly throughout the facility while reassociating with different access points.

Because the access points are less expensive, a "thin" solution is overall less costly to implement and support. Again, the sharing of the wireless intelligence in the switch results in lower TCO. The overall hardware costs are lower, and migrating to newer technologies is less expensive because of lower replacement costs.

The wireless switch implements effective rogue access point detection. If an employee or hacker plugs in a rogue on the wired side of the switch, the switch disallows access via the rogue access point to the network. The wireless switch containing all security configurations can also be kept in a locked server room, which prevents hackers from fiddling with the configurations to their advantage.

In addition to better security, a compelling reason to deploy the thin access point solution is centralized management. Administrators can maintain, monitor, and upgrade multiple access points and user access configurations through the central switch, enabling efficient management because of integrated support functions. Furthermore, this approach relieves a significant amount of overhead on the wireless LAN, which increases capacity and utility.

Another benefit of the switched wireless solution is that it is better understood by IT personnel. Wireless technologies are very new to most companies, and existing IT personnel are not familiar with the radio characteristics of wireless LANs. The switched wireless approach has less focus on radio waves and more emphasis on the switch, which is familiar territory for administrators.

Cisco offers the following wireless switch components:

- **Cisco 1000 Series Lightweight Access Points**—Formally an Airespace product, the Cisco 1000 Series Lightweight Access Point is an 802.11 a/b/g dual-band, zero-touch configuration and management access point for enterprise solutions. It works in conjunction with a Cisco Wireless LAN Controller and optional Cisco Wireless Control System (WCS) to support real-time intrusion monitoring in addition to data traffic.

- **Cisco 4100 Series Wireless LAN Controllers**—The Cisco Wireless LAN Controllers work in conjunction with the Cisco 1000 Series Lightweight access points and the Cisco WCS to provide systemwide functions, such as intrusion detection, RF management, and security policy management. Ideal for medium to large enterprise facilities.

- **Cisco 2000 Series Wireless LAN Controllers**—Similar to the 4100 Series, except the 2000 Series is best for small to medium enterprise facilities.

Case Study: Acme Furniture Selects Cisco's Wireless Switch Solution for Corporate Offices

Acme Furniture has existing Cisco wireless LANs in retail stores, distribution centers, and manufacturing plants. To deploy a complete VoWLAN solution, Acme Furniture must install a wireless LAN in its corporate headquarters. Headquarters consists of a two-story building with approximately 50,000 square feet. Based on preliminary analysis, 12 access points are needed to provide adequate signal coverage for wireless VoIP.

Because the company is installing a new wireless LAN in this area, it wants to take advantage of the benefits of wireless switches. So, Acme Furniture decided to install Cisco 1000 Series Lightweight Access Points and a 4100 Series Wireless LAN Controller. Doing so provides the company with an optimal solution for both voice and data traffic. Over time, the company will migrate existing traditional wireless LANs in retail stores, distribution centers, and manufacturing plants to the wireless switched network.

Mesh Networks

Many municipalities, such as Philadelphia, San Francisco, New York City, and a host of others, are deploying mesh networks that offer citywide Wi-Fi access. In general, mesh networking replaces traditional wireless LAN access points with "backhaul nodes" that are entirely wireless, except for the electrical cord. Figure 2-8 illustrates the Cisco wireless mesh network architecture. One side of the node interfaces with Wi-Fi users, typically using 802.11b/g. The Wi-Fi user associates with the mesh network node just as it does with an access point. The other side of the backhaul node has radios that interconnect the node to other backhaul nodes that make up the mesh network.

Figure 2-8 *Cisco Wireless Mesh Network Architecture*

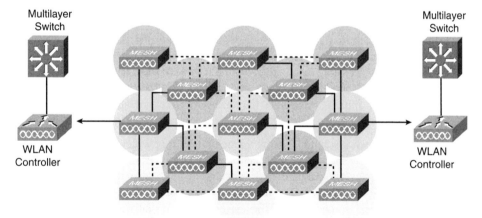

Mesh Access Points

The operation of a mesh network is fairly straightforward. For example, the URL request from a Wi-Fi user enters the mesh network at the backhaul node that the user associates with using Wi-Fi protocols. Then it hops from one node to the other until it reaches the node that connects to the Internet service provider (ISP). In some cases, the data packets may hop only a couple of nodes, but a greater number of hops may be necessary in larger networks.

Thus, the time taken for the corresponding web page to return to the user varies, depending on the layout of the network.

A mesh network offers multiple paths from source to destination. Intelligent routing algorithms allow each node to decide on which path to forward packets through the network to improve performance. If the link between a pair of nodes along one of the paths is clogged, for example, the algorithms establish another path that avoids the congested link. Also, if a node goes down, an alternate route is chosen based on the routing algorithms.

This feature makes mesh networks suitable for areas where installing a traditional wireless LAN consisting of access points is not feasible. For example, a mesh network approach makes sense to consider for residential and citywide Wi-Fi networks. The deployment of cabled access points over larger, open areas is a daunting task because of the massive amount of data cabling that requires installation and the countless permissions that you must receive. Other places where installation is difficult include convention centers, college campuses, stadiums, marinas, parks, and construction sites. Simply plop in the backhaul nodes where coverage is necessary, and automatic mechanisms connect the node into the network.

A mesh network is also worthwhile when installing a temporary wireless network because the backhaul nodes are faster to install and there is less to remove. For example, emergency crews can quickly establish a mesh network when working at a disaster site. Enterprises can also benefit from mesh networks when they need network connectivity in temporary work areas.

Another good fit for mesh networks is within buildings that do not have existing data cabling for access points. Instead of access points, the company installs mesh nodes. The costs of installing cable are relatively high, especially when requirements exist for conduit for enclosing the cabling, which is commonly the case. The conduit alone generally doubles the cost of installing access points. In this case, the deployment of a mesh network can save hundreds of dollars per access point.

The mesh network solutions on the market today differ widely. As a result, you must carefully analyze each solution and ensure that it satisfies requirements before moving forward. Latency, for example, may vary significantly, depending on the number of users and hops that are necessary for moving packets through the backhaul network. Roaming and routing delays may cause performance issues, especially for VoIP applications. Even if the data rate between the user and the local backhaul node is kept high, which many of the mesh network vendors claim, the delays across the network may be substantial. A mesh network in your application, though, will likely deliver much better performance than existing cell phone systems.

In some cases, the benefits of a mesh network far outweigh the issues. If you need a robust Wi-Fi solution where running cable to access points is not feasible, a mesh network is the answer. Lower installation costs because of less cabling and increased utility in difficult-to-wire areas make mesh networks shine. There are a few wrinkles to iron out with the standards and better provisions for VoIP, but mesh networks certainly have a permanent home in the wonderful world of wireless. Keep in mind, however, that without mesh network standards, you must install mesh nodes from the same vendor, such as Cisco.

The Cisco wireless mesh network solution includes the Cisco Aironet 1500 Series access point ("mesh node"):

- **Adaptive Wireless Path Protocol**—This patent-pending protocol dynamically forms optimal traffic routes between nodes. If RF interference occurs, the protocol automatically selects an alternate path.

- **Radio redundancy**—Each access point has two 802.11a/b/g radios for data integrity and throughput. One radio is dedicated to wireless communications between access points. The other radio can be dedicated to a specific application for segmentation or set to optimize performance of all users.

- **Security**—The solution offers a variety of security mechanisms, such as hardware-based Advanced Encryption Standard (AES) between access points and 802.11i, Wi-Fi Protected Access 2 (WPA2), and WEP for wireless clients. X.509 digital certification prevents unauthorized devices from joining the network.

- **Multiple SSIDs**—Each access point supports up to 16 SSIDs that can map into separate VLANs to support different wireless ISPs and private applications.

The Cisco mesh solution also includes wireless LAN controllers that implement the Cisco WCS, which offers scalable management, security, and support tools to manage a mesh network.

Case Study: City of Hope Chooses Cisco's Wireless Mesh Solution to Offer Wi-Fi Connectivity

Evan, the mayor of the city of Hope, learned about the benefits of wireless VoIP while golfing with Bob, president of Acme Furniture. Bob's company is deploying a wireless voice telephony solution. Evan liked the idea and envisioned similar applications for city employees. After researching citywide wireless networks, Evan realized that many other cities, such as Philadelphia and San Francisco, are deploying citywide Wi-Fi networks for both public and private applications. Hope is a medium-sized city with hundreds of employees (firefighters, police, and other staff) mobile throughout the city. The use of Wi-Fi for supporting voice communications would definitely enhance operations and save money. The city of Hope could not afford to install the mesh hardware, so arrangements were made with a local ISP to offer public, fee-based Wi-Fi access to the city's numerous business and vacation visitors.

The city of Hope decided to install a Cisco wireless mesh solution using Cisco Aironet 1500 Series access points and associated controllers. The city scheduled a preinstallation site survey to determine the presence of RF interference that might significantly impair the operation of the network. In addition, the site survey will include RF propagation tests to analyze impacts of buildings and other obstacles on RF signal coverage. These results are crucial for providing a basis for determining the required density of access points necessary for voice applications.

Chapter Summary

When building a wireless voice telephony system, you must include several components that are not typical of a standard data-only wireless LAN. For example, users need wireless IP phones to utilize voice services. The phone operates very similar to a cell phone, except that calls are made over a wireless LAN using VoIP signaling. In a wireless voice telephony system, a call manager replaces the traditional PBX. The resulting system can interconnect users in different facilities and cities using digital circuits, such as the Internet.

A key element of the wireless voice telephony system is a wireless LAN infrastructure, which routes calls to and from mobile users. A company's existing traditional ("thick") access points can support voice calls, assuming that the signal coverage and delays between access points are adequate. However, a wireless switched network using "thin" access points offers superior performance for voice applications. For example, the switch reduces the security issues resulting from someone connecting a rogue access point to the switch.

Cities can also deploy wireless mesh solutions to offer citywide voice services to employees and public users. Mesh networks can also be used indoors to reduce requirements for interconnecting access points with Ethernet cabling.

Chapter Review Questions

1   What are the primary components of a VoWLAN solution?

2   What are the two main Cisco wireless IP phone approaches?

3   What functions does a call manager have on a VoWLAN system?

4   What is the purpose of a voice gateway?

5   Why is a wireless switched network better for supporting voice applications?

6 Why would an existing "thick" access point solution not be the optimum solution for supporting voice applications?

7 What are examples of Cisco's traditional "thick" access points?

8 What Cisco access point is used with a wireless switch?

9 Why might a wireless mesh network not provide adequate performance for voice applications?

Objectives

Upon completing this chapter, you will be able to

- Understand the attributes of voice and video signals.

- Explain the basics of VoIP call control.

- Compare and contrast the various VoIP standards, such as H.323, SCCP, and SIP.

- Describe impairments that impact voice calls over wireless networks.

CHAPTER 3

VoWLAN Signaling Fundamentals

VoWLAN systems use voice signals, which are not well understood by the typical IT professional. As a result, this chapter is necessary to provide an overview of the primary elements of voice communications, such as voice characteristics, analog-to-digital conversion, compression techniques, call signaling standards, and so on. The idea is to provide the basics of Voice over IP (VoIP) communications as the basis to better understand interactions taking place over the wireless and wired network.

Voice Attributes

A wireless Internet Protocol (IP) phone transmits and receives signals that carry voice (audio) communications. This includes a combination of VoIP and wireless protocols. When someone speaks, the sound waves leaving his mouth mostly fit within a range of frequencies falling between 300Hz and 3,400Hz. As a result, telephone systems for many years have been designed to support this band of frequencies. Most humans can hear at somewhat higher frequencies. VoIP signaling supports voice conversations having sounds that fall within this band of frequencies as well.

Most VoIP phone systems are not designed to transport high-fidelity sound. A wider audio frequency band that extends up to 10,000Hz would offer better sound qualities, but it is not really necessary for most applications. This is especially true for systems supporting voice conversations between humans, which is the major trend in deploying wireless multimedia systems. In addition, the extra overall capacity needed to support the enhanced sound quality would consume a great deal of the capacity of the supporting system, especially wireless local-area network (LAN) interfaces. In some cases, though, transporting sound having higher-frequency components, such as high-fidelity music, might be necessary, but that is beyond the scope of this book.

A wireless IP phone, referred to by most VoIP standards as an endpoint, converts audible speech into analog electrical signals. The sound waves generated by the sending person's mouth enter a microphone that moves a small mechanical diaphragm back and forth inside the phone, which varies the frequency and amplitude of an electrical signal flowing through the diaphragm in a way that represents the speech. Amplifiers then boost the level of this tiny communications signal. With standard analog telephones, the analog signals are actually sent over wires either directly to the receiving person's telephone or to the local telephone exchange, which may route the call to the destination via multiple types of communications systems.

A wireless IP phone goes a step further than the standard analog phone. It uses an audio coder that converts the analog voice signal into a digital one that represents the voice using a series of logic 1s and 0s. This process is known as analog-to-digital conversion. The resulting data signal can then be transmitted via network protocols, such as those enabling VoIP communications. For example, an 802.11 data frame can carry portions of the digital voice signal in the frame bodies of the data frames. At the receiving endpoint, a decoder converts the digital stream of data into an audible analog signal that can be heard through a speaker. Each endpoint device, such as a wireless IP phone, includes the audio coder and decoder, referred to as an audio "codec."

The most popular analog-to-digital conversion mechanism is Pulse Code Modulation (PCM), which samples the amplitude of an analog signal 8,000 times every second. A PCM encoder assigns an 8-bit code to each sample, representing the amplitude of the sample. This code results in a 64-Kbps digital signal (8,000 samples per second times 8 bits per sample) that can be sent over the network via VoIP, offering an effective mechanism for portraying audio signals in the 300Hz to 3,400Hz range, such as human voice conversations. It makes high-fidelity music, however, sound a bit "tinny" due to cutting off much of the higher and lower tones that the music offers.

PCM alone does not offer any form of compression. The speech of someone with a dynamic voice (very little redundancy) or a constant tone (very redundant) both result in a 64-Kbps signal. Because of inherent redundancies in voice, it's possible to make effective use of compression techniques to provide a way to reduce this transmission rate to lower values for signals having redundant qualities.

Video Attributes

From watching television, we are all familiar with video, which is merely a series of still images (frames) sent sequentially at a rate that portrays movement of objects within a particular scene. In addition, it includes an audio channel. As compared to voice signals, video signals have much higher variation in bandwidth requirements depending on many factors. Attributes such as video frame rate, image resolution and size, and color affect the bit rate of the video signal. To restrict impacts on wireless LAN capacity, most Wireless Fidelity (Wi-Fi) video cameras implement maximum image resolutions of 640 × 480, 15 frames per second, and limited color depth per pixel. The quality of the image from Wi-Fi video cameras is not too bad for monitoring still or slow-moving scenes, but faster-moving objects, such as automobiles driving by at highway speed, appear choppy or in slow motion because the frame rate is relatively low. It is not fast enough to capture the motion. Thirty frames per second would offer video similar to television, which can keep up with even fast-moving objects. In fact, humans cannot detect differences in frame rates higher than 30 frames per second.

A raw video stream, even one constrained as already described, operates in the megabit-per-second range. Because most systems, especially wireless ones, have limited capacity, having video devices implement some sort of compression is important. This method reduces the bandwidth requirements needed to support the video streams. As a result, the codec in a wireless video camera compresses the digital video images before transmission over the communications medium.

Common compression algorithms for video fall within the Moving Picture Experts Group (MPEG) series of standards. MPEG-4 is a lossy compression algorithm, which means that the process of compression loses some of the video information content. This loss makes completely reproducing the video images at the destination endpoint impossible. In most cases, however, this small loss is not important. In fact, most people cannot distinguish the losses. MPEG-4 does a great job of compressing the images.

MPEG performs the compression by not sending the entire digital image of each subsequent video frame. For example, in a relatively still scene where a person is sitting at a desk with a wall behind her, MPEG has very little new information to send for each image, so it does not send much. The only parts of the image that may require the transmission of data to represent the changed image will be the immediate area around the person as she moves her head or hands. As a result, the signal rate of the video stream is low.

If the scene is dynamic, such as a basketball game, MPEG must send lots more data for each image because of the more dramatic changes in information. The players and fans are all moving throughout the scene. In addition, the camera may be panning up and down the court as the game progresses. The continual changes in the scene require lots of new video data to be sent to represent each image. For color images, MPEG-4 compression is from 20:1 for dynamic scenes to 300:1 for relatively still scenes.

Wi-Fi Video Camera Impacts on Network Utilization

Based on testing in a laboratory environment, a Linksys Wireless-G Internet Video Camera consumes an average of 3 percent of the capacity of an 802.11g wireless LAN with a still, unchanging scene streamed to a single wireless laptop. This particular camera uses MPEG-4 compression and offers 640×480 image resolution at 15 frames per second of video.

The movement of objects within the scene has significant effects on utilization. For example, standing in front of a camera and waving your hand causes a doubling of the utilization to an average of 6 percent. The reason for this increase is the decrease in image redundancy. The compression mechanism works better for redundant scenes as compared to dynamic scenes.

With two wireless laptops individually streaming the video, the utilization increases to an average of 5 percent with a still scene and 10 percent with a dynamic scene. With three wireless laptops individually streaming the video, the utilization for the still and dynamic scenes is 5 percent and 13 percent, respectively. The 802.11 date rate for this testing was mostly 54 Mbps due to relatively high signal and low noise amplitudes.

As a result of this testing, the inclusion of a single Wi-Fi video camera in a wireless LAN has significant impact on utilization and resulting performance of other wireless applications, especially if the scene includes continuous moving objects. Additional analysis should be done if you're implementing more than one camera to determine corresponding utilization levels.

VoIP Call Flow

The use of VoIP enables the transfer of voice packets through an IP network. When deploying VoWLAN systems, understanding the communications taking place over the wireless interface is most important, but knowing what happens at a top level throughout the entire system is also advantageous. The general VoIP call flow includes call signaling, which coordinates the placing, offering, and answering of a VoIP telephone call.

The call flow begins when a wireless IP phone user (Endpoint A) indicates the desire to place a call by taking his phone off the hook and dialing the phone number of another phone (Endpoint B). For example, Cisco CallManager receives this call request and extends the request to Endpoint B. This process sets up two VoIP endpoints to communicate directly with each other. When Endpoint B answers the call, the two endpoints negotiate a codec type and exchange Transport Control Protocol (TCP) port information to facilitate the connection. After establishing a connection, media exchange occurs whereby the two endpoints communicate directly with each other independent of Cisco CallManager. The sections "H.323" and "Session Initiation Protocol (SIP)" later in this chapter go into more detail on how this call coordination works with the various VoIP protocols.

When an active call is taking place, the endpoints send voice-encoded data via the Real-time Transport Protocol (RTP), which IETF RFC 3550 defines. RTP provides end-to-end functions suitable for applications transmitting real-time voice and video. RTP opens a TCP port for the audio stream and another for control (quality of service [QoS] feedback and media control). If video is associated with the audio, the video and audio streams are sent via different RTP sessions. The RTP packets have a header and payload containing the voice data.

With VoWLAN systems, TCP establishes the connection between the endpoints, but User Datagram Protocol (UDP), defined in IETF RFC 768, actually carries the RTP packets between end systems. The majority of packets relevant to voice calls flowing over the wireless link are these UDP packets being sent within the frame bodies of 802.11 data frames. In most cases, these frames are sent as unicast (directed) frames between the two endpoints.

Several standard and proprietary protocols exist for controlling calls over a VoIP system. H.323, Skinny Client Control Protocol (SCCP), and Session Initiation Protocol (SIP) are the most common and are covered in the following sections.

H.323

H.323 is an umbrella specification defined by the ITU-T (International Telecommunications Union—Telecommunications Standard Sector) that includes a group of protocols for voice and video over networks. H.323 is a well-established specification primarily designed by experts in the telephone industry. As a result, H.323 components and operation are similar to the standard analog telephone system. The biggest difference is that H.323 makes use of packet switching instead of circuit switching. Packet switching sends data representing the call in multiple packets, with each packet being sent independently through an end-to-end virtual TCP connection. Circuit switching, however, establishes a physical link between endpoints that supports a steady flow of a voice signal.

H.323 defines the following components:

- **Terminals**—These are endpoints, such as wireless IP phones, that may be audio-only; audio and video; audio and data; or audio, video, and data. The implementation of voice-only is the only one that is mandatory.

- **Gateway**—A gateway provides connections between terminals and the standard Public Switched Telephone Network (PSTN). It allows a warehouse clerk, for example, to use a wireless IP phone to call a customer having a standard analog telephone.

- **Gatekeeper**—A gatekeeper provides most of the call control actions, such as access control, bandwidth management, translation between telephone number and IP address, and call transfer. For example, Cisco CallManager provides gatekeeper functions.

- **Multipoint control units**—These devices enable conferencing to take place between multiple VoIP endpoints.

Traditional PSTN circuit-switched telephone systems implement signaling with various audible tones. You are likely familiar with the dial tone heard when taking a standard phone off the hook. As you dial a telephone number, you can hear the tone for each number. These dual-tone multifrequency (DTMF) tones enable components in the system to communicate control information, such as numbers dialed from the phone's keypad. Instead of audible tones, H.323 uses digital messages carried in packets to convey signaling information between components to process calls on a network. The dialed numbers, for example, are encoded into data carried in the RTP packet.

H.323 includes two primary standards that handle the calls: H.225 for call signaling and H.245 for call control. H.225 call signaling establishes a connection between endpoints, and H.245 communicates operational parameters for the connection. Also, H.225 Registration, Admission, and Status (RAS) may be incorporated if gatekeepers are in use.

The following defines each of the H.323 messages:

- **Registration Request (RRQ)**—H.225 RAS message sent from an endpoint to the gatekeeper after the endpoint powers up.

- **Registration Confirmation (RCF)**—H.225 RAS message sent from the gatekeeper to the endpoint requesting the registration to confirm that the registration is complete.

- **Registration Reject (RRJ)**—H.225 RAS message sent from the gatekeeper to the endpoint requesting the registration if the registration is not accepted.

- **Admission Request (ARQ)**—H.225 message sent by an endpoint to request admission to the network.

- **Bandwidth Change Request (BRQ)**—H.225 message sent by an endpoint to request a specific amount of network bandwidth.

- **Setup**—H.225 message sent by an endpoint to the remote endpoint to initiate a connection.

- **Call Proceeding**—H.225 message sent by the remote endpoint to indicate that the call is proceeding. The remote endpoint may be in the process of registering with the gatekeeper.

- **Alerting**—H.225 message sent by the remote endpoint to provide alert information.

- **Connect**—H.225 message sent by the remote endpoint to indicate that the connection is complete.

- **Terminal Capability Set**—H.245 messages sent between endpoints that include information on each endpoint, such as type of codec standard, sampling rate, and so on.

- **End Session**—H.245 message sent by the endpoint initiating the end of a call to the opposite endpoint to indicate the release of the call. This message is sent when someone hangs up his phone. The opposite endpoint responds with an End Session message.

- **Release Complete**—H.225 message sent from the endpoint initiating the end of the call to the opposite endpoint to indicate the completion of the call release.

For audio processing, H.323 requires the G.711 standard, which defines pulse code modulation of voice frequencies operating at 64 kbps that the codec implements. The following are optional audio standards:

- **G.722**—7-kHz audio coding at 64 kbps.

- **G.723.1**—Dual-rate speech coders for multimedia communication transmitting at 5.3 and 6.3 kbps.

- **G.728**—Coding of speech at 16 kbps using low-delay, code-excited linear prediction.

- **G.729**—Coding of speech at 8 kbps using conjugate-structure algebraic code–excited linear prediction.

After processing the audio, H.323 uses RTP and UDP to transport calls between endpoints. RTP Control Protocol (RTCP) works in conjunction with RTP and provides control services, such as feedback on the quality of the data distribution.

H.323 also includes the following supplementary services through the H.450 specification:

- **H.450.1**—Generic functions for the control of supplementary services in H.323
- **H.450.2**—Call transfer functions
- **H.450.3**—Call diversion functions
- **H.450.4**—Call hold functions
- **H.450.5**—Call park and pickup functions
- **H.450.6**—Call waiting functions
- **H.450.7**—Message waiting indication functions
- **H.450.8**—Name identification services functions
- **H.450.9**—Call completion services for H.323 networks

H.323 does not specify the type of network. The actual choice of network protocols, such as IEEE 802.11 or IEEE 802.3, is beyond the scope of H.323. Of course, for VoWLAN systems, IEEE 802.11 defines the network. Chapter 4, "Wireless LAN Technologies," provides details of the 802.11 standard that apply to VoWLAN systems. Most wired VoIP phones use IEEE 802.3, which is beyond the scope of this book.

Skinny Client Control Protocol (SCCP)

As a lightweight alternative to the full-blown H.323 standard, Cisco IP phones, such as the 7920 Wireless IP phone, use SCCP, which is a Cisco-proprietary protocol. The endpoints run Cisco's Skinny Client software, which implements SCCP. Cisco CallManager acts as an H.323 proxy and handles the H.323 protocols and takes on the majority of call control, which reduces the burden on the phone and wireless network. SCCP provides proprietary VoIP messaging between Cisco IP phones and Cisco CallManager. SCCP uses TCP/IP for data transport, but RTP and UDP convey the call directly between endpoints after a connection is made.

Table 3-1 documents the SCCP messages that are sent over TCP port 2000.

Table 3-1   *SCCP Messages Sent over TCP Port 2000*

Code	Station Message ID Message
0x0000	Keep Alive Message
0x0001	Station Register Message
0x0002	Station IP Port Message
0x0003	Station Key Pad Button Message

continues

Table 3-1 *SCCP Messages Sent over TCP Port 2000 (Continued)*

Code	Station Message ID Message
0x0004	Station Enbloc Call Message
0x0005	Station Stimulus Message
0x0006	Station Off Hook Message
0x0007	Station On Hook Message
0x0008	Station Hook Flash Message
0x0009	Station Forward Status Request Message
0x11	Station Media Port List Message
0x000A	Station Speed Dial Status Request Message
0x000B	Station Line Status Request Message
0x000C	Station Configuration Status Request Message
0x000D	Station Time Date Request Message
0x000E	Station Button Template Request Message
0x000F	Station Version Request Message
0x0010	Station Capabilities Response Message
0x0012	Station Server Request Message
0x0020	Station Alarm Message
0x0021	Station Multicast Media Reception Ack Message
0x0024	Station Off Hook with Calling Party Number Message
0x22	Station Open Receive Channel Ack Message
0x23	Station Connection Statistics Response Message
0x25	Station Soft Key Template Request Message
0x26	Station Soft Key Set Request Message
0x27	Station Soft Key Event Message
0x28	Station Unregister Message
0x0081	Station Keep Alive Message
0x0082	Station Start Tone Message
0x0083	Station Stop Tone Message
0x0085	Station Set Ringer Message
0x0086	Station Set Lamp Message
0x0087	Station Set Hook Flash Detect Message
0x0088	Station Set Speaker Mode Message

Table 3-1   *SCCP Messages Sent over TCP Port 2000 (Continued)*

Code	Station Message ID Message
0x0089	Station Set Microphone Mode Message
0x008A	Station Start Media Transmission
0x008B	Station Stop Media Transmission
0x008F	Station Call Information Message
0x009D	Station Register Reject Message
0x009F	Station Reset Message
0x0090	Station Forward Status Message
0x0091	Station Speed Dial Status Message
0x0092	Station Line Status Message
0x0093	Station Configuration Status Message
0x0094	Station Define Time & Date Message
0x0095	Station Start Session Transmission Message
0x0096	Station Stop Session Transmission Message
0x0097	Station Button Template Message
0x0098	Station Version Message
0x0099	Station Display Text Message
0x009A	Station Clear Display Message
0x009B	Station Capabilities Request Message
0x009C	Station Enunciator Command Message
0x009E	Station Server Respond Message
0x0101	Station Start Multicast Media Reception Message
0x0102	Station Start Multicast Media Transmission Message
0x0103	Station Stop Multicast Media Reception Message
0x0104	Station Stop Multicast Media Transmission Message
0x105	Station Open Receive Channel Message
0x0106	Station Close Receive Channel Message
0x107	Station Connection Statistics Request Message
0x0108	Station Soft Key Template Respond Message
0x109	Station Soft Key Set Respond Message
0x0110	Station Select Soft Keys Message

continues

Table 3-1 *SCCP Messages Sent over TCP Port 2000 (Continued)*

Code	Station Message ID Message
0x0111	Station Call State Message
0x0112	Station Display Prompt Message
0x0113	Station Clear Prompt Message
0x0114	Station Display Notify Message
0x0115	Station Clear Notify Message
0x0116	Station Activate Call Plane Message
0x0117	Station Deactivate Call Plane Message
0x118	Station Unregister Ack Message

Session Initiation Protocol (SIP)

SIP was developed by the Internet Engineering Task Force (IETF) and defined in RFC 2543. In contrast to H.323, SIP is based on existing Internet specifications, such as Hypertext Markup Language (HML) and Simple Mail Transfer Protocol (SMTP), and refers to VoIP components as clients and servers. Clients send SIP requests and receive SIP responses. Servers receive requests and service them. The different types of servers include a user agent server, which generates responses to SIP requests, a redirect server for redirecting a client to another server, and a registrar server that accepts and processes register requests. This environment is well understood by networking professionals. SIP is used with other IETF protocols, such as RTP, when deploying complete multimedia architecture.

SIP messages can be transmitted over either TCP or UDP. The messages have a syntax and header field that are similar to HTTP and include the following:

- **Register**—Endpoints send this message to the server to register an address with the server.
- **Invite**—This message is sent to invite another endpoint to participate in a call.
- **ACK**—The invited endpoint sends this message to confirm the Invite request message.
- **Bye**—When someone hangs up his phone, this message is sent by the applicable endpoint to indicate a call termination.
- **Cancel**—This message is sent to indicate a request cancellation.
- **Options**—This message is sent as an inquiry to determine the capability of a particular server.

SIP includes the following response messages:

- **1xx: Provisional responses**—Indicate that a particular request has been received.
- **2xx: Success responses**—Indicate that an action has been received, understood, and accepted.
- **3xx: Redirection responses**—Indicate that further action is required.
- **4xx: Client error responses**—Indicate that a request includes improper syntax and will not be processed by the server.
- **5xx: Server error responses**—Indicate that a server cannot fulfill a particular request.
- **6xx: Global failure responses**—Indicate that none of the servers can process the request.

SIP messages use the Uniform Resource Indicator (URI), which is an identification and addressing scheme. The SIP URI contains a username and hostname, just like an e-mail address. The following defines each of the SIP messages in a typical call:

- **Invite**—The endpoint initiating the call sends an Invite message to the remote (called) endpoint. This happens when the user takes his phone off the hook and dials the remote endpoint number.
- **180 Ringing**—The called phone rings, and it sends a 180 Ringing Response message to the endpoint initiating the call. This indicates that the called phone is ringing.
- **200 OK**—After the user of the called phone answers the call, the phone sends a 200 OK Response message to the endpoint initiating the call, indicating that the user has answered the call.
- **ACK**—This message is sent to acknowledge that the endpoint has received the 200 OK Response message.
- **Voice communications**—A two-way voice channel is established using RTP. At this point, a connection exists between the two endpoints for carrying voice conversations.
- **Bye**—When one of the users hangs up his phone, a Bye message is sent to the opposite endpoint.
- **200 OK**—After the opposite endpoint hangs up the call, the 200 OK message is sent to confirm the call termination.

Endpoints must communicate elements at the beginning of the session. The Session Announcement Protocol (SAP), defined in RFC 2974, and the Session Description Protocol (SDP), defined in RFC 2327, provide these elements. SAP advertises multimedia sessions, and SDP defines formatting for describing a communications session.

Radio Frequency (RF) Signals

Ultimately, voice packets are sent over a wireless link between the wireless IP phone and the nearest wireless access point.

Modulation

An RF signal has characteristics that enable it to be sent from an antenna, through the air medium, and be received by another antenna at the destination. RF signals are analog in nature. A computer, though, uses digital signals to represent bits of information.

Before transmitting data through the air, the transceiver within the radio cards and access points must convert digital signals into analog signals suitable for transmission through the air medium. As part of receiving an 802.11 frame, a radio card or access point must convert the analog signal back into a digital form that is understood by the computing device. This conversion process is known as modulation and demodulation, respectively.

The IEEE 802.11 standard defines several types of modulation, depending on which physical layer and data rate are in use by the 802.11 station. In general, modulating an RF carrier signal by changing its amplitude, frequency, or phase, as shown in Figure 3-1, is possible. For example, 802.11b uses phase shift keying (PSK) to represent digital data. The 802.11a and 802.11g standards, though, implement a combination of amplitude and phase shifts, which is referred to as quadrature amplitude modulation (QAM).

Figure 3-1 *Attributes of an RF Signal*

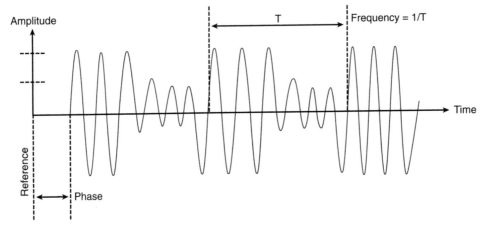

RF Signal Characteristics

RF signals are cyclic and vary in time continuously. The number of cycles that occurs in the signal per second is its frequency, which can vary throughout what is referred to as the frequency spectrum. The unit of frequency is Hertz (Hz), and wireless LAN signals fall roughly into the 2.4-GHz and 5-GHz portions of the frequency spectrum. The process of modulation causes the RF signal to occupy a portion of the frequency spectrum, which is known as bandwidth.

In addition to frequency, an RF signal at any time has specific amplitude. There are many ways to represent signal amplitude, but the most common with RF systems is signal power. The applicable unit for power is watt (W) or decibels relative to 1 milliwatt (dBm). The U.S. Federal Communications Commission (FCC) has rules for maximum transmitter output without licensing depending on the standard in use. For example, the maximum transceiver output for 802.11b in the United States is 1 W. In general, higher transmit power enables longer range operation. With special licensing, using amplifiers is possible.

Most wireless LAN systems have RF signals that fall into the milliwatt (mW) range, which makes the addition and multiplication of RF signals mathematically difficult. As a result, converting watts to dBm, which is a logarithmic value that references the signal power to 1 mW, is advantageous. The conversion formula is as follows:

$$dBm = 10 \log (mW)$$

For example, 100 mW equals 20 dBm.

Gain

The components of a wireless LAN offer varying degrees of *gain*, which represents how much a signal changes from one point to another. The gain in dB is simply the signal level at the output of a device (in dBm) minus the signal level at the input of the device (in dBm). The decibel is a unit that represents change in signal amplitude. A signal experiences a gain of 3 dB, for example, when it increases from 50 mW (17 dBm) to 100 mW (20 dBm). An amplifier or antenna may offer this gain to the signal.

Attenuation, or loss, is the inverse concept to gain. If the signal goes from 20 dBm to 17 dBm, the signal experiences attenuation of 3 dB. This can also be expressed as –3 dB gain. Antenna cabling and obstacles in a facility, such as walls and furniture, introduce attenuation. In addition, free space loss, which is dependent on frequency and path distance, is a form of attenuation. The free space loss occurs due to attenuation of the air medium and contributes to the majority of the total loss from the transmitter to the receiver. With wireless LANs, the RF signal amplitude must be of a specific minimum value before the radio card detects the signal. This value depends on the 802.11 physical layer and data rate in use but is approximately –85 dBm.

Antennas have gain, which impacts directivity of the RF signal. An omnidirectional antenna, for example, generally has a gain of 3 to 6 dB, or more, depending on the antenna design. Higher-gain antennas become more directive, with higher gains providing narrower beamwidths and longer range. Antenna gain comes from focusing a given amount of RF power into a narrower pattern, or beamwidth, much as a flashlight does.

Signal-to-Noise Ratio

If noise at the radio card is high, the radio card will have difficulty recovering the signal, which results in bit errors and retransmissions. An important signal measurement is the signal-to-noise ratio (SNR). The SNR (in dB) at a particular point in the network is simply the signal power (in dBm) minus the noise power (in dBm). A signal power of –65 dBm and noise power of –90 dBm yields an SNR of 25 dB. The noise power is anything other than signals corresponding to the access point or radio card.

Table 3-2 includes several SNR values and the resulting performance of an 802.11b network while using a Microsoft Windows XP laptop browsing websites and downloading files. The results depicted in Table 3-2 depict general end-user performance. The use of SNR to define the range boundary of an access point radio cell is more effective than either data rates or signal amplitudes. The higher degrees of noise cause more errors in frames and corresponding retransmissions. Note that Windows XP indicates the signal strength in a series of bars on a graph, showing no bars as poor quality and five bars as the best quality.

Table 3-2   *Correlation of SNR Values to Wireless LAN Performance*

SNR Value	Signal Indication (Windows XP)	Performance
> 40 dB	Excellent signal strength (five bars signal strength) and always connected with the access point	Extremely fast web browsing and file download
25–40 dB	Very good signal strength (three to four bars signal strength) and always connected with the access point	Very fast web browsing and file download
15–25 dB	Low signal strength (two bars signal strength) and always connected with the access point	Usually fast web browsing and file download
10–15 dB	Very low signal strength (one bar signal strength) and sometimes disconnected from the access point	Mostly slow web browsing and file download
5–10 dB	No signal strength (no bars) and not connected with the access point	No network services

NOTE   Cisco recommends a minimum of 25 dB SNR throughout the area where Cisco 7920 Wireless IP phones operate.

Spread Spectrum

In 1985, the FCC adopted regulations that specify the availability of license-free frequency bands in the 900-MHz, 2.4-GHz, and 5-GHz portions of the frequency spectrum. To be compliant with the rules for these bands, however, equipment must use spread spectrum or orthogonal frequency division multiplexing (OFDM) methods to spread the signal power over a relatively wide portion of the frequency spectrum. This approach promotes frequency reuse, otherwise known as sharing of these bands by multiple users with a low statistical probability of interference.

Spread spectrum was the first method in use by wireless LAN vendors. The two types of spread spectrum are

- **Frequency hopping spread spectrum (FHSS)**—With FHSS in the 2.4-GHz band, for example, the transceiver periodically tunes its transmitter and receiver to a different carrier frequency within approximately 84 MHz of bandwidth. Hopping from one frequency to another is done according to a hopping sequence programmed in each of the stations. The other stations receiving the frames tune their receivers to a specific frequency based on the hopping sequence. The RF signal occupies approximately a 2-MHz channel. Because the hopping occurs very often (many times per second) and uniformly over the entire band, the signal appears to occupy the entire 84 MHz. The 802.11 frequency-hopping physical layer standard enables data rates of 1 Mbps and 2 Mbps.

- **Direct sequence spread spectrum (DSSS)**—DSSS uses a coding technique to spread the signal over the frequency spectrum. The 802.11b standard uses direct sequence, which spreads the carrier signal over approximately one-third (30 MHz) of the 2.4-GHz band. With DSSS, a chipping code represents each data bit that needs transmission. This increases the signal rate by the number of bits in the chipping code (11 total). The increase in signal rate effectively spreads the RF signal. The differences between frequency hopping and direct sequence had been debated for a number of years, but the 802.11 working group finally selected direct sequence for extending the initial 1-Mbps and 2-Mbps 802.11 data rates to include rates up to 11 Mbps.

Orthogonal Frequency Division Multiplexing (OFDM)

OFDM is not a form of spread spectrum. Instead, OFDM divides a data signal across 48 separate subcarriers within a 20-MHz channel to provide transmissions of 6, 9, 12, 18, 24, 36, 48, or 54 Mbps. Data rates of 6 Mbps, 12 Mbps, and 24 Mbps are mandatory for all 802.11-compliant products. OFDM is extremely efficient, which enables it to provide the higher data rates. In addition, OFDM is highly immune to multipath propagation problems that cause significant performance issues with spread-spectrum techniques.

An 802.11a modulator converts the binary signal into an analog OFDM waveform through the use of different modulation types, depending on which data rate is chosen. For example, with 6-Mbps operation, 802.11a uses binary phase shift keying (BPSK), which shifts the phase of the transmit center frequency to represent different data bit patterns. The higher data rates, such as 54 Mbps, employ QAM to represent data bits by varying the transmit center frequency with different amplitude levels in addition to phase shifts.

Table 3-3 summarizes the primary attributes of the various wireless LAN technologies.

Table 3-3 *Wireless LAN Technology Comparison*

	Spread Spectrum?	**Maximum Data Rate**	**Standards**
FHSS	Yes	2 Mbps	802.11 FHSS
DSSS	Yes	11 Mbps	802.11b
OFDM	No	54 Mbps	802.11a and 802.11g

FCC Rules

In general, the FCC does not require users to license wireless LAN products, assuming that the user does not exceed certain emission limits. The FCC uses Effective Isotropic Radiated Power (EIRP) as a factor for determining whether a wireless LAN is in compliance with regulatory rules. EIRP equals the transmit power (in dBm) minus cable and connector losses (in dB) and plus the antenna gain (in dB). For 802.11b/g access points and radio cards, the EIRP can be up to 36 dBm, which includes a transmit power up to 30 dBm (4 watts) and 6 dBi antenna gain.

In addition, the user must obtain FCC licensing for the wireless LAN solution when using antennas or amplifiers that are not part of the access point vendor's products certified with the FCC. This licensing is necessary to ensure that the proposed wireless system will not interfere with existing systems at the location of operation. Regulatory agencies in other countries have similar rules, but they differ slightly depending on the country. As mentioned earlier, research your country's rules and deploy your systems based on them.

Wireless Impairments

The radio environment, which includes primarily the wireless LAN interface, is complex and presents several impairments to voice communications. The behavior of a wireless LAN is not as well understood and deterministic as a wired VoIP solution. The biggest problem with VoWLAN solutions is that wireless LANs may impair or disrupt the flow of UDP voice packets while calls are taking place. When deploying a VoWLAN system, understanding these impairments and trying to minimize them to maximize the capacity of the network and the quality of the voice calls is important.

Poor Signal Coverage

Signal coverage of a wireless LAN defines the space where wireless users can connect to the network and use the applications, such as carry-on voice communications from a wireless IP phone. Access points contribute to this coverage by forming overlapping radio cells. The actual cells generally have an irregular shape because of differing levels of attenuation caused by different physical environments. For example, the propagation of RF signals in one direction may be greater because nothing is in the way, but propagation in a different direction may have more walls and other objects, such as filing cabinets.

When defining coverage, you must understand what constitutes the edge of the radio cells, referred to as the range boundary (see Figure 3-2). The range boundary characterizes the circumference of the radio cell that each access point produces. With the boundaries known, a designer can make certain that the radio cells overlap enough to enable roaming and an adequate degree of redundancy. Knowing the boundaries may seem straightforward, but complications arise because of the nature of radio waves and the 802.11 protocol.

Figure 3-2 *RF Signal Coverage*

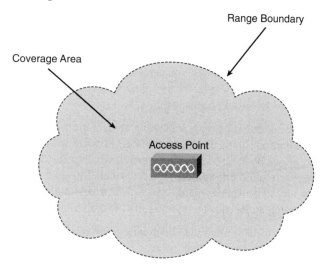

The range boundary of an access point based purely on connectivity indicates the point at which a user device can associate with an access point at a specific data rate. For example, you might define the connectivity range boundary to be at 11 megabits per second (Mbps), which means that the boundary exists where the associated data rate drops from 11 Mbps to 5.5 Mbps. Within this range boundary, all users have 11 Mbps associations. Similarly, you may define the boundary to be at 1 Mbps, which is when the associated data rate drops from 1 Mbps to the disassociated state. In general, you can define the connectivity range boundary to be any data rate that the access point supports.

Many companies deploying wireless LANs specify range boundary based only on connectivity, but this is not sufficient for systems needing to support many users or higher-end applications, such as voice. The issue is that data rate alone does not provide a true metric for user performance. The definition of range boundaries based on connectivity introduces significant risk when planning and managing the performance of the wireless LAN.

One user having an 11-Mbps association with an access point may be relatively free from RF interference and have nearly maximum throughput (approximately 6 Mbps for 802.11b). In this case, using range boundaries based on connectivity would probably be satisfactory, assuming the user conditions do not change. Users can carry on voice communications over wireless IP phones without any difficulties.

A more likely scenario, however, entails multiple users experiencing RF interference from a nearby microwave oven. Each user may have an 11-Mbps association with the access point, but the interference could cause each user to experience 50 percent frame retransmissions. This interference would significantly reduce the total throughput for users to unacceptable levels that do not adequately support the required number of simultaneous wireless voice calls.

With voice applications, signal coverage of a wireless LAN should define the space where wireless users can connect to the network and use the applications at a specific quality level. The signal coverage area should allow a wireless IP phone, for example, to connect to an access point and enable the user to carry on a conversation with another person using a different phone. This means that you need to ensure that frame retransmissions are kept to an acceptable level (preferably below 1 percent) and that enough channel capacity exists to support all simultaneous calls.

As a result, in addition to simply indicating association with an access point, the range boundary definition should also include effects of noise and interference. Doing so defines the useful service boundary of an access point, which is the distance at which the SNR is just high enough to provide sufficient performance. Designers should use this definition of range boundary when specifying the location of access points for voice systems, such as when performing an RF site survey to verify coverage.

The use of SNR for defining range boundaries with quality in mind generally produces smaller radio cells for each access point as compared to using connectivity alone to define the boundary. An acceptable SNR depends on the actual application, but 25 dB to 30 dB SNR generally provides optimum performance for maximum capacity wireless LANs.

A problem is that many existing wireless LANs have varying degrees of signal coverage throughout a facility. In some areas, signal coverage for a particular wireless LAN may be good enough to enable a wireless laptop to connect, but downloading a file from the Internet may take a considerable amount of time due to low signal levels. This kind of coverage results in high retransmissions and low data rates. This situation may suffice for data applications, but it is likely not good enough to carry on a quality voice call. The corresponding delay of voice packets causes the voice to sound poor.

NOTE   For optimum operation, a Cisco 7920 Wireless IP Phone requires a minimum signal level of –65 dBm and SNR of 25 dB.

Poor signal coverage is often found in existing wireless LANs, such as that shown in Figure 3-3. Coverage holes are usually present in particular areas, such as stairwells, elevators, and remote parts of the facility. These places generally are not where traditional wireless applications are planned to operate. As a result, these places within a facility pose connection problems when users try using their wireless IP phones. Fully defining required coverage areas and carefully designing the wireless LAN to provide enough signal strength is important.

Figure 3-3   *RF Signal Coverage Holes in a Facility*

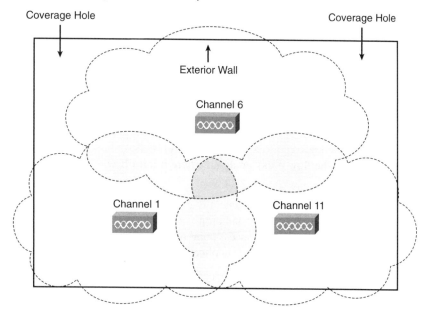

Poor signal coverage may appear in parts of the facility over time based on changes made within the radio environment. A company, for example, may install a long row of metal filing cabinets along a wall, which will significantly attenuate the propagation of radio signals. Or a warehouse may reconfigure the layout of storage racks, which may impact the coverage pattern.

As a result, performing an RF signal analysis of the locations where VoWLAN users will reside is very important. Doing so ensures that signal levels are high enough in all areas where users will operate wireless IP phones. Be certain to do this analysis whenever significant changes are made to the environment, and follow up with changes made to the configuration of the network. Refer to Chapter 8, "Installing, Configuring, and Testing a VoWLAN System," for details on how to perform an RF site survey for voice applications.

Latency

Because of medium access delays, standard 802.11 wireless LANs offer greater latency as compared to higher-speed wired Ethernet systems. Each wireless device, such as a wireless IP phone or access point associated with the same access point (same radio cell), must take turns sending data frames that carry information. Under high levels of utilization, the delays can become substantial and disrupt wireless voice applications.

In contrast, the delays resulting from a heavily loaded wireless network are not always a problem with data-only applications, such as e-mail or file transfer. A person sending e-mail, for example, probably does not care if it takes 150 ms or 3 s to send the e-mail. The longer and varying delays generally are not noticeable to the user. This delay can, however, impact the operation of real-time voice applications. In extreme cases, call connections may drop or the voice conversation will be choppy and unintelligible.

When users roam about a facility, their wireless IP phones periodically reassociate with access points having stronger beacon signals. This process supports any existing flow of 802.11 data frames. For example, a user may download a file from a server over the wireless network. The reassociation process disrupts the flow of the data frames for a period of time (referred to as roaming delay) while the reassociation process takes place, but then the flow picks up again where it left off when the reassociation is complete.

Interaccess point roaming delay generally goes unnoticed to users of data-only applications, but it may be disruptive and drop voice call connections if the delay is large enough. In most cases, an interaccess point roaming delay must be less than 100 ms to ensure effective operation of voice applications.

A mesh network, which is an interconnection of wireless LAN routers, may offer additional delays that may impact the operation of voice applications. For example, one voice user may associate via 802.11 with a nearby mesh node and communicate with a user associated with a mesh node several miles away. As a result, the voice packets hop through several nodes. This hopping may result in delays that are not acceptable for voice communications.

NOTE   Task Group R of the 802.11 Working Group is developing a new standard (802.11r) that addresses fast and secure transitions of wireless stations between access points.

RF Interference

Several sources of RF interference for wireless LANs can impact the performance of VoWLAN applications. As 802.11 data frames are in flight between the radio card and the access point carrying voice packets, the presence of an interfering RF signal may cause bit errors and resulting frame retransmissions. When interference is high, retransmission rates are relatively high, such as 20 percent. This rate produces a significant amount of overhead and consumes a great deal of the wireless LAN's capacity. In most cases, an interfering source may cause some distortion in the sound of the voice and limit the number of phones that can operate simultaneously. Severe RF interference can even block wireless IP phones from transmitting anything, but that is rare.

Most sources of RF interference, such as microwave ovens, cordless phones, frequency-hopping systems, and other wireless LANs, fall within the 802.11b/g 2.4-GHz band. The 802.11a 5-GHz bands are virtually free from RF interference. Figure 3-4 shows spectrum scans that provide signatures of various types of interfering sources.

Figure 3-4   *Various Signatures of RF Interference Sources*

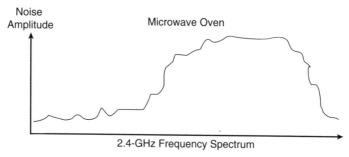

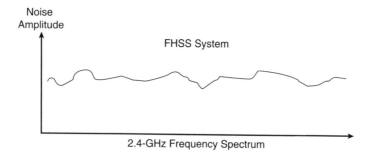

Microwave ovens emit damaging interfering signals at up to 25 feet or so of an operating oven. The interfering signals, however, only occupy approximately one-third of the 2.4-GHz band, depending on the type of microwave oven. This means that tuning the access point near a microwave oven to a noninterfering channel is possible. For example, the RF signal signature of the microwave oven depicted in Figure 3-4 covers the top third of the 2.4-GHz band. As a result, an access point closest to the microwave oven could be set to channel 1 and not suffer much impact from the interfering signals. Keep in mind that the microwave oven's interfering signal is present only while the oven is operating, which may not be very often. For example, a microwave oven in a break room may be in use only a few times during lunch and may be idle the rest of the day.

Microwave Oven Interference Testing

In a test laboratory, during a conversation between two Cisco 7920 Wireless IP Phone users, a microwave oven was turned on to introduce RF interference. The RF channel of the access point was set to channel 9, which is the part of the frequency band (for this particular oven) having the highest impact from the microwave oven interference. No noticeable difference was apparent in voice quality with and without the microwave oven operating. Throughput tests indicate that the capacity of the access point decreases by 30 percent, however. This decrease reduces the total number of wireless phones that this system can support while a microwave oven is operating, assuming that the access point in that area is set to a channel that conflicts with the microwave oven. Spectrum scans for this particular microwave oven indicate that most of the signals propagating from the oven are above channel 6. In fact, setting the microwave oven to channel 1 leads to only 5 percent degradation in access point capacity when the oven is operating. As a result, avoiding this form of interference by carefully analyzing the radio environment through the use of a spectrum analyzer is possible.

Bluetooth devices and some cordless phones and legacy wireless LANs use FHSS, which spreads the transmitted signal power over the entire 2.4-GHz band (refer to Figure 3-4). No matter what channel you set in an 802.11b/g access point, the FHSS signal is always present. An 802.11b/g signal only interferes with roughly one-third of the FHSS signal, however, which does not cause much damage to the FHSS signal. As a result, FHSS signals interfere much more with 802.11b/g systems rather than the opposite. At least Bluetooth devices operate at very low transmit power, which does not have much impact on the stronger signals of a well-designed wireless LAN. An existing wireless LAN implementing FHSS has relatively strong and continuous signals that have the greatest impact on 802.11b/g systems.

As part of the installation of a VoWLAN system, definitely analyze the RF spectrum of the environment, and determine whether sources of RF interference may disrupt the operation of the wireless LAN. In most cases, you can use the combination of a spectrum analyzer and knowledge of the potential interfering devices in the facility to characterize the interference. If microwave ovens are present, run them while observing the RF spectrum on the analyzer. Use this information to determine what nonconflicting channels to use for the access points. If interference is relatively high throughout the operating band of the wireless LAN, you may be able to compensate by placing the access points closer together and providing higher signal strength throughout the coverage areas.

NOTE   Wi-Spy is an inexpensive RF spectrum analyzer by Metageek (http://www.metageek.net) that consists of a USB-based dongle that interfaces with software running on a laptop or PC. User interface software displays the amplitude of signals across the 2.4-GHz band. Pre-recorded signals of various interference sources, such as microwave ovens and FHSS devices, illustrate typical corresponding interference signatures.

Limited Capacity

The existing usage of a wireless LAN affects available capacity for supporting voice calls. Without any existing utilization, only beacons and occasional 802.11 null data frames and probe requests are present on the network. Some client radio cards send a null data frame with the power-management bit set before scanning other channels, which causes the associated access point to buffer any downstream data frames while the client radio is scanning other channels. When scanning, some client radios send probe requests on each channel to receive immediate responses from access points that are within range of the client. In addition, some clients may send other packets, such as dynamic host configuration protocol (DHCP) packets. All of this activity, however, consumes only 1 to 3 percent of the capacity of an 802.11g access point. Under this somewhat idle condition, the wireless network can support the maximum number of simultaneous VoIP calls.

The number of calls that each access point can support depends on the wireless technology chosen. A typical RTP data packet carries a 20-ms voice sample, and the total size of the packet is 228 bytes (1824 bits). RTP traffic is generally sent at 50 pps in each direction, or 100 pps for a full-duplex conversation, which results in 22,800 bytes per second (182,400 bps). The theoretical maximum throughput available from a single 802.11b channel operating at an 11-Mbps data rate, for example, is 324,573 bytes per second (2,596,588 bps), which results in support for a maximum of 14.235 calls (324,573 / 22,800). When planning a VoIP deployment, however, you should only count on approximately 60 percent of the total capacity being available for calls. With this percentage in mind, the total number of calls supported would be 8.54.

As utilization from nonvoice applications increases, not as much room remains for the voice calls. As a result, the total number of simultaneous calls that the access points can support decreases. The degradation in call capacity is difficult to model because it depends on many factors. For example, 10 wireless users may be downloading very large files from a web server on the Internet. The utilization from this activity may consume only 10 percent of the capacity if the Internet connection speed is relatively low, but it could be 70 percent if the Internet connection speed is high. In addition, a raw, high-resolution video stream may consume nearly all the capacity of an access point, or it may consume very little if the video stream has low resolution and is implementing compression.

You need to measure the utilization of an existing wireless network with typical usage of nonvoice applications as the basis for determining the remaining capacity for supporting simultaneous voice calls. Keep in mind that if the utilization of the wireless LAN is high resulting from non-VoWLAN traffic, such as frequent file downloads and video streaming, the retransmission rates will be higher than if the load on the network were lighter. These additional retransmissions can consume a significant additional amount of the overall capacity. The best way to assess utilization and available capacity is to actually measure it.

NOTE   Airmagnet Analyzer includes a feature for measuring the channel utilization of a wireless LAN. You can click any 802.11 channel and view the percent utilization and throughput for that particular channel.

The existence of neighboring wireless LANs may also impact the available capacity of the wireless LAN supporting voice applications. The degree of interference, however, depends on the RF channel settings and utilization of the neighboring wireless LAN. Interference is possible if access points of the neighboring network are set to channels that overlap with access points of the voice network, and the conflicting access points are within radio range of each other. Figure 3-5 illustrates this scenario.

Figure 3-5   *Interference from Neighboring Wireless LANs*

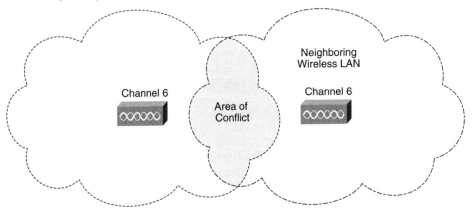

With the neighboring wireless LAN somewhat idle (no significant data traffic), the majority of the interference comes from the neighboring access point beacons. This ends up consuming only about 2 percent of the wireless LAN's capacity. The interference does become significant, however, as the utilization of the neighboring wireless LAN increases. If a neighboring wireless user begins downloading a file, the activity consumes some of the capacity of the users and access points near the neighbor (if both networks are set to conflicting channels). Roughly speaking, the degradation in capacity of the voice system will be approximately equal to the utilization of the neighboring access point.

To minimize impacts of neighboring wireless LANs, determine the operating channels of nearby access points, and avoid using these channels where conflicts will occur. Some access points, such as the Cisco 1200, support a configuration whereby the access point automatically selects the least-congested RF channel. This feature makes installation and configuration of the network much easier. Be certain, though, that the access point does not change channels too often, because that forces associated clients, such as wireless IP phones, to reassociate. Frequent reassociations can cause disruption to voice calls.

Multipath

Multipath interference occurs when an RF signal takes different paths when propagating from one wireless station to another. While the signal is en route, walls, chairs, desks, and other items get in the way and cause the signal to bounce in different directions. A portion of the signal might go directly to the destination, and another part might bounce from a chair to the ceiling, and then to the destination. As a result, some of the signal encounters delay because it has to travel over a longer path to the receiver.

Multipath interference causes the information symbols received by an 802.11 signal to overlap, which causes the receiver to have difficulty demodulating the signal. This effect is often referred to as intersymbol interference (ISI). Because the shape of the signal conveys the information being transmitted, the receiver demodulates errored data. If the delays are great enough, bit errors in the packet occur. The receiver cannot distinguish the symbols and interpret the corresponding bits correctly. As a result, the sending station must retransmit the affected frames.

Because of retransmissions, users encounter lower throughput when multipath interference is significant. The reduction in throughput depends on the environment. For example, 802.11 signals in homes and offices might encounter 50-nanosecond multipath delay spread whereas signals in a manufacturing plant could encounter delay spread as long as 300 nanoseconds. As the delay spread increases, the effective radio cells become smaller. Based on these values, multipath interference is not too much of a problem in homes and offices. Metal machinery and racks in a plant, however, provide a lot of reflective surfaces for RF signals to bounce off of and take erratic paths from. As a result, be wary of multipath problems in warehouses, processing plants, and other areas full of irregular metal obstacles. In-high-multipath environments, you should analyze range boundaries with an actual wireless IP phone.

Antenna diversity can aid in combating multipath propagation. An access point may implement a spatial diversity antenna system that consists of two antennas that interchangeably receive and transmit radio signals. An access point will receive a signal on both antennas, but many times, because of multipath propagation and interference, the same signal does not reach both antennas at the same time and strength. The access point then performs internal calculations to optimize the received signal. The main benefits of spatial diversity antenna systems are improved coverage and signal reception.

Chapter Summary

In contrast to traditional data-only applications, such as e-mail and file downloads, voice and video require a real-time transfer of information. Voice and video systems must use a codec to convert analog voice and video into digital signals that can be placed into packets. PCM is one of the most common types of codecs; it converts a voice signal into a 64-Kbps stream of data. Raw video streams, even those having limited frame rates and resolution, require much higher data rates, but video uses compression, such as MPEG-4, to significantly reduce capacity requirements.

Most VoIP systems allow endpoints, such as wireless IP phones, to communicate signaling information (off hook, number dialed, and so on) to one another through the transmission of messages. This type of communication is in contrast to the standard PSTN, which uses audible tones. After a call is established between two VoIP endpoints, UDP and RTP packets carry the voice data, which is the majority of traffic related to the VoIP communications taking place over the wireless link.

VoIP technologies include H.323, SIP, and SCCP. H.323 is a relatively old standard developed from the ground up primarily by PSTN telecom companies. SIP is a newer specification developed by the IETF and based primarily on existing IETF specifications, such as HTTP and SMTP. To reduce impacts on the wireless network, Cisco implements SCCP in all its wireless IP phones, which is similar to H.323.

Various impairments reduce the performance of voice communications over wireless networks. Poor signal coverage reduces the quality of phone calls, and significant inter-access point delays can drop calls. RF interference may also produce a substantial amount of overhead that reduces the capacity of the wireless network in supporting simultaneous calls. As a result, you must pay close attention to the radio environment when deploying wireless voice applications.

Chapter Review Questions

1 What is the audible frequency range that VoIP systems support?

2 What is the function of a codec?

3 In what scenario does compression offer the greatest savings in capacity?

4 What protocol provides the end-to-end network transport functions for real-time streaming of data?

5 What are the biggest differences between VoIP and standard analog telephone systems?

6 What is the purpose of a gateway in an H.323 system?

7 What VoIP is used between Cisco VoIP phones and Cisco CallManager?

8 What is the signal-to-noise ratio if the noise is –90 dBm and the signal is –65 dBm?

9 How much delay can most wireless IP phones tolerate to avoid dropping a call when roaming from one access point to another?

10 How can you design a wireless LAN to minimize the impact of microwave oven interference and neighboring wireless LANs?

Critical Technologies

Objectives

Upon completing this chapter, you will be able to

- Describe the operation of a wireless LAN.
- Define typical wireless LAN configuration settings.
- Differentiate pros and cons of 802.11a, 802.11b, and 802.11g.

CHAPTER 4

Wireless LAN Technologies

To effectively design a VoWLAN system, ensuring that you fully understand the operation of 802.11 wireless LANs is important. This chapter describes applicable elements, such as Media Access Control (MAC) layer frames and Physical (PHY) layer options. It focuses on how these elements impact the operation of VoWLAN applications and system design. Special attention is given to options that govern the behavior of a VoWLAN system.

The IEEE 802.11 standard, which is similar in scope and functionality to IEEE 802.3 (Ethernet), is a common basis for wireless LAN operation. As with 802.3, the 802.11 standard defines a common MAC and multiple physical layers, such as 802.11a, 802.11b, and 802.11g.

Infrastructure Mode

An infrastructure wireless LAN (sometimes referred to as infrastructure mode) is what most companies, public hotspots, and home users implement. An infrastructure wireless LAN, as shown in Figure 4-1, offers a means to extend a wired network. In this configuration, one or more access points interface wireless mobile devices to the distribution system, which interconnects the access points and connects them to the rest of the network. Each access point forms a radio cell, also called a Basic Service Set (BSS), which enables wireless users located within the cell to have connectivity to the access point.

Each access point in the infrastructure wireless LAN creates a radio cell, with a coverage area that depends on the following variables:

- Facility construction
- Chosen 802.11 physical layer
- Transmit power
- Antenna type

The range of the coverage area is typically 150 feet in most enterprise facilities. The desired level of performance, however, can impact the effective range of the access points. For example, the use of fixed 11-Mbps data rates can limit range considerably as compared to 1 Mbps. Also, when the client radios are configured for automatic data rate, the data rate generally decreases as you operate the client farther away from the access point. So, you might have coverage at farther distances, but the performance will likely be less.

Figure 4-1   *Infrastructure Wireless LAN*

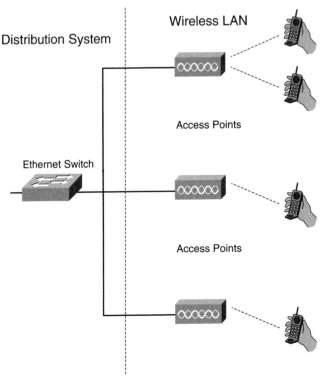

With the infrastructure configuration, data traffic going from one wireless user to another user must travel through the access point. The access point determines whether the traffic is destined for the distribution system or another wireless user. If the traffic is destined for the distribution system, the access point forwards the applicable data to the wired side of the access point. This is the route that Voice over Internet Protocol (VoIP) traffic takes between a Cisco 7920 wireless Internet Protocol (IP) phone and Cisco CallManager, shown in Figure 4-2 as Route A. It is also the route for traffic between two wireless IP phones connected to different access points, which Figure 4-2 illustrates as Route B.

When calls are taking place between two users connected to the same access point, as shown in Figure 4-3, the impact on utilization doubles as compared to users connected to different access points. The reason for the increase in utilization is because users on a common access point must share the same radio frequency (RF) channel, whereas users connected to different access points operate on nonoverlapping channels. This scenario assumes that proper channel reuse is kept in mind when installing the wireless LAN.

Figure 4-2 *Packet Routing Through an Infrastructure Wireless LAN*

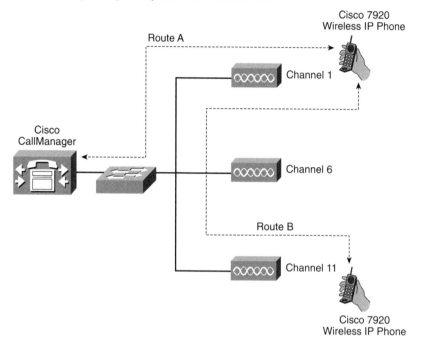

Figure 4-3 *Packet Routing Between Wireless IP Phones Connected to the Same Access Point*

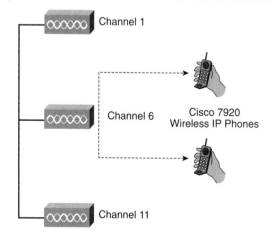

Figure 4-4 illustrates the three possible 802.11 radio cell configurations, which include partial overlap, collocated, and disjointed cells. If a company installs access points with overlapping radio cells, as shown in part A of Figure 4-4, users can roam throughout the facility. This solution is necessary to support use of the network while users are moving throughout a facility. The radio card within the user's mobile device automatically reassociates with access points having stronger signals. For example, a user might begin a phone call when associated with access point A. As the user walks out of range of access point A and within range of access point B, the wireless LAN automatically reassociates the user to access point B, and the user's call continues through access point B.

Figure 4-4   *Various 802.11 Radio Cell Configurations*

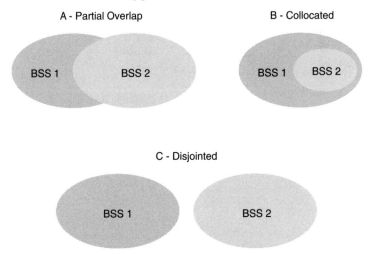

The 802.11 standard also supports collocated (part B of Figure 4-4) and disjointed radio cells (part C of Figure 4-4). A company might install disjointed access points because complete coverage throughout the facility is not necessary. For example, the company might install an access point in each conference room and not the rest of the building. This method allows users to make calls from only the conference room while away from their wired desk phones.

If the radio cells are disjointed, users temporarily lose the network connection and then reassociate when roaming within range of another access point. An 802.11 network supports this form of network, which is similar to the roaming with the overlapping radio cells. The reassociation delay is a function of the time it takes the user to move into range of the next access point. The wireless application in use, however, might or might not be able to tolerate this longer roaming delay. The longer delays might not support mobile voice applications; however, users can at least initiate and carry on calls from the covered areas.

The collocated radio cell configuration is useful if a company needs greater capacity than what a single access point can deliver. In this scenario, two or more access points are set up so that their radio cells overlap significantly. This setup works well, assuming that the access points are set to nonconflicting radio channels. A portion of the users in the area, for example, associate with access point A, and the other users associate with access point B. This setup boosts the wireless LAN capacity in that particular area. In this case, you effectively get 2 times 11 Mbps for performance in that particular area of the facility.

The collocation of access points is a good method of increasing capacity for supporting a greater number of voice users. A single 802.11b access point can support eight simultaneous users. If the simultaneous call density in a particular area is 16, you can install two access points. For this technique to work effectively, you must set the access points to nonoverlapping channels and implement a method to balance the load across the two access points.

Scanning

In an infrastructure wireless LAN, each radio card implements a scanning function to find access points. Scanning occurs after the user device boots, and periodically afterward to support roaming. The 802.11 standard defines two scanning methods:

- Passive scanning
- Active scanning

Passive Scanning

The following list describes how a radio card uses passive scanning:

1 The radio card automatically tunes to each RF channel, listens for a period of time, and records information it finds about access points on each channel.

2 By default, each access point transmits a beacon frame every 100 m on a specific RF channel, which the administrator configures.

3 While tuned to a specific channel, the radio card receives these beacon frames if an access point is in range and transmitting on that channel.

4 The radio card records the signal strength of the beacon frame and continues to scan other channels.

5 After scanning each of the RF channels, the radio card decides which access point it will associate with.

In general, the radio card selects the access point with the strongest beacon signal. Some radio vendors might include other parameters, such as noise levels and utilization, when deciding which access point to associate with.

Active Scanning

The following list describes how a radio card uses active scanning:

1 The radio card sends probe request frames on each RF channel.

2 Access points that can receive the probe request respond by sending a probe response. The probe response is similar to a beacon frame. Active scanning, however, enables the radio card to receive information about nearby access points in a timely manner, without waiting for beacons.

3 The radio card uses the signal strength and possibly other information corresponding to the probe response frame to decide which access point it will associate with.

Each radio card vendor implements scanning differently. The chosen method of scanning significantly impacts the speed at which the radio roams between access points. The radio card in use with the Cisco 7920 wireless IP phone implements scanning that minimizes roaming delays.

Connecting with a Network

After obtaining a list of potential access points via either passive or active scanning, the radio card moves forward with joining the network by tuning to the RF channel of the chosen access point. To initiate association, the radio card sends an authentication request frame, and the access point responds with an authentication response frame. This is the default authentication that 802.11 refers to as open system authentication. In most cases, this form of authentication is desirable. 802.11 offers the optional shared key authentication, which uses a wired equivalent privacy (WEP) key to authenticate the radio card, but WEP is relatively easy to hack. Therefore, companies should use stronger forms of authentication, such as 802.1x, that rely on authentication servers.

After performing the authentication handshake, the radio card sends an association request frame to the access point. This request contains information about the radio card, including the service set identifier (SSID) and the radio card's supported data rates. The SSID must match the one configured in the access point for association to complete. The access point replies to the radio card with an association response frame containing an association identifier (AID), which is a number that represents the radio card's association. At this point, the radio card is considered associated with the access point, and the radio card can then begin sending data frames to the access point and communicating with other nodes on the network.

Data Transfer

The exchange of data in an infrastructure network is bidirectional between the radio card and access point. As mentioned earlier, data frames in an infrastructure wireless LAN do not travel directly between wireless users. Instead, the access point relays the data.

A radio card or access point (802.11 station) having the destination MAC address of the data frame replies with an acknowledgment (ACK) frame. This frame adds significant overhead to a wireless LAN as compared to an Ethernet network that does not require ACKs for every data frame. The ACKs are necessary with 802.11 due to the nature of the shared radio medium; data loss is much more likely with the wireless medium, so wireless LANs perform error detection and error correction at Layer 2.

If an 802.11 station sending a data frame does not receive an ACK after a specific period of time, the station retransmits the frame. These retransmissions occur up to a particular limit, which is generally three to seven times. After that, higher-layer protocols, such as Transmission Control Protocol (TCP), must provide error recovery.

To allow for extended range, 802.11 includes automatic data rate shifting. For example, an 802.11 station generally lowers its transmission data rate if a retransmission is necessary. Access points support multiple data rates to facilitate this kind of operation, where different remote stations might transmit data upstream at different rates. With voice applications, however, operating with fixed data rates, such as 11 Mbps, is often beneficial. This method reduces issues with latency.

NOTE Cisco recommends disabling data rates less than 11 Mbps to ensure effective performance of the 7920 Wireless IP Phone.

Roaming

Periodically, each radio card performs scanning, either active or passive, to update its access point list. Some radio cards might limit the scanning function first to only RF channels where access points formerly had been found. This feature enables the radio card to offer higher throughput because the card cannot send or receive data frames while scanning other channels.

If the associated access point signal becomes too weak, the radio card implements a reassociation process. The radio card sends a reassociation frame to the new access point and a disassociation frame to the old access point. 802.11 does not require the authentication frame handshake when reassociating. If the old access point has buffered data frames destined for the radio card, the old access point forwards them to the new access point for delivery to the radio card.

As discussed in Chapter 3, "VoWLAN Signaling Fundamentals," excessive roaming delays severely disrupt wireless VoIP calls. An issue is that the existing 802.11 standard does not specify a roaming function. As a result, Task Group R of the 802.11 Working Group is developing a standard specifying fast transitions between Basic Service Sets (BSS). The 802.11r standard should be ratified by the IEEE in 2007 and will significantly improve roaming for wireless voice communications across multiple vendor access points.

Ad Hoc Mode

Instead of forming an infrastructure wireless LAN, the 802.11 standard allows users to optionally connect directly to each other in what is referred to as Ad Hoc mode, as shown in Figure 4-5. The rationale behind this form of networking is to enable users to spontaneously set up wireless LANs. This optional mode is available to users on most radio cards. With Ad Hoc, no need exists for access points. The wireless connection is made directly between the users in a peer-to-peer fashion.

Figure 4-5   *Ad Hoc Wireless LAN*

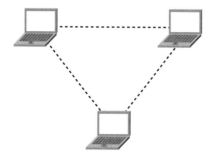

Ad Hoc mode is beneficial when a user needs to send a file to another user within the same room, and no other networking is practical. Both users can enable Ad Hoc mode on their radio cards, and the users can communicate wirelessly. The use of an Ad Hoc wireless LAN is also valuable when users need to rapidly establish a wireless network when responding to emergencies in areas where no network is in place.

Because Ad Hoc wireless LANs have no access points, the radio cards must send beacons. The Ad Hoc mode of operation transpires as follows:

1 After a user switches to Ad Hoc mode, the radio card begins sending beacons if one is not received within a specific period of time.

2 After receiving a beacon, each radio card waits a random period of time.

3 If a beacon is not heard from another station in this time, the station sends a beacon. The random wait period causes one of the stations to send a beacon before any other station. Over time, this distributes the job of sending beacons evenly across all 802.11 stations.

The sharing of the transmission of beacons among all Ad Hoc stations is necessary to ensure that beacons are still sent if a particular station becomes unavailable. If a station becomes disassociated with the network, another station sends the beacon.

With pure Ad Hoc networks, there is no direct connection to a wired network, which, of course, limits applications. In fact, Cisco's voice telephony system is not designed to operate over ad hoc wireless networks. A user, however, can configure an 802.11-equipped device as an Ad Hoc station, such as a PC, to provide a shared connection to a wired network. Thus, with specialized software or functions within the PC operating system, the PC can offer functions similar to those of an access point. All the other Ad Hoc stations needing to reach devices on the wired network route their packets through the PC's connection to the network.

Wireless Medium Access

Before transmitting frames, a station must gain access to the medium, which is a radio channel that stations share. The 802.11 standard defines two forms of medium access:

- Distributed coordination function (DCF)
- Point coordination function (PCF)

The following sections detail these two functions.

DCF

DCF is mandatory and is based on the Carrier Sense Multiple Access with Collision Avoidance (CSMA/CA) protocol. With DCF, 802.11 stations contend for access and attempt to send frames when no other station is transmitting. If another station is sending a frame, stations are polite and wait until the channel is free.

The following are details on how DCF works:

- As a condition of accessing the medium, the MAC layer checks the value of its network allocation vector (NAV), which is a counter resident at each station that represents the amount of time that the previous frame needs to send its frame. The NAV must be zero before a station can attempt to send a frame. Before transmitting a frame, a station calculates the amount of time necessary to send the frame based on the frame's length and data rate. The station places a value representing this time in the duration field in the header of the frame. When stations receive the frame, they examine this duration field value and use it as the basis for setting their corresponding NAVs. This process reserves the medium for the sending station.

- An important aspect of the DCF is a random back-off timer that a station uses if it detects a busy medium. If the channel is in use, the station must wait a random period of time before attempting to access the medium again. This feature ensures that multiple stations wanting to send data do not transmit at the same time. The random delay causes stations to wait different periods of time and avoids the situation where all of them sense the medium at exactly the same time, find the channel idle, transmit, and collide with each other. The back-off timer significantly reduces the number of collisions and corresponding retransmissions, especially when the number of active users increases.

- With radio-based local-area networks (LAN), a transmitting station cannot listen for collisions while sending data, mainly because the station cannot have its receiver on while transmitting the frame. As a result, the receiving station needs to send an acknowledgment (ACK) if it detects no errors in the received frame. If the sending station does not receive an ACK after a specified period of time, the sending station assumes that a collision (or RF interference) occurred and retransmits the frame.

PCF

For supporting time-bounded delivery of data frames, the 802.11 standard defines the optional PCF where the access point grants access to an individual station to the medium by polling the station during the contention-free period. Stations cannot transmit frames unless the access point polls them first. The period of time for PCF-based data traffic (if enabled) occurs alternately between contention (DCF) periods.

The access point polls stations according to a polling list and then switches to a contention period when stations use DCF. This process enables support for both synchronous (for example, video applications) and asynchronous (for example, e-mail and web-browsing applications) modes of operation. No known wireless NICs or access points on the market today, however, implement PCF.

802.11 Physical Layer Standards

The initial 802.11 wireless LAN standard, ratified in 1997, specifies the use of both direct sequence spread spectrum (DSSS) and frequency hopping spread spectrum (FHSS) for delivering 1-Mbps and 2-Mbps data rates in the 2.4-GHz band. DSSS and FHSS are different forms of transmitting data over a wireless LAN. This bandwidth was plenty for supporting bar code applications, which was the first commercial use of wireless LANs.

802.11a

In 1999, the 802.11 group ratified the 802.11a standard, which offers data rates up to 54 Mbps in the 5-GHz band using Orthogonal Frequency Division Multiplexing (OFDM). Even though the 802.11a standard was available in 1999, 802.11a access points and radio cards did not become commercially available until several years later. The primary reasons for the delay to market were the difficulties in developing 5-GHz 802.11 hardware and the weak market potential for wireless LAN components that do not interoperate with existing DSSS wireless LANs. 802.11a products are available now, but their use is somewhat limited to specialized applications, especially where high performance is necessary. An issue is that most wireless IP phones do not currently interface with 802.11a access points.

A significant advantage of 802.11a is that it offers very high capacity as compared to the other physical layers. The reason is that the 802.11a 5-GHz spectrum defines 12 RF channels that do not overlap in frequency. As a result, having up to 12 802.11a access points set to different channels and operating within the same room is possible. This setup produces up to 12 separate radio cells that can support their own group of wireless users. Most indoor 802.11a access points implement only eight of these RF channels, but that still provides a large potential capacity as compared to 802.11b and 802.11g.

Another advantage of 802.11a is that it operates in the 5-GHz band, which is mostly free from sources of RF interference. Microwave ovens, Bluetooth devices, most cordless phones, and the majority of neighboring wireless LANs operate in the 2.4-GHz band of frequencies. The lower noise floor in the 5-GHz band affords lower retransmission rates and higher resulting throughput as compared to 802.11b and 802.11g systems.

On the other hand, 802.11a has limited regulatory acceptance around the world. In fact, some countries do not yet allow 802.11a networks. This situation could certainly impact the selection of the 802.11 physical layer (a, b, or g) for products that you want to use worldwide.

802.11b

To provide higher data rates when operating in the 2.4-GHz band, the 802.11 group ratified the 802.11b physical layer in 1999, enhancing the initial DSSS physical layer to include additional 5.5-Mbps and 11-Mbps data rates. Very soon after ratification of the 802.11b standard, 802.11b access points and radio cards began shipping. It was a fairly easy modification for existing 802.11 DSSS devices to become 802.11b-compliant. In fact, most users could upgrade their existing access points and radio cards with simple firmware upgrades. For several years, 802.11b devices were the best ones on the market, so they proliferated throughout the industry and became the most common installed wireless LAN hardware.

An advantage of 802.11b, then, is that it interoperates well with the majority of installed wireless LANs. That is why most wireless user devices include 802.11b. It is not compatible with 802.11a, but 802.11b does interface with 802.11g systems.

Much more RF interference, however, resides in the 2.4-GHz band, which impacts 802.11b users. As mentioned earlier, a microwave oven can cause significant degradation in throughput because radio waves from the oven can block 802.11b and 802.11g radio cards from accessing the medium or create bit errors in the 802.11 frames in transit. The potential for RF interference in the 2.4-GHz band is one reason why a company should strongly consider using 802.11a solutions.

A limiting factor of 802.11b is that it supports only up to three nonoverlapping radio cells in the same area. The 2.4-GHz frequency spectrum is roughly 84 MHz wide, and an 802.11b radio card or access point uses approximately 30 MHz when transmitting. To avoid interaccess point interference, 802.11b access points must be set to specific channels. For example, access points in the United States can be set to channels 1, 6, and 11 to avoid overlap and mutual interference. This factor is especially important to consider if there are many active wireless users. As a result of this frequency plan and limited data rates, 802.11b has limited capacity.

802.11g

802.11g, ratified in 2004, is the most recent 802.11 physical layer, which further enhances 802.11b to include data rates up to 54 Mbps in the 2.4-GHz band using OFDM. 802.11g is backward-compatible with 802.11b, which is referred to as *802.11b/g mixed-mode operation*. For example, an 802.11b radio card can associate with an 802.11g access point. Most organizations today are deploying 802.11g wireless LANs. Because of its support for data rates up to 54 Mbps, 802.11g offers higher performance than 802.11b systems. Capacity is still somewhat limited, however, because 802.11g operates in the 2.4-GHz band, which limits the number of nonoverlapping channels to three, as with 802.11b. As a result, 802.11g systems have less capacity than 802.11a wireless LANs. 802.11g, for example, can have up to three nonoverlapping channels with 54 Mbps per channel. 802.11a, however, can have up to 12 nonoverlapping channels with 54 Mbps per channel.

A single 802.11b station associating with an 802.11g access point invokes the use of protection mechanisms, such as request-to-send/clear-to-send (RTS/CTS). The reason that these mechanisms are necessary is that 802.11b and 802.11g use different modulation, which means that they cannot interoperate and coordinate transmissions according to the 802.11 protocol. The access point informs all stations that an 802.11b station is present by setting an applicable bit in the body of each beacon frame. As a result, all stations begin using protection mechanisms.

The RTS/CTS protection mechanism requires each station to implement the entire RTS/CTS process for each data frame needing transmission. The problem with this requirement is that throughput suffers because of the RTS and CTS frames. Thus, a mixed environment of 802.11b and 802.11g users significantly degrades the throughput of the wireless LAN, often by as much as 30 percent, which reduces the number of simultaneous voice calls that the network can support.

This reason is why most vendors allow administrators to configure access points to allow only 802.11g station associations, referred to as 802.11g-only mode. Of course, the problem with this restriction is that all users must have 802.11g radio cards. 802.11b-equipped devices will not be able to associate with the access point. But at least the throughput will remain relatively high.

Some vendors also allow you to disable protection mechanisms in mixed mode, which supports both 802.11b and 802.11g connections. This approach is good if there are a limited number of active users because the probability of 802.11b and 802.11g devices transmitting at the same time is minimal.

If the need exists to effectively support 802.11b and 802.11g users, especially when there are larger numbers of active users, you should consider a "dual-mode" access point. These access points provide separate 802.11b and 802.11g radios in the access points that are set to different, nonoverlapping RF channels. The 802.11g radios in the access points in this case are set to 802.11g-only. This setting forces the 802.11b users to associate with the 802.11b side of the access point, and the 802.11g users associate with the 802.11g side of the access point. Because each side is to a different channel, protection mechanisms are not needed.

802.11n

The 802.11 working group is actively developing a new physical layer known as 802.11n. In fact, products based on the draft version of the standard are already being sold. This standard will be the basis of the next generation of wireless LANs, with data rates well above 100 Mbps and much better throughput. At this point, no decision has been made about which proposal for this standard will move forward as the draft standard, but it will certainly include multiple input-multiple output (MIMO) antenna technology. MIMO enables multiple antennas to create simultaneous RF channels that increase the performance of wireless LANs, similar to serial-to-parallel conversion techniques used with wired networks. The 802.11 working group is expected to ratify this standard in 2007.

Comparison of 802.11 Standards

Table 4-1 compares the different characteristics of the 802.11a, 802.11b, and 802.11g standards.

Table 4-1   *802.11 Standards Comparison*

	RF Spectrum	Maximum Speed	Compatibility	RF Interference Impact	Year Ratified
802.11a	5 GHz	54 Mbps	Does not work with 802.11b or 802.11g	Slight	1999
802.11b	2.4 GHz	11 Mbps	Works with 802.11g	Moderate	1999
802.11g	2.4 GHz	54 Mbps	Works with 802.11b	Moderate	2004

Wireless Configuration Parameters

The 802.11 standard specifies several configuration parameters, which are set in the radio card or the access point (or both). To optimize performance and security of a wireless LAN, you must choose configuration settings that best satisfy application requirements. Most of these configurations apply to the access points, but some settings are necessary on the radio cards within the end-user devices, such as wireless IP phones.

SSID

The SSID is an alphanumeric value set in access points and radio cards to distinguish one wireless LAN from another. For example, the default SSID for most Cisco access points is "tsunami." The SSID provides a name for the wireless LAN. The beacon frame includes the SSID. The operating system extracts the SSID from the radio card, which obtains SSIDs from the beacon frames. Windows displays a list of available wireless networks (by SSID) to the user. If the user chooses to connect to one of the wireless LANs, Windows initiates the association process.

NOTE   Keep in mind that not all radio cards support the feature that Microsoft Windows offers. When using mobile device operating systems or radio cards that do not extract the SSID from beacons, the user must manually configure the radio card with the SSID of the access points that he or she wants to associate with.

When installing a wireless LAN with multiple access points, such as in the case of an enterprise network, set all access points to the same SSID. Doing so minimizes issues with users having incorrect SSIDs and ensures roaming between access points works as smoothly as possible and without user intervention.

Some access points, such as the Cisco 1200 Series, allow administrators to set the access point to disable SSID broadcasting. When SSID broadcasting is disabled, the access point does not include the SSID in beacon frames. As a result, Windows cannot obtain the SSID and display it as a candidate network for association. This feature is beneficial in corporate networks to keep casual snoopers and war drivers from finding the network. For example, a user with a Windows-based laptop would not see the corporate network as an association option.

With SSID broadcasting disabled, however, a user must manually configure the radio card with the correct SSID to associate with the access point. With wireless IP phones, the administrator can do this task when setting up the phone for use. The disabling of SSID broadcasting is beneficial in corporate and home environments, but it is not desirable with public wireless hotspots. Public hotspots need to use the SSID broadcasting for advertising their service. For example, T-Mobile uses the SSID "T-Mobile" to inform users (through Windows) that their network is available and to distinguish their service from competitors. Disabling SSID broadcasting in public networks would keep users from determining that wireless LAN coverage for a particular service provider was available.

Keep in mind that the disabling of SSID broadcasting is not a strong security mechanism. An eavesdropper, for example, can easily monitor 802.11 frames on the wireless LAN and wait until an association frame is sent by a radio card as a mandatory part of the association process. The hacker will find the SSID in association request frames and some probe requests. In fact, commercial wireless LAN analyzers look inside association frames and automatically display SSIDs after finding them.

The 802.11 standard specifies the need for each access point to have an SSID, but several vendors, including Cisco, allow multiple SSID assignments for each access point. Administrators can map each SSID to a different virtual LAN (VLAN), which makes supporting diverse applications on a common wireless LAN infrastructure possible. This creates multiple virtual wireless LANs operating over the same physical layer.

NOTE   Cisco recommends that voice applications be assigned an SSID and VLAN separate from data applications.

For example, an airport might want to share the same wireless LAN infrastructure to support both voice applications for airport personnel and wireless service providers offering public Internet access to passengers. The airport can disable SSID broadcasting for the voice applications and map this SSID to a VLAN accessible only through strong security mechanisms. As a result, passengers would not see the airport's SSID through Windows. Each access point can be set to broadcast the SSIDs of the public service providers so that users can find the service offerings. Each SSID would interface to a VLAN that connects only with the applicable service provider.

With Ad Hoc wireless LANs, the first radio card in the area that is set to Ad Hoc mode includes its SSID in the beacon. Doing so establishes an Ad Hoc wireless LAN that other users (set to Ad Hoc mode) can join. As with an infrastructure network, each radio card must be set to the same SSID to associate in an Ad Hoc network. As with infrastructure wireless LANs, Windows displays a list of SSIDs corresponding to Ad Hoc networks. With some radio cards and when using non-Windows operating systems, it might be necessary for each Ad Hoc user to manually configure their radio card with the desired SSID. SSID disabling is generally not available to Ad Hoc users.

RF Channels

Each 802.11 physical layer defines a set of RF channels. For example, the 802.11b/g standard defines 14 RF channels in the 2.4-GHz band, with varying numbers of these channels available in specific countries. In the United States, for instance, the FCC's rules allow the use of only channels 1 through 11. In the case of 802.11b/g, these channels overlap each other, as shown in Figure 4-6. As a result, companies installing 802.11b/g wireless LANs should set adjacent access points (where their radio cells overlap) to nonconflicting channels. These channels do not overlap each other, such as channels 1, 6, and 11 in the United States. This technique minimizes interaccess point interference, which can significantly reduce throughput when user traffic is high. Other 802.11 standards, such as 802.11a, define separate RF channels that do not overlap.

Figure 4-6   *Overlapping 802.11 RF Channels in the 2.4-GHz Band*

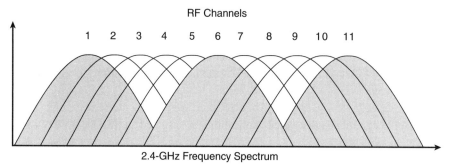

Defining the appropriate RF channels by first conducting an RF site survey is important, as explained in Chapter 8, "Installing, Configuring, and Testing a VoWLAN System." The survey provides information necessary to identify the most optimum channels for avoiding interference sources, such as microwave ovens and neighboring wireless LANs. In infrastructure wireless LANs, the RF channel is set in the access point only. Cisco access points include automatic channel selection as an option. When this feature is enabled, the access point automatically listens to each RF channel and decides which channel to use to avoid interference. As conditions change, the access point responds accordingly. This feature significantly reduces the time necessary to initially determine optimum channel settings and make applicable updates when supporting the network.

In Ad Hoc networks, the first radio card active on the network is set by the user to a specific channel. After joining a particular Ad Hoc wireless LAN, each radio card belonging to that particular Ad Hoc network stays on the same channel. The channel in use by the Ad Hoc network is the one that the first Ad Hoc user selected.

Transmit Power

Most access points and radio cards allow the setting of transmit power. The highest value is generally 100 mW (0.1 W), with increments of lower power available. Some devices enable settings as low as 1 mW. In most cases, it's best to set all wireless LAN devices to the highest transmit power, which is generally the default setting.

NOTE   Cisco recommends that the access point and the 7920 Wireless IP Phone be set to the same transmit power. Doing so makes the range in both directions equivalent and avoids scenarios where one-way audio transmission can occur.

To configure a wireless LAN for optimum capacity, you can set the transmit power to a lower value, which effectively reduces the size of the radio cells surrounding each access point and radio card. More access points are necessary to cover an entire facility, as compared to using higher transmit power levels, but fewer wireless users then associate with each access point. The result is better performance due to fewer users competing for access to the medium. The use of lower power settings and a greater number of access points is beneficial for supporting voice-over-Wi-Fi applications, assuming that roaming delays between the access points are kept to a minimum by careful system design. Keep in mind, however, that the greater density of access points increases costs for hardware.

Some access points, such as those from Cisco, have configurations whereby the access point automatically tunes to the least congested RF channel. The problem with this type of configuration is that the automatic changing of channels causes wireless clients, such as wireless IP phones, to roam, which introduces delays and possible dropped calls. With voice applications, do not use this feature. Instead, set each access point and phone to a static RF channel that does not overlap with neighboring access points.

Data Rates

The default data rate setting on access points is generally **auto**, which allows radio cards to use any of the data rates of the given physical layer. For example, 802.11b allows data rates of 1, 2, 5.5, and 11 Mbps. The 802.11g standard extends these data rates up to 54 Mbps. The radio card usually attempts to send data frames at the highest supported rate, such as 11 Mbps for 802.11b stations and 54 Mbps for 802.11g stations. When set to **auto**, the radio card automatically rate-shifts to the highest data rate that the connection can support. A lower data rate, for example, might be necessary if the radio card encounters too many retransmissions.

Setting the access point to a specific data rate, such as 1 Mbps, is possible. Doing so forces the access point to send all frames at 1 Mbps, which effectively increases the range of the access point, because 802.11 stations can detect access points over longer ranges. In general, a radio card can communicate successfully with lower data rates over longer ranges.

The access point data rate setting, though, does not affect the data rate of the radio cards. If the radio card is set to **auto** data rates (the default setting), the radio card can still use the highest possible data rate when sending frames to the access point. To maximize the range with fewer retransmissions, set the radio cards to lower, fixed data rates. These data rate settings impact only the transmit data rate. The radio card can still receive frames at higher data rates if necessary.

Power-Save Mode

Most radio cards employ an optional 802.11 power-save mode that users can enable. Access points do not implement power-save mode, except for the buffering functions necessary to support power-saving functions of the radio cards. If power-save mode is enabled, the radio card enters sleep mode, which draws much less current than when the card is operating actively. Thus, power-save mode can conserve batteries on mobile devices. In fact, power-save mode often lengthens battery life by 20 to 30 percent. The actual savings, however, depend on the applications and other variables.

Before switching to power-save mode, the radio card notifies the access point by setting the power management bit in the frame control field of an upstream frame. The access point receives this frame and starts buffering applicable data frames. The buffering takes place until the radio card awakens and requests that the access point send the saved frames to the radio card.

After entering sleep mode, the radio card keeps track of time and wakes up periodically to receive each beacon coming from the access point. The radio card must wake to discover whether the access point is buffering any frames that need delivery to the radio card. The access point notifies radio cards about buffered packets through what the 802.11 standard defines as the *traffic indication map (TIM)*.

A radio card set to power-save mode wakes just in time to receive the TIM, which resides in the beacon frames. The TIM indicates the AID of the 802.11 stations that have data frames buffered at the access point. If a station discovers it has frames at the access point, the station stays awake and sends a power-save poll frame to the access point, requesting that the data frames be forwarded to the station. The station stays awake long enough to receive all the buffered frames. The amount of time required to transfer all the buffered frames depends on the current utilization of the access point and the radio link quality. A large number of stations implementing power-save mode can cause a surge in traffic after each beacon due to power-save poll frames and corresponding data frames.

After the access point delivers the buffered frames, the radio card enters sleep mode again, unless the beacon frame corresponds with the delivery traffic indication map (DTIM). The DTIM is set in the access point to determine how many beacons must pass before the access point delivers multicast frames. A common default DTIM interval is 3, which means that the access point sends multicast frames after every third beacon. The DTIM interval, however, can be set to other values, such as 1, which enables the access point to send multicast frames after every beacon. Based on the DTIM interval setting, a station implementing power-save mode stays awake long enough after the beacon transmission to receive the multicast frames in addition to unicast frames.

The use of power-save mode can make batteries last longer in user devices, but throughput decreases for data moving from the access point to the user device. The radio card awakens immediately and sends data going from the user device to the access point, however. As a result, upstream throughput remains unchanged in low-power mode.

NOTE   If the wireless client is obtaining electrical power from an alternating current (AC) outlet, disable power-save mode to improve throughput.

RTS/CTS

The 802.11 standard defines request-to-send/clear-to-send (RTS/CTS) as an optional function of 802.11 to regulate the transmission of data on the wireless LAN. RTS/CTS can be set in the access point or a radio card individually, or on both devices at the same time. In most cases, the RTS/CTS function is helpful in counteracting collisions between hidden nodes. To gain access to the shared wireless medium, a station can transmit only if no other station is transmitting. Within a particular access point radio cell, two stations associated with the same access point might possibly be out of range with each other.

For example, Figure 4-7 illustrates this scenario where Station A is either far away from Station B, or a barrier is blocking the radio signals between the two stations. The problem is that Station A might be in the middle of transmitting a frame to the access point when Station B wants to send a frame. Station B listens to the medium to determine whether another station is already transmitting. Because Station B cannot hear Station A, Station B starts transmitting the frame. A collision then occurs at the access point, which destroys both frames. As a result, the access point does not acknowledge reception of the frames. Both stations have to retransmit their respective frames, which likely result in another collision.

Figure 4-7 *Hidden Node Problem in Wireless LANs*

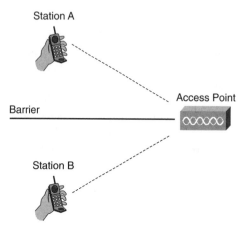

The RTS/CTS function is a handshaking process that minimizes collisions when hidden nodes are operating on the network. In addition, protection mechanisms may use RTS/CTS to avoid collisions between 802.11b and 802.11g radio cards. If hidden nodes are not causing significant retransmissions or hidden nodes are not present, RTS/CTS is generally not necessary (unless protection mechanisms are in use). RTS/CTS works by enabling each station to explicitly request a time slot for data transmission. For example, if RTS/CTS is enabled in the radio cards of Station A and Station B, Station A sends an RTS frame to the access point before attempting to transmit a data frame. The access point receives the RTS frame and responds with a CTS frame. Both stations receive the CTS frame. This process gives clearance for Station A to transmit a data frame. The CTS frame carries a duration value that informs all other stations, including Station B, to not transmit during the specified time interval. This delay equals the amount of time that Station A requires to send the data frame and for the access point to respond with an acknowledgment. As a result, collisions due to hidden nodes are much less likely. The only time collisions are possible with RTS/CTS enabled is when hidden nodes also miss CTS frames from the access point because of interference or weak signals.

Enabling RTS/CTS requires setting RTS/CTS to a specific threshold value in the access point or radio card. The threshold is the frame length that invokes the RTS/CTS process. If the data frame needing transmission is larger than the threshold, the station implementing RTS/CTS uses the RTS/CTS process.

If you suspect hidden nodes might be causing collisions on the network and degrading network performance, consider activating RTS/CTS. First setting the threshold to approximately 750 bytes, which is roughly the halfway point (50 percent of the maximum frame size), and assessing changes in throughput is best. If throughput increases, the use of RTS/CTS is beneficial. If throughput decreases, RTS/CTS likely is not worthwhile.

If RTS/CTS is in fact improving performance, consider tweaking the threshold value to maximize throughput.

Keep in mind that the use of RTS/CTS adds overhead to the network because the transmission of data frames might require RTS and CTS frames as well. As a result, the lessening of collisions by using RTS/CTS might not offer enough improvement in throughput to compensate for the additional overhead of RTS/CTS frames. The ultimate goal of using RTS/CTS is to improve throughput. If RTS/CTS causes throughput to decrease due to the additional overhead, do not use it. Even if the use of RTS/CTS improves performance, changes within the facility and users who are roaming to other areas will change the hidden node situations. Thus, RTS/CTS might not be necessary and can even cause degradation in throughput as conditions change. 802.11 does not offer adaptive mechanisms that automatically adjust RTS/CTS thresholds.

Fragmentation

A radio card or access point can be set to optionally use fragmentation, which divides 802.11 data frames into smaller pieces (fragments) that are sent separately to the destination. Each fragment consists of a MAC layer header, a frame check sequence (FCS), and a fragment number indicating its ordered position within the frame. Because the source station transmits each fragment independently, the receiving station replies with a separate acknowledgment for each fragment.

An 802.11 station applies fragmentation only to frames having a unicast destination address, including any data frame directed toward a specific station. To minimize overhead on the network, 802.11 does not fragment broadcast and multicast frames.

The destination station reassembles the fragments into the original frame using fragment numbers. After ensuring the frame is complete, the station hands the frame to higher layers for processing. Even though fragmentation involves more overhead, its use can result in better performance if you tune it properly.

Fragmentation can increase the reliability of frame transmissions when significant RF interference is present. When transmitting smaller frames, collisions are less likely to occur. In addition, frames that do encounter errors can be retransmitted faster because they are smaller. The fragment size value can typically be set between 256 and 2048 bytes, although this value is user-configurable. In fact, you activate fragmentation by setting a particular frame size threshold (in bytes). If the frame that the access point is transmitting is larger than the threshold (similar to RTS/CTS), it triggers fragmentation. If the packet size is equal to or less than the threshold, the access point does not use fragmentation.

Consider enabling fragmentation on radio cards and access points. As with configuring RTS/CTS, first set the fragmentation threshold to 750 bytes. If throughput increases, fragmentation is beneficial. If throughput decreases, fragmentation probably is not worthwhile. Because of the additional overhead required for frame headers on each fragment, the reduction in frame retransmissions might not be enough to counteract the additional overhead necessary.

RTS/CTS and Fragmentation Summary

Table 4-2 summarizes some of the benefits and drawbacks of both RTS/CTS and fragmentation when trying to improve throughput in a wireless network.

Table 4-2   *Improving Throughput Using RTS/CTS and Fragmentation*

	RTS/CTS	**Fragmentation**
Method to improve throughput	Reduce collisions	Reduce percentage of frames with transmission errors
How to enable	Configuration on access points and radio cards	Configuration on radio cards and access points
Subset of data frames	Frames under a statically defined length	Frames under a statically defined length
Overhead created	RTS/CTS process frames	Addition of fragmentation headers

Chapter Summary

The wireless LAN is a critical component of a VoWLAN solution by providing the wireless interface for wireless IP phones to place telephone calls. An infrastructure wireless LAN is the most common architecture for voice applications. You can set many configuration settings, such as transmit power, RF channel, RTS/CTS, and fragmentation, in ways to optimize performance. For example, you can set RF transmit power to relatively low values to reduce the radio cell size, which requires a higher density of access points to cover a particular area. Doing so increases the capacity of the network and supports a greater number of simultaneous voice calls in the same physical area. The proper setting of RF channel, RTS/CTS, and fragmentation improves operation by reducing retransmissions.

Chapter Review Questions

1 How do 802.11 frames flow from one wireless IP phone to another wireless IP phone in an infrastructure wireless LAN?

2 Explain at least two methods for increasing the capacity of a wireless LAN.

3 Which IEEE 802.11 standard is being developed to standardize and improve roaming between access points?

4 Which 802.11 physical layer theoretically has the greatest capacity for supporting voice calls?

5 Why is it an advantage to set the wireless IP phone and access point to operate at the highest fixed data rate?

6 What are some disadvantages of using 802.11b/g wireless LANs for supporting voice communications?

7 Why is the disabling of SSID broadcasting not a foolproof security mechanism?

8 What are nonconflicting RF channels relevant to 802.11b/g?

9 What is a reason to implement RTS/CTS?

10 What is a problem that will occur when 802.11b clients associate with an 802.11g access point?

Objectives

Upon completing this chapter, you will be able to

- Identify the security risks of VoWLAN systems.
- Differentiate the various encryption and authentication solutions.
- Understand tips for implementing VoWLAN systems.

CHAPTER 5

VoWLAN Security Solutions

Because VoWLAN systems make use of wireless technology, you must consider security issues and corresponding countermeasures. This chapter addresses security issues and provides an overview of the security mechanisms available for protecting VoWLAN systems.

Security Implications

To fully appreciate the need for security for VoWLAN systems, you need to understand the risks of not implementing security beyond the default wireless LAN configuration. The primary implications are unauthorized access, passive monitoring, and denial of service, as shown in Figure 5-1. When deploying a VoWLAN system, assess the potential harm that can be done based on these implications, and determine which security solutions will provide the most effective countermeasures.

Figure 5-1 *Primary Wireless LAN Security Implications*

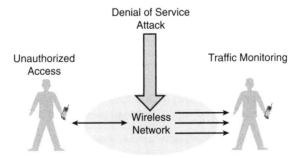

Passive Monitoring

A wireless LAN access point set to factory defaults likely has no security mechanisms enabled. As a result, all data sent between the access point and the client device, such as a wireless Internet Protocol (IP) phone or a wireless-equipped computer, is sent "in the clear" without any encryption. Of course, this poses a significant security issue. A hacker using a packet-sniffing tool, such as Ethereal, can passively monitor the transmissions of the wireless clients and access points and capture passwords and contents of e-mails, documents, HTTP messages, and voice conversations. In addition, an access point with default configuration also has default usernames and passwords, which are well known. Also, firmware usually is outdated and needs updating to be fully secure.

A legitimate user, for example, may use her favorite username and password to log in to a fitness website. The hacker can record the packets containing the username and password as the data travels wirelessly from the user's client device to the access point. The hacker likely doesn't care about getting access to the fitness site but realizes that the user likely makes use of the same password for other, more important sites, such as banks and corporate applications. These systems generally encrypt the exchange of passwords, so the hacker wouldn't be able to monitor them. But the hacker can continue to monitor the user's transmissions and determine the address of where these logins take place. With the user's favorite and likely common password, the hacker can then access the user's bank account and applications.

To avoid falling into this trap, users should always use different passwords on each account. In addition, the wireless system should implement a strong form of encryption to ensure that hackers can't make any sense of the wireless data that they may be monitoring.

Unauthorized Access

With no security enabled on an access point, just about anyone with a wireless-equipped laptop in the parking lot can connect to a wireless local-area network (LAN) located in an office building, manufacturing plant, or hospital. The unsecured access point continually broadcasts a beacon that the wireless laptop receives, and the Microsoft Windows operating system displays the Service Set Identifier (SSID) found within the beacon as an available wireless network. The laptop owner, possibly a hacker, can then readily connect to the access point, which makes the hacker part of the company's network. This feature allows the hacker to use strategies and tools to steal and corrupt corporate data located on servers in the building. For example, the hacker could run a Transmission Control Protocol (TCP) port scanner and uncover unsecured HTTP administrative interfaces of applications and support tools on servers. This could allow the hacker to create an account on the system for himself and then start stealing and corrupting files and applications.

As a result, you must enable effective access control on the wireless LAN to block hackers from accessing the system.

Denial of Service

A denial of service (DoS) attack is an assault that can cripple or disable a wireless LAN. It blocks users from using their wireless IP phones. The possibility of such an attack occurring is something that all companies deploying wireless LANs should consider.

One form of DoS attack is the "brute-force" method, which can come in two forms: either a flood of packets uses up all the network's resources and forces it to shut down, or a very strong radio signal dominates the airwaves and renders access points and wireless clients useless. A hacker can perform a packet-based brute-force DoS attack by using other computers on the network to send the useless packets to the server. This method adds significant overhead on the network and takes away useable bandwidth from legitimate users.

The use of very strong radio signals to disrupt the network is a rather risky attack for a hacker to attempt. Because a very powerful transmitter at a relatively close range must be used to execute this type of attack, the owners of the wireless LAN can find the hacker through the use of homing tools, such as AirMagnet.

Sometimes a DoS occurrence on a wireless network may not be intentional. The spectrum that 802.11b operates is very crowded. Other 2.4-GHz devices, such as cordless phones, microwaves, Bluetooth, and more, may cause a significant reduction in 802.11b performance.

To protect against DoS attacks, you must give careful attention to the design of the wireless LAN in a way that limits the propagation of radio waves into the company's building.

Encryption

As shown in Figure 5-2, encryption is a process that alters data bits of packets before transmission. The opposite end of the wireless link decrypts the data. This process acts to "hide" the data from hackers.

Figure 5-2   *Process of Encryption*

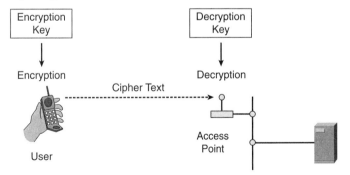

Figure 5-3 illustrates the portion of the network that encryption protects, depending on whether the encryption is implemented by the wireless LAN or an end-to-end process. Wireless LAN encryption protects only data between the wireless client and the access point, whereas end-to-end encryption protects data between the wireless client and the endpoint of the system, such as a server within an enterprise system.

Figure 5-3   *Differences Between Encryption Approaches*

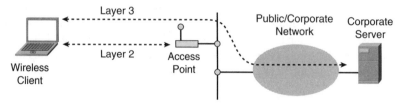

Encrypting the data flowing over the wired portion of a corporate network is not generally necessary because it is located within physically controlled space. As a result, wireless LAN encryption alone is generally sufficient. Someone connecting to the corporate network over a public wireless LAN, such as from within a hotel, should use a virtual private network (VPN) client that provides end-to-end encryption.

The following are several encryption techniques that wireless LANs use:

- Wired Equivalent Privacy (WEP)
- Temporal Key Integrity Protocol (TKIP)
- Advanced Encryption Standard (AES)
- Wi-Fi Protected Access (WPA)
- 802.11i
- Virtual Private Network (VPN)

Each of the preceding techniques, except VPN, provide encryption only between the wireless client and the access point. The following sections examine each of these encryption techniques in more detail to show how you might use them to protect a VoWLAN system.

WEP

WEP is an encryption method using RC4 encryption. It has been part of 802.11 (as an option) since the standard was first ratified in 1997. WEP makes use of a common key to encrypt and decrypt data frame contents between 802.11 stations, such as wireless IP phones, at the data link layer. Each sending station encrypts the body of each frame with a WEP key before transmission, and the receiving station decrypts it using an identical key upon reception. This process reduces the risk of someone passively monitoring the transmission and gaining access to the information that the frames are carrying. Only 40-bit keys were implemented initially due to U.S. export limitations, but later 128-bit keys were added for additional security.

An issue is that the 802.11 standard doesn't define a mechanism for distributing WEP keys to the stations. This requires the administrator or users to manually configure their wireless clients with the encryption key, and changing the key is not practical. Thus, WEP keys remain the same on most wireless LANs for months or years, which gives a hacker enough time to exploit the vulnerabilities of WEP and crack the encryption.

WEP has been a target for hackers for several years. In fact, tools freely available from the Internet, such as WEPCrack and Airsnort, can crack the WEP encryption mechanism using either 40- or 128-bit keys. Another problem is that someone can steal a wireless client configured with WEP and then access the network. An administrator won't know that the device is stolen until it is reported, giving someone enough time to steal and possibly corrupt corporate data. As a result, WEP is not strong enough for enterprise security.

NOTE   For more information on the weaknesses of WEP, refer to the paper at the following link: http://www.isaac.cs.berkeley.edu/isaac/wep-faq.html.

TKIP

TKIP fixes the key distribution problem of WEP. The TKIP process begins with a 128-bit "temporal key" shared among clients and access points. TKIP combines the temporal key with the client's Media Access Control (MAC) address and then adds a relatively large 16-octet initialization vector to produce the key used to encrypt data. This procedure ensures that each station uses different key strings to encrypt data.

TKIP uses RC4 to perform the actual encryption of data frames, which is the same as WEP. A major difference from WEP, however, is that TKIP changes temporal keys periodically according to a setting configured in the access point by an administrator. This feature provides a dynamic distribution method that significantly enhances network security and makes cracking it very difficult, if not impossible, for a hacker.

AES

AES offers much stronger encryption than WEP and TKIP. In fact, the U.S. Commerce Department's National Institute of Standards and Technology (NIST) chose AES to replace the aging Data Encryption Standard (DES). AES is now a Federal Information Processing Standard, FIPS Publication 197. It defines a cryptographic algorithm for use by U.S. Government organizations to protect sensitive, unclassified information. The Secretary of Commerce approved the adoption of AES as an official government standard in May 2002. Some of the older access points and client cards, however, do not support AES because of requirements of a specialized math coprocessor. Keep in mind that regulations exist that prohibit exporting wireless LAN equipment with AES to some countries.

WPA

Before the ratification of the 802.11i standard, the Wi-Fi Alliance released the WPA (version 1) standard that most wireless LAN vendors rapidly adopted. WPA is actually a snapshot of the preratified 802.11i standard involving TKIP and IEEE 802.1x standards. Eventually, the Wi-Fi Alliance released WPA version 2 (WPA2), which includes AES. This mirroring of standards has been effective for end users because the Wi-Fi Alliance requires special interoperability testing before a wireless LAN vendor can claim that its wireless clients and access points are Wi-Fi certified.

802.11i

The 802.11i standard was ratified and became final in mid-2004. The final version specifies the use of TKIP with 802.1X (refer to the later section "IEEE 802.1X"), as well as AES as an option. WPA2 is the same as 802.11i.

Virtual Private Networks

To fully secure wireless connections, many companies require the use of VPN software on each user device. This software encrypts all communications between the user device and the remote system at higher layers. The use of VPN software is especially important when users are communicating over public wireless LANs. Public Wi-Fi hotspots, for example, do not implement any encryption over the wireless portion of the network. In this case, the VPN protects the data traffic.

In fact, some companies treat all wireless users as though they are operating from a public network, even though users are inside the company's building. In this case, the wireless LAN access points connect to a distribution system that falls outside the firewall. This approach, however, might require an impractical number of VPN connections, which can be costly to deploy and support. For internal communications, fully securing wireless users is possible through the use of mechanisms, such as WPA, that encrypt data only between the wireless client and access point.

Authentication

Authentication is a process that identifies a particular person or network component based on credentials, as shown in Figure 5-4. Authentication makes sure that a particular user or component is authorized to communicate with another user or device. This process is analogous to someone showing his driver's license when entering a secure facility. The guard ensures that the person's name is on the access list and verifies that the photo on the license matches the person. If everything checks out okay, the guard opens the door so that the person can enter the facility. A network implements authentication in a very similar manner, except identification is given through the use of a password, digital certificate, or some other element that verifies identity. In addition, an authentication server provides the means for authorizing access to the network.

Figure 5-4   *Process of Authentication*

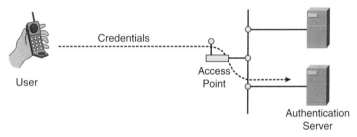

Network systems go a step further and implement mutual authentication. In this case, an access point verifies that a wireless client device wanting access is authorized, and the client device ensures that the access point is legitimate. If this authentication were not done, a hacker could power up a fake access point near the user and issue a special 802.11 packet that disconnects the user's client device from the legitimate access point. The user's client device then reconnects to the hacker's fake access point. It's possible that the hacker can configure this access point to funnel the user's data traffic (unknown to the user) to the hacker's computer, giving the hacker access to possibly sensitive information, such as passwords. The implementation of mutual authentication, though, can prevent this breach from happening.

The following are several authentication techniques that wireless LANs use:

- Open system authentication
- Shared key authentication
- IEEE 802.1X
- Cisco LEAP

The next few sections cover each of these authentication techniques and uncover which ones might make sense for protecting a VoWLAN system.

Open System Authentication

Open system authentication is the default mode that 802.11 uses for authenticating wireless clients to an access point, as shown in Figure 5-5. In this mode, a wireless client sends an authentication frame to the access point, and the access point returns an authentication response.

Any wireless client with the correct SSID can authenticate. This is easily done by the user selecting the applicable wireless network through the Microsoft Windows Wireless Network Connection feature if the SSID is broadcast. Or it can be found through sniffing 802.11 association frames from other users if the SSID is not broadcast. This form of authentication provides an open system, not really a form of authentication. It is mainly part of the standard as a baseline operational mode.

Figure 5-5 *Open System Authentication*

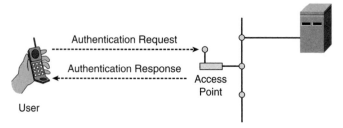

With open system authentication, no credentials except the SSID are passed to the access point; however, some vendors might implement provisions that must be met to authenticate stations when using 802.11 open system authentication. For example, most access points do not allow wireless clients configured for open system authentication to connect with the access point unless a valid WEP key is provided. This form of authentication is primarily used when the wireless LAN is to implement WEP encryption. For smaller networks, MAC address filtering can be fairly effective at allowing only authorized users (ones having acceptable MAC addresses) to access the network. MAC address filtering on larger networks can be difficult to manage, however, due to difficulties in adding new users.

Shared Key Authentication

The 802.11 shared key authentication goes a step further than open system authentication by using the common WEP key to authenticate wireless clients. It is a four-way handshaking process, as shown in Figure 5-6:

1 The wireless client sends an authentication request.

2 The access point responds with an authentication frame containing challenge text, which is a string of unencrypted text.

3 The wireless client encrypts the challenge text with the WEP key and sends the result to the access point.

4 The access point decrypts the challenge text with the common WEP key. If the challenge text is the same as the access point initially sent, the access point assumes that the wireless client has the correct WEP key and that the wireless client is a legitimate user.

Unfortunately, shared key authentication is easy to crack. In fact, a hacker can use freely available tools to readily find even the WEP key by detecting both the unencrypted challenge text and the WEP-encrypted challenge text. As a result, not using shared key authentication is strongly advised.

Figure 5-6   *Shared Key Authentication*

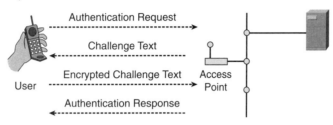

IEEE 802.1X

The use of IEEE 802.1X offers an effective framework for authenticating and controlling user traffic to a protected wired or wireless network, as well as dynamically varying encryption keys. 802.1X ties a protocol called EAP (Extensible Authentication Protocol) to both the wired and wireless LAN media and supports multiple authentication methods, such as token cards, Kerberos, one-time passwords, certificates, and public key authentication. For details on EAP specifically, refer to Internet Engineering Task Force (IETF) RFC 2284.

Initial 802.1X communication begins with an unauthenticated supplicant (that is, client device) attempting to connect with an authenticator (that is, 802.11 access point). The access point responds by enabling a port for passing only EAP packets from the client to an authentication server located on the wired side of the access point. The access point blocks all other traffic, such as Hypertext Transfer Protocol (HTTP), Dynamic Host Configuration Protocol (DHCP), and Post Office Protocol 3 (POP3) packets, until the access point can verify the client's identity using an authentication server, such as Remote Authentication Dial-In User Service (RADIUS). After authentication, the access point opens the client's port for other types of traffic.

To get a better idea of how 802.1X operates, the following are specific interactions that take place among the various 802.1X elements:

1 The client sends an EAP-start message, which begins a series of message exchanges to authenticate the client. Think of this process as a group of visitors approaching the front gate of a theme park and the group's leader (the client) asking the gatekeeper (the access point) whether they can enter.

2 The access point replies with an EAP-request identity message. In the case of the theme park, the gatekeeper asks the leader for his name and driver's license.

3 The client sends an EAP-response packet containing the identity to the authentication server. The leader in our example provides his name and driver's license, and the gatekeeper forwards this information to the group tour manager (the authentication server), who determines whether the group has rights to enter the park.

4 The authentication server uses a specific authentication algorithm to verify the client's identity. This could be through the use of digital certificates or another EAP authentication type. In our example, this process simply involves verifying the validity of the leader's driver's license and ensuring that the picture on the license matches the leader. For this example, assume the leader is authorized.

5 The authentication server sends either an accept or reject message to the access point. The group tour manager at the theme park tells the gatekeeper to let the group enter.

6 The access point sends an EAP-success packet (or EAP-reject packet) to the client. The gatekeeper informs the leader that the group can enter the park. Of course, the gatekeeper would not let the group in if the group tour manager had rejected the group's admittance.

7 If the authentication server accepts client, the access point transitions the client's port to an authorized state and forwards additional traffic. This process is similar to the gatekeeper automatically opening the gate to let in only people belonging to the group cleared for entry.

The basic 802.1X protocol provides effective authentication. Most major wireless LAN vendors, however, offer proprietary versions of dynamic key management using 802.1X as a delivery mechanism. If configured to implement dynamic key exchange, the 802.1X authentication server can return session keys to the access point along with the accept message. The access point uses the session keys to build, sign, and encrypt an EAP key message that is sent to the client immediately after the success message is sent. The client can then use the contents of the key message to define applicable encryption keys. In typical 802.1X implementations, the client can automatically change encryption keys as often as necessary to minimize the possibility of eavesdroppers having enough time to crack the key in current use.

It is important to note that 802.1X does not provide the actual authentication mechanisms. When using 802.1X, you need to choose an EAP type, such as Transport Layer Security (EAP-TLS) or Tunneled Transport Layer Security (EAP-TTLS), that defines how the authentication takes place.

The important point to know at this point is that the software supporting the specific EAP type resides on the authentication server and within the operating system or application software on the client devices. The access point acts as a "pass through" for 802.1X messages, which means that you can specify any EAP type without needing to upgrade an 802.1X-compliant access point. As a result, you can update the EAP authentication type as newer types become available and your requirements for security change.

The use of 802.1X has become the industry standard for an authentication framework for networks, and you would be wise to include it as the basis for your wireless LAN security solution. Microsoft Windows XP implements 802.1X natively, and some vendors support 802.1X in their 802.11 access points.

NOTE   To download the 802.1X standard, go to http://www.ieee802.org/1/pages/802.1x.html.

Cisco LEAP

Cisco's LEAP wireless authentication process helps eliminate security vulnerabilities by supporting centralized, user-based authentication and the ability to generate dynamic WEP keys. LEAP is easy to implement and contains compelling features:

- **Mutual authentication**—In wired networks, a direct physical connection exists between the client and device; therefore, the client is relatively sure that it is communicating with the right network. This is not the case, however, in a wireless LAN. Because no physical connection exists between the two, the client must authenticate the network, and the network needs to authenticate the client—hence mutual authentication. With LEAP, mutual authentication is provided by a shared secret, which is the user's network password.

- **User-based authentication**—Traditional 802.11 authentication verifies only radio devices, not actual users. Because of this, an unauthorized user can very easily access the network through a preauthorized piece of equipment—for example, an employee's laptop. LEAP eliminates this vulnerability by authenticating the user through usernames and passwords, rather than just the device.

- **Dynamic WEP keys**—Cisco LEAP uses 802.1X to continually generate unique WEP keys for each user. Every 802.1X session timeout forces clients to reassociate to the network, which is when the new WEP keys are generated. The reassociations are not noticeable by users and are very important to keep all sensitive data constantly encrypted.

The following steps take place with LEAP:

1 The client device associates with the access point. This is done via the regular 802.11 connection process, often referred to as the association process.

2 The access point blocks client device access to the network, and a LEAP-compliant RADIUS server, such as the Cisco Access Control Server (ACS), issues an authentication challenge to the client device.

3 The user provides login credentials, which is a user-supplied password. LEAP performs a one-way hash of the password before sending it to the RADIUS server.

4 The RADIUS server authenticates the user by verifying the user's credentials located in the database.

5 The user authenticates the RADIUS server similarly to how the RADIUS server authenticated the user. After this task is completed, the RADIUS server sends an EAP-success message to the client device.

6 The client device and RADIUS server derive a unicast WEP key.

7 The RADIUS server delivers the unicast WEP key to the access point.

8 The access point delivers a broadcast WEP key encrypted with the unicast WEP key to the client device.

9 The client device and access point activate WEP and use the broadcast and unicast WEP keys.

When deploying the ACS, be sure to minimize the delays between the access points and the ACS. Doing so is necessary because the LEAP authentication process must take place every time the client device roams to another access point. Cisco IOS Release 12.2(11)JA introduced support for the Cisco access point to authenticate LEAP users without having to access an external ACS. This functionality supports up to 50 usernames for small deployments. In addition, the Cisco ACS can either store the username and password database locally, or it can access that information from an external Microsoft Windows NT directory. If users are fairly mobile and roam between access points frequently, not using an external database is best, because associated delays may cause poor voice quality.

Also, segment the voice and data traffic by placing the voice traffic on one VLAN and data traffic on the other VLAN. With the voice traffic pointed to only a particular VLAN, a hacker who steals a wireless IP phone cannot use the phone's password to access the data network—assuming, of course, that the user has a different password on the phone compared to the one used on the data network.

NOTE   When using LEAP, be certain to use strong passwords, which have between 10 and 12 characters and can include a mix of uppercase, lowercase, and special characters. Also, use passwords on wireless IP phones that are different than other passwords. Doing so helps make the overall system more secure, because wireless IP phones, containing the user's phone password, may be compromised if the phone is stolen or lost.

Cisco freely licenses its wireless LAN security suite, which includes LEAP, to chipset and wireless client manufacturers. Because not all 802.11 products support LEAP, though, you may run into interoperability issues in a mixed-vendor environment. If you are sure that all products on the network will support LEAP—for example, a Cisco-only network— LEAP is a viable security measure. Keep in mind, however, that LEAP does have some issues. The asleap tool threatens the security of LEAP by exploiting the challenge/response technique when authenticating a client connecting to the wireless network. The tool enables a hacker to run a dictionary attack against the system and uncover the network passwords. For more details, refer to http://asleap.sourceforge.net/.

Cisco 7920 IP Phone Security

The Cisco 7920 wireless IP phone has the following security features:

- 40- and 128-bit WEP
- TKIP
- WPA
- IEEE 802.1X
- EAP-LEAP
- EAP-FAST
- Optional password prompt at power up
- Automatic key lock

When WEP or WPA is implemented, the signaling (Skinny Client Control Protocol [SCCP]) and media (Real-time Transport Protocol [RTP]) data is encrypted between the Cisco 7920 phone and the access point.

NOTE   Cisco recommends that you design the security of the wireless LAN based on the Cisco SAFE architecture. Refer to the following document for more information: http://www.cisco.com/en/US/netsol/ns340/ns394/ns171/ns128/ networking_solutions_package.html.

Tips for Enhancing Security

The use of effective encryption and authentication mechanisms goes a long way toward securing a wireless LAN. But good overall security results from a combination of many elements. The more roadblocks you put in the way, the tougher it is for a hacker to harm your company through the network. Consider implementing the tips given throughout this section when deploying a VoWLAN system.

SSID Broadcasting

Some access points, such as the Cisco 1200, allow administrators to disable the access point from broadcasting the SSID. The 802.11 standard specifies that the access point include the SSID in the body section of beacon frames, which the access point broadcasts regularly. When SSID broadcasting is disabled, the access point does not include the SSID in beacon frames. As a result, Windows cannot obtain the SSID and display it to the user as a possible wireless network to associate with. This feature is beneficial to corporate networks to keep "casual snoopers" and war drivers from finding the network. For example, a user with a Windows-based laptop would not see that the applicable company has a wireless network.

In addition, with SSID broadcasting disabled, each user must manually configure his or her wireless client device with the correct SSID that matches the one configured in the access point to associate with the access point. This is why disabling SSID broadcasting with public wireless hotspots is not desirable. Public hotspots need users to easily find the right network to connect to. In fact, the SSID is a form of advertising for hotspots. For example, T-Mobile uses the SSID "T-Mobile" to inform users (through Windows) that its network is available and to distinguish its service from competitors. The disabling of SSID broadcasting in public networks would keep users from finding out that wireless LAN coverage for a particular service provider is available.

For corporate networks, the disabling of SSID broadcasting is not a strong security mechanism. A hacker, for example, can easily monitor 802.11 frames on the wireless LAN and wait until an association frame is sent by a wireless client when a user connects to an access point or when the user roams from one access point to another. The hacker can find the SSID in the association request frames and some probe requests even when SSID broadcasting is disabled on the access point. In fact, wireless LAN analyzers, such as AirMagnet, Cain & Able, and Ethereal, look inside association frames and automatically display SSIDs when they are found.

When deploying VoWLAN systems in corporate environments, disabling SSID broadcasting is a good idea, primarily to keep causal snoopers from finding the network. Doing so provides some added protection. However, keep in mind that it is not a full-proof security technique.

Systems Management

The following are several security tips related to the management of the VoWLAN system:

- **Choose strong SNMP community strings**—The community string is sort of a Simple Network Management Protocol (SNMP) security password that allows administrators (and hackers) to configure network components, such as access points. Most SNMP agents have default community strings of "public" and "private," which a hacker will try first when trying to break into a network. As a result, be certain to change the community strings of all network components to "strong" community strings. Use strings that would not be easy to guess, are at least six characters in length, and use a mix of alphanumeric and uppercase/lowercase characters. Also, be sure to change the community strings often.

- **If practical, configure all SNMP ports as Read Only**—Some hackers attempt to change the configuration of access points by turning off security, which then allows the hacker to associate with the access point without needing to know encryption keys or passwords. The hacker then has access to the rest of the corporate network and can possibly harm servers and users. With the SNMP ports set to Read Only, a hacker may be able to read the configuration information, but she will not be able to change it. Thus, the security of the access point will stand unchanged, keeping the hacker from getting onto the corporate network.

- **Use secure management protocols**—For example, Secure Shell Protocol 2 (SSH2) offers a very secure way of configuring network components, such as access points. SSH provides an encrypted tunnel between the administrator's computer and the network component.

- **Keep software and hardware up to date**—Track updates of software and firmware for phones, access points, and other network components to be sure that you have the latest, most secure versions. When security holes are found, vendors often write patches to fix the problems. The vendor then includes these patches in future updates. Cisco, for example, noticed that its 7920 wireless IP phone had SNMP service with fixed community strings, which could allow remote users (such as hackers) to read, write, and erase the phone's configuration. Cisco then made free software available to address these vulnerabilities for affected customers. Therefore, keep an eye on the updates!

Access Point Installation

When installing the network, consider concealing the access points. A good location to install the access points is above the ceiling tiles, referred to as the plenum. In most cases, even the antennas can be mounted above the ceiling tiles without significantly disturbing radio signal propagation. The idea is to ensure that an unauthorized person cannot locate the access point and cause damage or connect a terminal cable from a laptop and disable security settings. Of course, when hiding access points, you must keep an accurate record of the locations to find them later for support purposes.

Something to keep in mind, however, is that a wireless LAN based on wireless switches can automatically detect an access point being configured by an unauthorized person. The wireless switch is smart enough to keep track of the configuration of the access points and alert an administrator when the configuration of the access point does not match security policies. In addition, the switch can block access to the network through the affected access point until an administrator has time to investigate and correct the problem.

Rogue Access Points

One of the most critical security concerns of IT managers today is the possibility that rogue wireless access points may be present on the corporate network. A rogue access point is one that the company does not authorize for operation. The trouble is that a rogue access point often does not conform to wireless LAN security policies. This enables an open, insecure interface to the corporate network from outside the physically controlled facility, as shown in Figure 5-7.

Within a properly secured wireless LAN, rogue access points are more damaging than rogue users. Unauthorized users trying to access a wireless LAN likely will not be successful at reaching valuable corporate resources if effective authentication mechanisms are in place. Major issues arise, however, when an employee or hacker plugs in a rogue access point. The rogue allows just about anyone with an 802.11-equipped device on the corporate network, which puts them very close to mission-critical resources.

Figure 5-7   *Open Access via a Rogue Access Point*

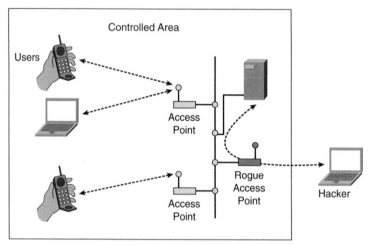

Employees have relatively free access to a company's facility, which makes it possible for them to inadvertently (or mischievously) install a rogue access point. An employee, for example, may purchase an access point at an office supply store and install it without coordinating with the IT organization to support wireless printing or access to the network from a conference room. Also, developers working on wireless applications may connect an access point to the corporate network for testing purposes.

In most cases, employees installing these types of access points do not understand the security issues involved. These scenarios often lead to access points that do not conform to adequate security practices. As a result, the corporate network is left wide open for a casual snooper or criminal hacker to attack the network by stealing corporate information or Internet service.

To avoid this situation, implement security policies that mandate conformance with effective security controls and coordination with the IT organization before installing access points. This method is effective only if you clearly inform employees of the policies.

A hacker can install a rogue access point to provide an open, nonsecure interface to a corporate network. To do so, he must directly connect the access point to an active network port within the facility, which requires him to pass through physical security. However, this task is easy to do in most companies. It is unlikely that a hacker would go to this trouble if the company has worthwhile resources. But many others would be willing to give this technique a try just to enable access to free wireless Internet service through the corporate system.

Really, no effective way exists to eliminate the possibility of a rogue access point from cropping up on your network. As a result, you must implement processes and mechanisms to constantly monitor for rogue access points as part of your ongoing security assessments.

One method of detecting rogues involves the use of wireless sniffing tools that capture information on access points that are within range of where you are using the tool. This method requires you to walk through the facilities to capture the data. With this method, you can scan the entire facility, but doing so can be very time-consuming for larger companies with many buildings or that span a large geographical area. Neverless, consider performing these types of scans each week.

Capturing data in this fashion is valid only at the time of capture. Someone could activate a rogue seconds after you turn off the sniffing device, and you will not have any idea that it is present. Still, this method is often the most common and least expensive way of finding rogues. It just takes a lot of time and effort.

When using wireless sniffing tools, look for access points that have authorized MAC addresses, vendor names, or security configurations. Create a list of MAC addresses of the authorized access points on the LAN and check whether each one you find is on the list. An access point with a vendor name different from your authorized access points is the first alert you to a possible rogue. Improper security settings (that is, WEP disabled) could indicate a rogue, but it may also be authorized but wrongly configured.

If you find an access point that looks suspicious, consider it to be a rogue, and then try locating it through homing techniques. To do so, walk in directions that cause the signal strength of the access point's beacons to increase. Eventually, you can narrow down the location to a particular room, which often requires you to do some looking. In some cases, the "rogue" is simply an active access point that is not connected to the corporate network—which doesn't cause any security harm. When you find one that actually interfaces to the corporate network, immediately shut it off.

The ideal method of detecting rogue access points is to use a central console attached to the wired side of the network for monitoring. Some of the more advanced wireless management tools have this feature. This feature eliminates the need to walk through the facilities.

Low-Cost Centralized Method for Finding Rogues

A fairly crude but inexpensive method for finding potential rogue access points from the wired side of the network is to use a free TCP port scanner, such as SuperScan, that identifies enabled TCP ports from various devices connected to the network. You run the software from a laptop or desktop PC connected to the corporate network. The tool uncovers all Port 80 (HTTP) interfaces on the network, which includes all web servers, some printers, and nearly all access points. Even if an access point's Port 80 interface is disabled or protected by a username and password, the access point generally responds to the port scanner's ping with the vendor name and its corresponding IP address.

You can download a free copy of SuperScan at the following link: http://www.foundstone.com/resources/proddesc/superscan.htm.

You can scroll through the list of found Port 80 interfaces and discover potential rogues if their vendor names are different from those authorized in your wireless LAN. With the

IP address of a suspected access point, attempt to open its administration screen. You will quickly notice whether an access point is legitimate. The difficult chore is determining the physical location of the rogue; router table entries may help.

In addition, consider using APTools, which is available at http://winfingerprint.sourceforge.net/aptools.php.

Signal Propagation

Another method to increase the security of a wireless LAN is to control the transmission and reception of the radio signals. The idea is to significantly reduce or eliminate signal coverage in areas outside the physically controlled area of the facility. These areas are where hackers may be lurking and possibly attempting to access your wireless LAN.

The ability to control radio signal propagation depends a great deal on the construction of the facility. For example, a building with exterior walls made of steel-reinforced concrete introduces a much greater amount of attenuation between the wireless LAN inside the building and potential hackers outside the building. A facility located inside a large physically controlled area also provides some protection, because radio signals need to propagate over greater distances before getting outside the controlled area.

To reduce signal transmission and reception of access points, set the access points near the perimeter of the building to lower transmit power and use lower-gain antennas. Directional antennas aimed inward focus more of the transmission and reception of radio signals inside rather than outside the building. This focus makes the radio cell of the access point smaller. To fully take advantage of this approach, however, you also need to decrease the transmit power of the client devices. Otherwise, the client device will still transmit radio signals outside the physically controlled area.

Another method to improve security is to paint the interior or exterior walls of the building with a metallic-based paint. For example, Force Field Wireless makes a special latex paint that significantly attenuates RF signals. You can paint the walls and ceiling of a room with this paint and block wireless LAN signals from escaping outside and keep RF interference and jamming signals from getting in. Also available is metallic-based film for putting on windows. The use of these protection measures, though, leaves your cellular phones useless inside the building because the cell phone system signals will no longer penetrate the walls and windows.

By carefully controlling signal propagation, you can decrease the chance of DoS attacks; however, the only completely effective way to counter DoS attacks is to isolate your computer in a room with heavy security and unplug it from all networks, including the Internet. Of course, this means not using a wireless network. The U.S. government uses this method to protect its most sensitive data, but this solution is not practical for any enterprise or home application where benefits exist for deploying wireless networks.

The most fundamental protection is developing and maintaining strong security practices. Actions such as implementing and updating firewalls, maintaining updated virus protection, installing up-to-date security patches, ensuring strong passwords, and turning off network devices when they are not needed should be routine practices for all companies.

After installing and configuring the wireless LAN, be sure to run tests to determine how far the signal actually leaks outside the building and then adjust transmitter power until the leakage is eliminated or reduced to the point that it would not be easy for a hacker to access the system.

Chapter Summary

When deploying a VoWLAN system, implementing effective security mechanisms is very important. The most important elements are encryption and authentication. Some encryption methods, such as WEP, are not very secure. Others, such as WPA and 802.11i, ensure that a hacker cannot compromise the data and voice being sent over the wireless network. Authentication plays a crucial role on a wireless network as well by significantly minimizing the possibility that a hacker can gain access to the network.

In addition to encryption and authentication, you should strive to harden the wireless network through effective configuration of the access points and control of the radio signals. The disabling of SSID broadcasting, for example, can keep your network more secure by reducing its exposure to potential hackers. In addition, adjusting the transmit power on access points and using directional antennas can help keep signals inside the building and out of the hands of unauthorized people.

Chapter Review Questions

1 What are the primary security implications of a wireless LAN?

2 When WEP is implemented, all users of the wireless LAN must use the same encryption key. True or false?

3 What encryption type does TKIP use?

4 What version of WPA implements AES encryption?

5 What is the primary difference between WPA and 802.11i?

6 What part of the network do WEP, WPA, and AES protect?

7 Which two forms of authentication are part of the 802.11 standard and are not effective for protecting wireless LANs?

8 The disabling of SSID broadcasting prevents a hacker from obtaining the SSID of the wireless LAN. True or false?

9 Why should you use strong SNMP community strings?

10 What are methods that you can use to keep the radio signals inside the building?

PART III

Implementation Steps

Objectives

Upon completing this chapter, you will be able to

- Identify potential requirements for a VoWLAN system.
- Verify and validate requirements for a VoWLAN system.
- Document requirements for a VoWLAN system.

CHAPTER 6

Analyzing VoWLAN Requirements

Before designing a VoWLAN system, you must fully understand requirements, such as number of users, existing data traffic, roaming needs, security needs, and anything else that will provide a basis for the design. A designer uses these requirements when making decisions about which technologies to use and how to configure the network. This chapter describes each type of requirement that needs definition to implement a quality VoWLAN system.

Overall Requirements Analysis Steps

No matter the size of the wireless network, be certain to complete the following steps when defining requirements:

Step 1 **Identify potential requirements**—This provides the opportunity to identify a starting set of requirements based on researching user needs, talking with managers, and reviewing documentation of existing systems. Generally, a system analyst completes this step and presents the results to stakeholders of the system.

Step 2 **Verify and validate requirements**—Before solidifying the requirements, gaining consensus from all stakeholders is crucial. This step ensures that the requirements are accurate and provide the right solution.

Step 3 **Document requirements**—The documentation of requirements provides a basis for designing the solution. The same people may not be available throughout the life cycle of the VoWLAN system deployment, so be complete in recording the requirements.

Identifying Potential Requirements

When you are first analyzing requirements, define a set of potential requirements that offers a basis for discussion. At this stage of the project, the requirements definition should be flexible enough to allow changes based on the thoughts of all stakeholders. For example, you may identify a certain number of users who will be using voice IP phones. After meeting with managers of the company, however, you may find that budget limitations allow for fewer voice IP phones. Or you may include as a preliminary requirement that the wireless LAN use 802.11 frequency-hopping technologies because the company has a policy that all new applications use this type of technology for new applications. However, after reviewing this technical requirement, a decision may be made to make an exception and allow 802.11b technologies. At first, the requirements must be fluid and accommodate these types of changes.

Case Study: Acme Furniture Gets Started with Analyzing Requirements

As shown in Chapter 1 in the hypothetical case study, Acme Furniture has decided to move forward with deploying a VoWLAN solution. To kick off the requirements analysis effort, Debbie, the IT manager for Acme, assigns Madison, one of her IT staff, the task of identifying preliminary requirements. Debbie asks Madison to first review preliminary requirements defined by Eric, the consultant hired to help Acme decide whether to move forward with the project, to offer some initial starting requirements. Madison finds, though, that these requirements only offer enough detail, such as number of potential users and presence of wireless LANs in some of the facilities, to base cost estimates. These preliminary estimates are not complete enough to provide the basis for the design. As a result, Madison schedules interviews with each of the department heads and also reviews all existing system documentation to prepare for identifying potential requirements.

Applications

The identification of applications as requirements is very important to ensure that the system will satisfy the needs of users. Ultimately, a VoWLAN system must support voice traffic, which may be the primary application. In fact, it may be the only application. With a wireless LAN in place, though, supporting other data applications will likely be beneficial. These could be general office applications, such as web browsing, e-mail, and file transfer. Or they could be wireless patient monitoring in a hospital or price marking in a retail store. Be as specific as possible by defining all information types, such as data, video, and voice, and how they will flow throughout the facility.

Case Study: Acme Furniture Defines Applications

Madison, assigned to define requirements for Acme Furniture, includes voice telephony as the primary application. Eric did a thorough job of analyzing the related benefits, which were very favorable for deploying a VoWLAN system. In addition to voice telephony, Madison found that the company can benefit by making use of the wireless LAN for mobile computing throughout the corporate facility in Columbus. Many of the executives and managers have laptops, and they often meet in the conference room at staff meetings and project reviews. To stay in touch with e-mail and have the ability to access corporate applications and the Internet, Madison includes these types of applications as potential requirements.

Users

Identify the number of users who will have access to the wireless LAN. This number includes the total number of voice IP phones and other wireless client devices, such as laptops. Even though not all users will access the wireless LAN at the same time, designers need to know the total number of users to ensure proper configuration of the network. Also, indicate where users will likely access wireless applications. This helps you decide where signal coverage is needed and properly size the network. Identifying the geographic distribution of users on a floor plan is often beneficial, as shown in Figure 6-1.

Figure 6-1   *Geographic Distribution of Users*

Case Study: Acme Furniture Identifies the Number of Users

Madison finds existing documentation that identifies the projected numbers of voice IP phones that were used for defining the cost of the system. She double-checks with the department heads to ensure that these numbers are still accurate and then includes them as potential requirements. As defined before, the following are the number of voice IP phones needed:

- Five for each distribution center
- One for each store manager
- Ten for line supervisors in the manufacturing plant
- Seven for IT staff
- Ten for corporate office executives

The total count of voice IP phones is 127. It is an initial number; the company will likely need more as its workforce grows. The voice telephony user locations will vary uniformly throughout distribution centers, stores, the manufacturing plant, and the corporate offices. The reason for the system is that all personnel are highly mobile and need to handle calls from just about anywhere within the facilities. The only personnel who roam outside their facilities are the IT staff.

In addition, Madison finds that a need exists for supporting up to 25 wireless laptops within the conference room for executives needing to send and receive e-mail, access corporate applications, and surf the web.

Utilization

Because of the way wireless LANs operate, users share the medium. Wireless users connected to the same access point cannot transmit signals simultaneously. As a result, users must take turns transmitting signals, which limits the performance as the number of active users grows. Thus, assessing the activity rate or utilization of users accessing the wireless LANs is very important. A single active wireless IP phone in one particular area, for example, would not pose any issues with performance. But 20 managers talking on voice IP phones from a conference room through a single access point would probably not work. Each access point offers limited capacity. Thus, designers need to know the number and utilization of users in each of the areas of the facility to ensure that the wireless LAN is sized adequately.

Case Study: Acme Furniture Identifies the Number of Simultaneous Active Users

By interviewing the department heads, Madison learns enough about the operations to understand the approximate frequency and duration of each call. This information provides a foundation for forecasting the activity rate of each user. The following is a summary that

Madison prepares on the maximum number of predicted simultaneous voice telephony calls for each of the facility types:

- Two for each distribution center
- One for each retail store
- Three in the manufacturing plant
- Three within the general corporate offices
- Five within the corporate office conference room
- Three for IT personnel, which may occur within the corporate offices, distribution centers, retail stores, or manufacturing plant

In addition, the wireless LAN needs to support up to five wireless laptops having simultaneous access to e-mail, corporate applications, or web browsing from within the corporate office conference room.

All in all, a VoWLAN system can easily handle this level of activity, except that supporting five simultaneously active voice IP phones within the corporate conference room may be a bit challenging to designers.

Coverage Areas

After you know where users will need access to the wireless LAN, defining the signal coverage areas is possible. By properly specifying the coverage area, you avoid the unnecessary expense of installing access points where they are not needed. Also, identify the country in which the wireless LAN will operate. The location impacts channel planning and product availability.

In addition to the obvious coverage areas, such as conference rooms, offices, and outdoor areas, consider the following places:

- **Elevators**—Providing reliable signal coverage inside elevators is often difficult, so carefully assess the need for enabling access to the wireless LAN from inside elevators. When deploying a VoWLAN system in a hospital, for example, access in elevators will likely be a requirement. Nurses and doctors are very mobile and often use elevators when rushing to care for patients. A corporate office, however, may not have critical needs to warrant usage from inside elevators.

- **Stairwells**—Stairwells are also very difficult to provide signal coverage for. The construction of the facility around the staircases usually includes fireproofing material and steel-reinforced concrete, which greatly attenuates radio waves. In most cases, you need an access point inside each stairwell on each floor to offer adequate signal levels for voice applications, which can lead to tremendous cost. If it is absolutely necessary, however, the benefits may exceed the higher costs.

- **Restrooms**—This area might seem silly to cover, but critical areas, such as hospitals, generally need to supply instant communications to essential people. However, in general, the need to cover restrooms will likely be limited.

- **Utility rooms**—If the applications warrant, the need may exist for providing signal coverage in utility rooms. For example, an IT person may need to communicate with a manager or engineer while troubleshooting the network from inside a wiring closet.

- **Basements**—Many facilities have basements, and including signal coverage there may or may not make sense. In some cases, the basement is where a company stores old equipment that eventually will be thrown away or sold to a scrap yard. Some companies, however, make better use of the basement by using it to house exercise areas, extra inventory, and so on. Because of the varied uses for basements, carefully consider whether you need signal coverage there.

After considering all areas of the facility, be certain to indicate on a floor plan where signals do not need to go, as shown in Figure 6-2. Doing so is beneficial to the people who will eventually be performing radio frequency (RF) testing.

Figure 6-2 *Coverage Area Throughout a Facility*

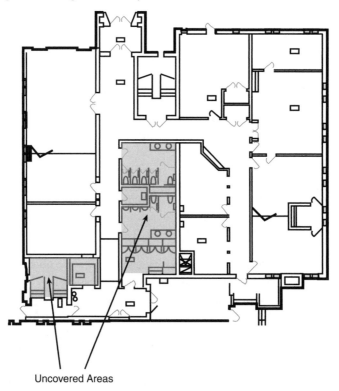

Uncovered Areas

Case Study: Acme Furniture Identifies Coverage Areas

After reviewing the location of users and their likely roaming habits, Madison identified the coverage area for the VoWLAN system as potential requirements. All facilities, such as the corporate headquarters, distribution centers, retail stores, and the manufacturing plant, need RF coverage in offices, hallways, lobbies, and operational areas to accommodate local staff and the IT personnel who need voice telephony services throughout the facilities. Corporate headquarters has elevators and stairwells, but Madison found through interviewing the executives and managers who will be using voice IP phones that calls will not need to take place in elevators. Thus, coverage is not needed in the elevators and stairwells. Calls will primarily take place throughout the offices, hallways, and the main conference room in corporate headquarters. In addition, there is no need to provide coverage in restrooms in any of the facilities. The utility rooms that contain networking equipment, however, need coverage so that IT personnel can communicate using voice calls and surf the web while installing and troubleshooting network problems. On AutoCAD diagrams of the buildings, Madison shades the areas that will not have coverage, such as restrooms, elevators, stairwells, and the utility rooms not containing networking equipment.

Roaming

Be sure to identify whether users are mobile or stationary; this offers valuable information to designers when they configure the network to support roaming. Mobile users need to move about the facility and possibly roam across Internet Protocol (IP) domains, creating a need to manage IP addresses dynamically. Some users, however, may be stationary and make use of wired IP phones from their desktops.

In most cases, there is no need to specify a speed of roaming if you're defining the network for only pedestrian traffic. If you're deploying an outdoor network, for example, for vehicle traffic, determine the maximum speed at which users will need to roam. For example, a wireless network supporting access from moving vehicles may have a requirement for up to 60 miles per hour.

Another aspect of roaming is to specify the need for "seamless connectivity." This requirement is somewhat vague, and you should take care when using it. Instead, giving more details about allowable disruptions is best. For example, requirements for voice telephony may state that calls should not be dropped while users move about the covered areas of the facility. Also consider specifying an acceptable roaming delay. Voice IP phones can generally accept a roaming delay of only 100 milliseconds or less. With data applications, the delays can be much greater, depending on the type of application.

Case Study: Acme Furniture Identifies Roaming Requirements

Through the interviewing process, Madison learned that the typical behavior of voice telephony users is to place calls from stationary locations. For example, most calls within the corporate headquarters are placed from inside the conference room or offices. In the retail stores, a single access point will probably cover most of the store area, so movement within that area will not generally require roaming from one access point to another. Some cases will occur, though, where calls will need to take place while users move about the larger facilities, such as corporate headquarters, the manufacturing plant, and the distribution centers. These cases require roaming from one access point to another while the users walk throughout the facility. Madison makes note of these scenarios as potential requirements.

Environment

As part of the requirements, documenting aspects of the environment that may impact the design is a good idea. These types of requirements generally cannot be changed, so they are considered constraints. Describe all facilities where coverage will be present. Include the floor plans, type of wall and ceiling construction, and possible locations for mounting access points. Find or create building drawings and walk throughout the facility to verify accuracy. Also, take some photographs that show areas that will raise issues when designing and installing the system. For example, Figure 6-3 is a photograph of the ceiling of a warehouse that shows available structures for mounting access points.

Visualizing the interior construction of walls will likely not be possible, so ask the facility manager for details. Try to determine whether the walls are constructed with wood and drywall or concrete with steel reinforcement. The latter case offers much greater attenuation to RF signals, which makes designing the system with a higher density of access points necessary.

At this point of the deployment, you do not need to identify the exact installation of access points, but at least mention the options. For a warehouse, for example, mention in the requirements that the environment includes vertical posts spaced approximately 25 feet apart, with horizontal beams elevated at 40 feet. With an office building, you may identify that the ceiling consists of removable tiles. The main idea is to offer enough details to designers so that they know the options for mounting access points. Be sure to take applicable photos to characterize the types of mounting locations and include them in the requirements documentation. Be sure to point out any issues related to antenna clearances, especially in tight spaces.

Figure 6-3   *Mounting Environment for Access Points in a Warehouse*

In addition to a visible inspection of the facility, consider performing a preinstallation RF survey to understand existing RF signals. In most cases, a company needs to hire someone to do this survey because it requires the use of specialized equipment. With a spectrum analyzer and wireless LAN analysis tool, walk through the facilities and record the presence of existing wireless LANs and other RF signals. Figure 6-4, for example, indicates the existing signals found at a particular point in a facility. In this case, some existing 802.11b/g systems are around channels 1 and 11. There are no existing 802.11a wireless systems.

Figure 6-4   *Signals Found by AirMagnet Analyzer*

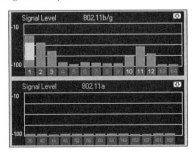

Take note of the noise floor levels within each facility, which generally are between –95 dBm and –85 dBm for the 2.4–2.5-GHz band (802.11b/g). Noise floors in the 5.0–6.0 band (802.11a) generally are much lower because of fewer interfering sources that operate in that band. High noise floor, greater than –85 dBm, requires a higher density of access points to accommodate the noise levels and allow the signal-to-noise ratio to be high enough for voice telephony.

Case Study: Acme Furniture Identifies Environmental Requirements

Earlier on in the Acme Furniture project, RF signal testing was done, but primarily to determine whether the signal coverage of the existing wireless LAN within the retail stores, manufacturing plant, and distribution centers would support a VoWLAN system. Indeed, sufficient signal strength already exists in those areas. So Madison noted that in the requirements documentation and focused on characterizing the environment of the corporate headquarters. This work was already done in the other facilities when the wireless LANs were installed.

Madison walked through the corporate headquarters building and took several photos of the ceilings and made notes that the ceiling consisted of removable tiles. The mounting location of access points here will be above the tiles. Based on previous remodeling work, Madison knows that at least some of the interior walls are constructed with wood and drywall. She talked to the facility manager, though, to verify that most office walls are constructed the same. The load-bearing walls, which run along the hallways and periodically throughout the facility, include concrete with steel reinforcement.

To understand the presence of existing RF signals, Madison contracted with a consultant, Kimberlyn, to test the signals within the corporate headquarters. Kimberlyn walked through the entire building while observing a spectrum analyzer and wireless LAN analyzer tuned to the 2.4–2.5-GHz and 5.0–6.0-GHz bands. Kimberlyn found that the noise floor in the 2.4–2.5-GHz band varied from –96 dBm to –89 dBm, which is within an acceptable range. Noise floor in the 5.0–6.0 band was less than –100 dBm. Several 802.11b/g wireless LAN access points were found, but the signal levels were less than –80 dBm, which means that they are likely wireless LANs installed in neighboring buildings. In fact, one of the network names was "JavaExpress," which is a coffee shop located across the street. Kimberlyn provided a report of the findings. No 802.11a wireless LANs were found. Overall, the presence of existing RF signals does not pose any big issues with the deployment of a VoWLAN system.

Madison noted all of these particulars as environmental requirements.

Security

When defining requirements, document the sensitivity of the information being stored and sent over the wireless network. You might need to identify a need for encryption if users will be transmitting sensitive information, such as credit card numbers. Be certain to include protection from hackers who can access files on your laptop through the wireless LAN by including requirements for personal firewalls. Give security requirements plenty of thought so that you design a solution that will protect the company's valuable information. Refer to Chapter 5, "VoWLAN Security Solutions," for more information on how to secure a wireless LAN.

Case Study: Acme Furniture Defines Security Requirements

Madison spent considerable time with the Acme Furniture security manager, Jake, discussing the needs for wireless security. Because of the sensitivity of the telephone calls, Jake wanted to ensure that effective encryption and authentication are put in place for all voice calls and data communications. The company cannot take the chance of company information getting into the wrong hands.

Jake also explained the security policies that they have in place for the existing wireless LANs in the retail stores, manufacturing plant, and distribution centers. These policies include the use of Wi-Fi Protected Access (WPA). All access points do not broadcast Service Set Identifiers (SSID), and they use Cisco Lightweight Extensible Application Protocol (LEAP) authentication. The security for the VoWLAN system must be at least as good as what is deployed in the existing system. New advancements in security standards, however, should be explored to ensure that optimum security is deployed.

Madison made applicable notes in the requirements documentation and wrote that the design team will need to look further into security options and select the best solution.

Client Devices

The type of client devices, if known at this point in the project, should be clearly defined in the requirements to ensure the design solution accommodates these devices effectively. For example, you could specify that users will have laptops running the Microsoft Windows XP operating system or a particular brand of PocketPCs having Microsoft WindowsCE with CompactFlash interfaces. These device specifications provide a basis for deciding on the type of 802.11 radio cards and drivers to use, as well as assessing the type of wireless middleware that may be necessary. Keep in mind that the choice of client operating system will impact the type and level of security provided to the client devices.

Or, more specifically for voice systems, the requirements should indicate the exact model of voice IP phone that the company would like to use so that designers can integrate the phones into the system design. If using proprietary protocols, such as Cisco Skinny, the selection of phones will constrain the design to including the call control gateways made by the same vendor as the phone. If the phones are based on SIP, the capability to integrate the phones into different platforms will be much broader.

In some cases, a company may not know which phones or vendor to use. In this case, only partial requirements may be needed for client devices for data-only applications.

Case Study: Acme Furniture Identifies Client Device Requirements

Madison recalled that Eric, the consultant hired to assist Acme Furniture with deciding on whether to move forward with a VoWLAN solution, recommended the use of Cisco 7920 IP Phones. As a result, Madison included this model of phone as a potential requirement. She did spend some time, however, researching the latest features of the 7920 and competing phones as well. No noticeable changes had occurred to the 7920 since Eric had completed his work. But she wanted to be prepared to at least mention the other vendor phones again when verifying the requirements with the stakeholders, mainly because when Eric made his recommendation, not all the requirements were known. Madison also acquired some Cisco 7920 phones from the local Cisco sales representative and let a few of the users handle the phones and provide feedback. She was most interested in understanding whether the look and feel of the phone was appropriate for the users and their applications. Because the IP phone is a crucial part of the solution, she wanted to be sure the most effective one is chosen to satisfy all accepted requirements.

Existing Systems

In many cases, users need to access information located on existing servers on the wired side of the system. As a result, describe applicable end systems and interfaces so that you can properly design the wireless system interfaces. For example, you may find that, in addition to call gateways, users may need to interface with a warehouse management system on an IBM AS/400 already in place for nonvoice applications. Figure 6-5 illustrates this scenario. Having the end system and interface descriptions will later prompt you in the design phase to consider interface alternatives, such as 5250 terminal emulation and middleware connectivity for interfacing with the AS/400.

Something else to include in the requirements is the location of existing wiring closets and communications rooms. These places are where access point wiring needs to terminate. You need to identify whether access points can be installed throughout the facilities and still be within 100 meters (300 feet) of these termination locations, which is a limitation based on the use of Category 5 cable. Annotate the locations on facility diagrams and measure the distances. Keep in mind that the 300-foot limitation is the distance that the cable must travel, which will likely be farther than the direct distance between the termination location (switches) and the access point. You may need to look up in the ceiling or refer to cable installation documentation to determine the actual distances. On the facility drawings, mark the areas that are beyond the 300-foot range of the termination locations. These distances may require designers to specify optical fiber connections between the access points in the affected areas and the switches. In case specifying optical fiber is not feasible (likely due to cost), determine whether it's practical to install switches in additional locations to ensure that all access point installation locations will be within 300 feet of a switch.

Figure 6-5   *Existing System Impacting a Wireless LAN System*

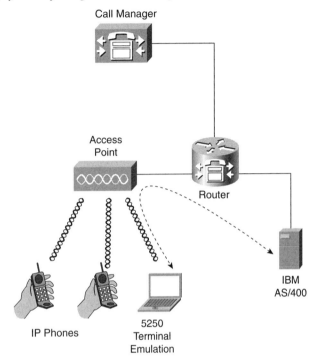

Call Manager

Access
Point

Router

IBM
AS/400

IP Phones

5250
Terminal
Emulation

Case Study: Acme Furniture Defines Existing System Requirements

Madison reviewed all system documentation for the company and also spent quite a bit of time talking with Debbie, the IT manager for Acme, about existing systems that wireless users will need to access. Of course, the design will specify some new systems, such as the voice call management server, but users will need to have access to some existing file servers and corporate applications via wireless laptops. Madison includes these servers in the requirements. One is a Microsoft Windows 2000 server and another is an AS/400, and both are located at the corporate headquarters. Users will need access to files stored on the Windows 2000 server and run distribution center applications on the AS/400. As with the other requirements, Madison notes all of this in the requirements documentation and includes references to more detailed system descriptions located in other documents.

Policies and Preferences

Some companies have policies and strong preferences that will impact the system design. For example, some companies have existing wireless LANs based on 802.11b/g and do not want to change to a different technology. As a result, this would likely become a requirement instead of a design specification to use 802.11b/g for deploying a VoWLAN solution. Also, based on budget constraints, the company may want to maximize the coverage from each access point, which minimizes the number and cost of access points needed to cover the entire facility. If this is the case, include it as a requirement. Keep in mind, however, that this approach will limit performance and possibly reduce the number of simultaneous voice calls that can take place through a particular access point.

Also, a company may have policies or preferences for working with a single vendor, such as Cisco, for networking equipment. The use of a single vendor is generally easier to manage because upgrades and new features will generally work across the entire system, and support for the entire system can be obtained through a single point of contact.

Case Study: Acme Furniture Defines and Identifies Policies and Preferences as Requirements

Acme Furniture already has 802.11b/g wireless LANs installed in the retail stores, manufacturing plant, and distribution centers. And the company definitely wants to take advantage of these existing systems to support the VoWLAN system. In addition, the company would like the wireless LAN needing installation in corporate headquarters to be 802.11b/g as well to provide interoperability with laptops already having integrated 802.11b/g radio cards. Madison includes this requirement, as well as the security policies that Jake gave her previously, in the requirements documentation.

Budget

The requirements stage of a wireless LAN project is a good time to ask how much money is available. If funding limits are known, you will know how much you have to work with when designing the system. In most cases, however, a company will ask how much the system will cost. You then need to define the requirements and design the system before giving a cost estimate.

Case Study: Acme Furniture Identifies Budget Requirements

Madison read the reports that Eric provided earlier in the project that outlined projected costs for the system. The total first-year cost of deploying the VoWLAN solution is $264,500, which includes $119,500 in capital costs and $145,000 in operational costs. The company will also incur an annual cost of $20,000 for ongoing operational support. After talking briefly with the company president, Bob, Madison discovers that the company has already allocated the funds for the project. The total budget will be $300,000 for the first year, which is a bit higher than the projected cost, but an additional amount was included for unforeseen costs. The company will also allocate $20,000 each year for support. Madison includes this information in the requirements documentation.

Schedules

Of course, a company generally wants the wireless LAN installed "yesterday," but we all know that this is not possible. You do need to nail down a realistic completion date, though, and plan accordingly. For example, you may be defining your requirements in July, and a retail store will likely demand that a wireless price marking application be installed by the end of September. This deadline makes it possible to make use of the system during the Christmas holiday season. Be sure to probe for the realistic dates.

**Case Study: Acme Furniture Establishes a Preliminary Schedule
for Deploying the VoWLAN Solution**

Madison spent some time talking with others in the IT department and came up with a preliminary schedule for deploying the VoWLAN system. This schedule consists of the following:

- Finalize requirements analysis: 3 weeks

- Design: 4 weeks

- Installation and testing: 3 weeks

Madison met with the IT manager, Debbie, and learned that this schedule will suffice. The department heads at the last staff meeting that Debbie attended mentioned that they wanted the system operational within three months.

Verifying and Validating Requirements

Before finalizing requirements, be certain to ensure that all stakeholders agree. You can achieve this task by documenting all the requirements, labeling them "preliminary," and distributing them to all applicable people to review. After giving enough time for review, schedule a meeting with all stakeholders to discuss each of the requirements. Through the meeting, identify and resolve any discrepancies and edit the requirements documentation to reflect any changes. In some companies, you may need to process the requirements through a configuration management board for approval, but in most cases, a simple meeting with the stakeholders is sufficient.

When reviewing the requirements, make sure that all requirements are needed and accurate. In some cases, some prototyping or pilot testing may be necessary to ensure that specific applications really do have enough benefits and should be included as system requirements.

Case Study: Acme Furniture Approves the Requirements

After documenting all potential requirements and reviewing them with her boss, Debbie, Madison e-mailed the requirements document to the company president, Bob, and each of the company's department heads. These people have the most knowledge about the requirements. In fact, they are the same people Madison interviewed when collecting the data for the requirements. The reason for sending them the requirements documentation is to ensure that all requirements are accurate and fulfill all needs. Madison also scheduled a requirements review meeting to occur three days after sending out the document. At the meeting, some debate occurred about whether coverage should include elevators and stairwells. Some thought it was needed to ensure that everyone could be in continual contact with each other as they roamed between floors within corporate headquarters, the only facility that has elevators and closed stairwells. Others, however, argued that there would be very few times that this would be necessary, and accepting a possible dropped call in this situation would not be a huge problem. The group concluded that this requirement would be left open for now, and a decision would be made later after designing the system. If the additional cost to cover the elevators and stairwells was too high, they would not cover these areas. Other than that, the group accepted all the requirements.

Documenting Requirements

After you have identified, verified, and validated potential requirements for a VoWLAN system, the last step in defining system requirements is to document the requirements.

The life cycle of the VoWLAN system deployment can be long; consequently, the people who are working on the system deployment may move on to other career opportunities, locations, projects, and so on. Documentation can easily get lost in the shuffle.

Thus, thoroughly documenting and recording the requirements for the VoWLAN system is important to provide a basis for designing the solution, as well as to serve as a written record of the design process.

If you identify, verify, validate, and document requirements for a VoWLAN system, no matter the size of the wireless network, defining the requirements will help create a solid foundation from which you can build your VoWLAN system.

Chapter Summary

Requirements are very important because they provide a foundation for the design. Without accurate requirements, the design will not yield a system that best satisfies the needs of users. When analyzing requirements, start by identifying potential requirements for various elements, such as applications, coverage areas, roaming, and security. To identify requirements, you need to interview company stakeholders, such as managers and potential users. Also, review any related project reports and documents describing existing systems. After you have nailed down the requirements, gain acceptance from the stakeholders by allowing them to review and comment on the requirements.

Chapter Review Questions

1   What are the steps of analyzing requirements?

2   Who should review and comment on the requirements?

3   Why is defining requirements crucial?

4   What are examples of requirements elements that you should define?

5   What type of testing should you consider performing when analyzing the environment?

6   What areas of the facility may be questionable to include as covered areas?

7   Why are stairwells difficult to cover?

8   What are typical noise floor values for the 2.4–2.5-GHz band (802.11b/g)?

9   Why should you identify the location of equipment and wiring closets?

10   What is a typical policy or preference that a company may have regarding requirements?

Objectives

Upon completing this chapter, you will be able to

- Define an effective VoWLAN system architecture.
- Identify an appropriate VoWLAN deployment model.
- Explain optimum roaming and security strategies.
- Describe effective network infrastructure elements.
- Identify the optimum placement of access points.

CHAPTER 7

Designing a VoWLAN Solution

This chapter discusses the technical elements that need consideration when designing a VoWLAN system. This includes definition of the system architecture, effective configuration of access points, optimum location of access points, applicable configuration settings for voice gateways, and configuration of wireless Internet Protocol (IP) phones.

Overall Design Steps

The design process of any system uncovers technical elements that together explain how the system will satisfy requirements. Thus, be certain that you have thoroughly analyzed and documented the requirements before moving on with the design. The requirements provide the basis for making crucial decisions about which technologies and configuration settings will make up the system. Refer to Chapter 6, "Analyzing VoWLAN Requirements," for details on how to define requirements for VoWLAN solutions.

The steps for designing a VoWLAN system are as follows:

Step 1   Specify the overall system architecture. This step involves selecting a well-tested model that indicates how the necessary components will interact, specifying how roaming will work, determining security and Quality of Service (QoS) elements, and defining the network infrastructure.

Step 2   Identify access point installation locations. This step involves active testing within the facility to identify the optimum installation location for each access point.

Step 3   Document the design. Documenting the design is very important. This documentation is a valuable reference when installing the system and also when supporting the system.

Deployment Models

When you deploy wireless voice systems, it's strongly recommended that you base the system on a well-tested model, preferably one that is outlined by the manufacturer of the wireless IP phones that you plan to use. For example, if you plan to use Cisco 7920 wireless IP phones, Cisco offers the following deployment models:

- Single-site architecture
- Multisite WAN with centralized call processing
- Multisite WAN with distributed call processing

The following sections provide more details on each of these models.

Single-Site Architecture

Figure 7-1 illustrates the single-site architecture model for Cisco VoWLAN systems. This model consists of a call processing agent (that is, Cisco CallManager) located at a single site that has a wireless local-area network (LAN) for carrying voice traffic. Any calls that interface outside the wireless LAN must use the Public Switched Telephone Network (PSTN). This model is ideal for a single campus or site having fewer than 30,000 phone lines.

The primary benefit of this architecture is that it is relatively easy and inexpensive to deploy. For example, no need exists for a wide-area network (WAN) to interconnect users to the call processing agent. All call control and voice traffic occur over a common local infrastructure.

The following are tips for deploying the single-site model architecture:

- Analyze calling patterns of your company. The single-site model is best when most of the calls stay within the same site or calls are destined for PSTN users outside the company. For example, an operational support call center would likely fit this model.

- Include G.711 codecs for all endpoints. Doing so reduces the phone's processor consumption for transcoding signals, which enables the processor to be available for other functions.

- If no need exists for H.323 functionality, use Media Gateway Control Protocol (MGCP) gateways for the PSTN. Doing so simplifies the dial plan configuration.

Multisite WAN with Centralized Call Processing

Figure 7-2 illustrates the architecture model for Cisco VoWLAN systems having multiple sites with centralized call processing. This model includes a single call processing agent at a centralized site. As a result, the call processing packets must flow over the WAN equipped with QoS. Thus, a WAN outage will disrupt calls within each site. The WAN must support speeds of at least 768 kbps per connection. The WAN can use just about any technology, such as leased lines, Frame Relay, and Asynchronous Transfer Mode (ATM). This model is best for sites with more than 30,000 phone lines.

Figure 7-1   *Single-Site Model for the Cisco VoWLAN System*

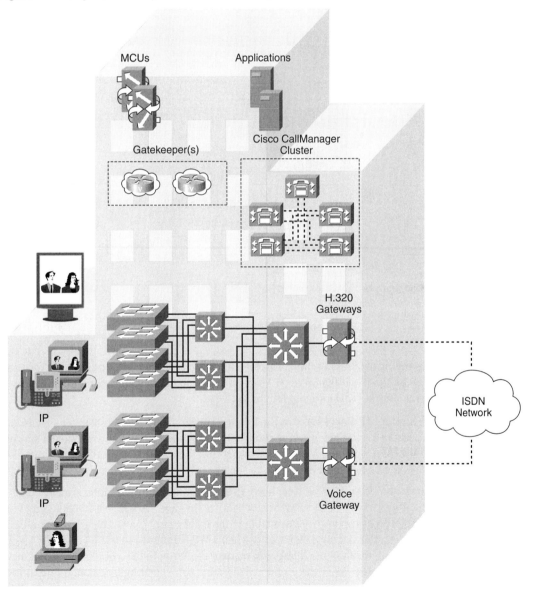

Figure 7-2 *Multisite WAN Model with Centralized Call Processing*

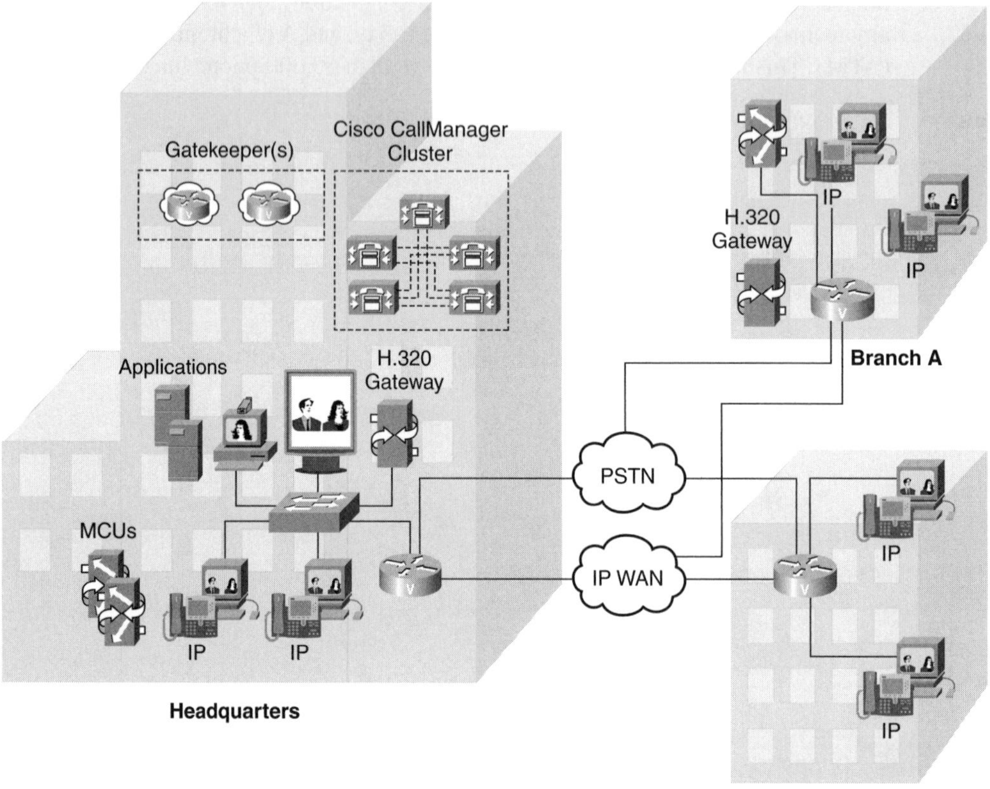

When deploying the multisite model architecture with centralized call processing, focus on strengthening the reliability of the WAN. The following are recommended methods that you can implement for improving reliability:

- **Redundant IP WAN links in the branch router**—This low-cost strategy enables the system to continue working if one of the WAN links goes down. It cannot survive the loss of a branch router, however. As a stronger solution, consider deploying redundant branch routers.

- **Survivable Remote Site Telephony (SRST)**—This approach alone provides high reliability for only voice services, not data. In this case, the wireless IP phones rehome to call processing functions available in the local router if a WAN failure occurs. Figure 7-3 shows how SRST works when a WAN failure occurs. When the WAN is operational, the branch office connects over the WAN to Cisco CallManager at the central site. The WAN carries the voice traffic, call signaling, and data traffic. If the WAN fails, the wireless IP phones register with the branch router, which allows calls to take place internally within the branch office and which routes external calls over the PSTN. In this case, the phones display the message "Unified CM fallback mode" to the user. Some of the advanced phone features will be grayed out and not available due to the limitations of the PSTN. When the WAN is reestablished, the wireless IP phones at the branch office automatically reregister with Cisco CallManager at the central site.

Figure 7-3   *SRST Operation in the Presence of a WAN Failure*

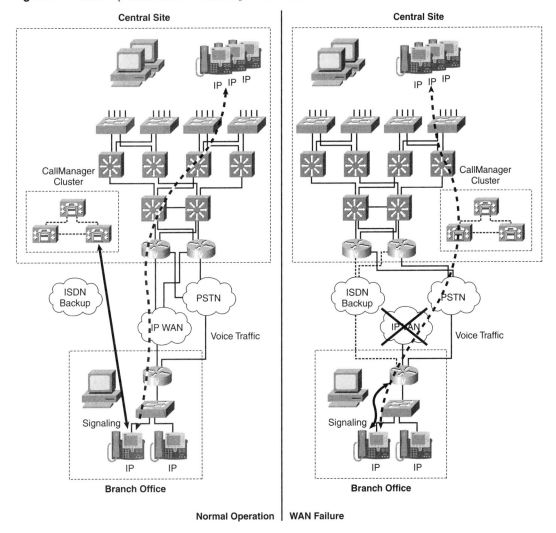

- **SRST with ISDN backup for data**—In addition to SRST, you can interface the branch router to an Integrated Services Digital Network (ISDN) connection to provide data backup. If you use this method, be certain to configure the ISDN connection to not allow Simple (Skinny) Client Control Protocol (SCCP) traffic from the wireless IP phones to enter the ISDN interface. This configuration keeps signaling from the wireless IP phones from reaching Cisco CallManager at the central site.

- **Data and voice ISDN backup**—With this approach, Survivable Remote Site Telephony (SRST) is not used. Instead, the branch router provides a backup connection to the ISDN, which maintains voice traffic, call signaling, and data flowing between the branch and central office if the primary WAN goes down. This approach, however, is effective only if the bandwidth requirements of the voice traffic are equal to or less than the ISDN bandwidth allocation. In addition, the interface between the branch router and the ISDN must implement Cisco's QoS for network infrastructures.

Multisite WAN with Distributed Call Processing

Figure 7-4 illustrates the architecture model for Cisco VoWLAN systems having multiple sites with distributed call processing. This model involves a call processing agent, such as Cisco CallManager, at each site. As a result, the disruption of the WAN does not disrupt all calls. This model best serves a maximum of six large sites with a maximum of 30,000 phone lines total.

Figure 7-4 *Multisite WAN Model with Distributed Call Processing*

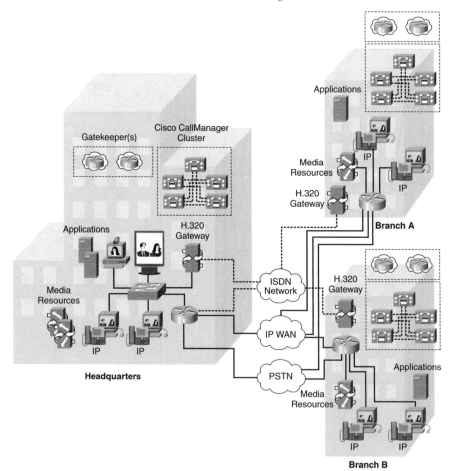

In addition to the tips and strategies provided for the other models in the preceding sections, consider implementing the following:

- **Gatekeepers**—A gatekeeper is an H.323 device that provides Call Admission Control (CAC) and E.164 dial plan resolution. To provide high reliability of the gatekeeper, use Hot Standby Router Protocol (HSRP) gatekeeper pairs, gatekeeper clustering, and alternate gatekeeper support. In addition, use multiple gatekeepers to provide redundancy within the network.

- **Session Initiation Protocol (SIP) proxies**—Ensure adequate redundancy for the SIP proxies, and ensure that the SIP proxies have the capacity for the call rate and number of calls required in the network.

- **Call processing agents**—Using different processing agents at each site is possible. Table 7-1 recommends which processing agent to use based on requirements.

Table 7-1   *Recommended Call Processing Agents*

Call Processing Agent	Recommended Size	Comments
Cisco Unified CallManager Express (CME)	Up to 240 phones	For small remote sites Capacity depends on Cisco IOS platform
Cisco Unified CallManager	50 to 30,000 phones	Small to large sites, depending on the size of the Cisco Unified CallManager cluster Supports centralized or distributed call processing
Legacy PBX with Voice over Internet Protocol (VoIP) gateway	Depends on PBX	Number of IP WAN calls and functionality depend on the PBX-to-VoIP gateway protocol and the gateway platform

Roaming

Because of the mobile aspect of wireless voice telephony, ensure that the VoWLAN system architecture you select supports effective roaming. The voice user must be able to move about the facility, and the system needs to allow roaming at both Layer 2 and Layer 3 (see Figure 7-5). Without smooth roaming, users will experience dropped calls.

Figure 7-5   *Layer 2 and Layer 3 Roaming*

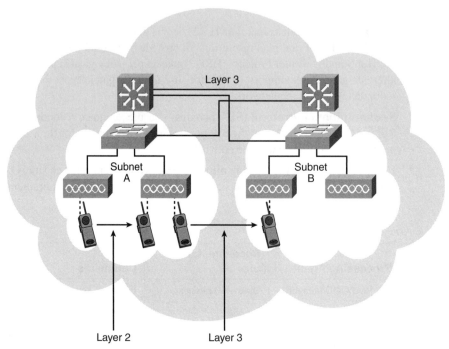

With VoWLAN systems, roaming may take place before a user places a call, which is commonly referred to as precall roaming. In this case, the user may traverse the boundaries of Layer 2 virtual local-area networks (VLAN) and layer subnets. If the wireless IP phone stays within the same subnet, the phone's IP address remains the same. If the phone moves into an area associated with a different VLAN, the wireless IP phone should automatically use Dynamic Host Configuration Protocol (DHCP) to obtain an applicable IP address.

Is Wi-Fi Roaming Really Seamless?

An extremely beneficial aspect of Wi-Fi networks is mobility. For example, a person can walk through a facility while carrying on a conversation over a Wi-Fi phone or when downloading a large file from a server. The Wi-Fi radio inside the user device automatically roams from one access point to another as needed to provide seamless connectivity. At least that is what one hopes will happen!

To determine how well roaming works with conventional wireless clients, I performed some testing. The test configuration included two access points, with one access point (AP-1) set to channel 1 and the other access point (AP-2) set to channel 6. Other settings were default values, such as beacon interval of 100 milliseconds, RTS/CTS disabled, and so on. The access points were installed in a typical office facility in a manner that provided a minimum of 25-dB signal-to-noise ratio throughout each access point's radio cell, with about 20 percent overlap between cells. This is somewhat the industry standard for wireless voice applications. The roaming client in this case, though, was a laptop equipped with an internal Centrino Wi-Fi radio (Intel 2915ABG).

While standing with the wireless client within a few feet of AP-1, I used AirMagnet Laptop Analyzer (via another Wi-Fi card inserted into the laptop's PCMCIA slot) to ensure that I was associated with AP-1. I then kicked off a File Transfer Protocol (FTP) transfer of a large file from the server to the laptop and started measuring the 802.11 packet trace using AirMagnet Laptop Analyzer. With the file downloading throughout the entire test, I walked toward AP-2 until I was directly next to it. With the packet trace, I was able to view the exchange of 802.11 frames, calculate the roaming delay, and see whether any significant disruption occurred to the FTP stream.

After the client radio reassociated, it issued several 802.11 disassociation frames to AP-1 to initiate the reassociation process. The radio then broadcast an 802.11 probe request to get responses from access points within range of the wireless client. This process is likely done to ensure that the client radio has up-to-date information (beacon signal strength) about candidate access points before selecting which one to reassociate with.

AP-2 responded with an 802.11 probe response. Because the only response was from AP-2, the client radio card decided to associate with AP-2. As expected, the association process with AP-2 consisted of the exchange of 802.11 authentication and association frames (based on 802.11 open-system authentication).

The reassociation process took 68 milliseconds, which is the time between the client radio issuing the first disassociation frame to AP-1 and the client receiving the final association frame (response) from AP-2. This time is quite good, and I have found similar values with other vendor access points.

The entire roaming process, however, interrupts wireless applications for a much longer period of time. For example, based on my tests, the FTP process halts an average of 5 seconds before the radio card initiating the reassociation process (that is, issuing the first disassociation frame to AP-1). I measured 802.11 packet traces indicating that the client radio card retransmits data frames many times to AP-1 (due to weak signal levels) before giving up and initiating the reassociation with AP-2. This substantial number of retransmissions disrupted the file download process, which makes the practical roaming delay in my tests an average of 5 seconds! The Centrino radio card I tested is notorious for this problem, but I found this to be the case with most other radio cards as well.

Vendors are likely having the radio cards hold off reassociations to avoid premature and excessive reassociations (access point hopping). Unfortunately, this disrupts some wireless applications. If you plan to deploy mobile wireless applications, be sure to test how the roaming impacts the applications.

Every model of radio card behaves differently when roaming due to proprietary mechanisms, and some cards do better than others. Just keep in mind that roaming may take much longer than expected, so take this delay into account when deploying wireless LAN applications, especially wireless voice, which is not tolerant of roaming delays exceeding 100 milliseconds.

Roaming that occurs during a call is referred to as mid-call roaming. For example, a user may be walking from one building to another building while talking on the phone. To avoid having the call dropped due to latency, it is very important that the mid-call roaming be accomplished as quickly as possible. This requires careful attention to the design of the network infrastructure. Strive for mid-call roam times of 100 milliseconds (ms) or less. The mid-call roam time is the amount of time that elapses after the last Reliable Transport Protocol (RTP) packet is seen from the current access point and the first RTP packet is seen from the access point that the wireless IP phone associates with.

Layer 2 roaming, which is a data link layer operation, takes place when a wireless IP phone moves out of range of an access point and reassociates with a different access point. Because this type of roaming occurs frequently as users move about a facility, such as a warehouse or hospital, be certain that Layer 2 roaming is fast. In most cases, the speed at which Layer 2 roaming occurs is highly dependent on the client radio. For example, some client radios found integrated in laptops may take anywhere from a couple seconds to several minutes to roam. These speeds are not fast enough to support roaming without dropping calls. When selecting wireless IP phones, be certain that they support fast roaming. The Cisco 7920 wireless IP phones, for example, are specially designed to make Layer 2 roaming fast enough to avoid dropped calls. For example, a Cisco 7920 phone initiates a reassociation process with a different access point if the phone doesn't receive three consecutive beacons from the existing access point and its unicast frame to the access point is not acknowledged. The 7920 also periodically scans for better access points and maintains a list of potential access points. A decision to roam is made on signal strength and signal quality metrics. The quality metric makes use of information provided by each access point in its beacon about the utilization of the access point. As a result, the phone can avoid attempting to reassociate with access points that have high utilization and may not be able to effectively support voice traffic. With these mechanisms, the 7920 generally can complete Layer 2 roaming within 100 ms.

In addition to needing Layer 2 roaming, someone using a wireless IP phone may roam into a different subnet of the network, thus requiring Layer 3 roaming to occur. The addition of Layer 3 roaming to Layer 2 roaming often causes substantial delays that may drop voice calls. As a result, avoid having wireless IP phones perform mid-call Layer 3 roaming. If possible, define a single subnet for the entire wireless LAN, which avoids Layer 3 roaming. If using this method is not possible, at least minimize the possibility of Layer 3 mid-call roaming. For example, you may have a different subnet on each floor of a hospital. When performing the RF survey, ensure that signals from one floor do not overlap at such an extent that the wireless IP phones roam to the floor above (or below) while the user is walking throughout a particular floor.

Security

The VoWLAN system architecture must ensure that voice traffic is secure. To deploy an effective security solution, refer to Chapter 5, "VoWLAN Security Solutions," for more details on encryption and authentication techniques and best practices for securing wireless networks. Carefully assess each of these security mechanisms, and include the ones that will best satisfy requirements as part of the VoWLAN architecture.

In addition, minimize delay between access points and authentication servers. For example, when a Cisco 7920 wireless phone implementing LEAP roams between access points (that is, Layer 2 roaming), the phone must perform LEAP authentication. This can cause dropped calls if the communications with the access control server (ACS), which performs the authentication, incorporate too much delay. The RTP voice traffic will not flow until the LEAP authentication has finished. Therefore, you need to minimize the delay between the access points and the ACS. To lessen delays, consider distributing ACSs (in lieu of a centralized approach) locally to place an ACS as close as possible to users. This technique is especially necessary if the WAN offers slow speeds or becomes congested from time to time. In some cases, as with Cisco access points, hosting the authentication server at the access point may be possible. This provides the fastest form of authentication, which significantly decreases the possibility of dropped calls. However, it is effective only for small deployments (fewer than 50 phones) or when used as a backup if the primary authentication server becomes unavailable.

Network Infrastructure

Several design aspects of the network infrastructure require careful consideration to ensure that the VoWLAN system performs effectively.

Virtual LANs

With VLANs, segmenting networks into one or more broadcast domains is possible. Keeping data and voice applications on different VLANs is important because it enables the network to provide priority queuing at the Layer 2 access switch port, which makes certain that appropriate QoS is provided for various classes of traffic and helps resolve issues such as IP addressing, security, and network dimensioning.

For example, the Cisco Aironet 350, 1100, and 1200 Series access points support up to 16 VLANs. The access point connects to a Cisco Catalyst Switch via 802.1Q trunks. Each VLAN maps to a unique Service Set Identifier (SSID) on the access point. Assigning users of wireless IP phones to the applicable VLAN by configuring the corresponding SSID in the phone is then possible. With multiple VLANs supported, you can create different security domains, such as open, Wired Equivalent Privacy (WEP), Lightweight Extensible Authentication Protocol (LEAP), Protected Extensible Authentication Protocol (PEAP), and Extensible Authentication Protocol–Transport Layer Security (EAP-TLS).

Multicasting

Avoid using wireless IP phones that use Layer 2 multicast transport for the following reasons:

- Multicast does not use acknowledgments; therefore, quality is less due to the relatively high bit error rate of wireless networks.

- Multicast frames are transmitted at the rate supported by the device associated at the lowest data rate.

- When a client device, such as a wireless IP phone, implements power-save mode, the access point buffers all multicast frames and sends them periodically when all devices are awake. This introduces delays, which can degrade voice quality.

NOTE   The Cisco 7920 wireless IP phone does not support multicast traffic to improve voice quality.

Switch Recommendations

With voice applications, the access points sometimes operate near capacity. As a result, there might be times when the number of voice users could exceed the capacity of a particular access point, and the access point begins dropping packets and may degrade the voice quality of all users. To avoid this situation, take advantage of rate limiting available on the switch. For example, the Cisco Catalyst 3550 has policing and rate-limiting capabilities. You can set the 3550, for example, to rate-limit at the maximum throughput level of the access point. This setting keeps the access point from dropping voice packets. Table 7-2 identifies the maximum throughput of various access point types.

Table 7-2   *Maximum Throughput Values of Different Access Point Types*

Access Point Type	Maximum Throughput
802.11a	42 Mbps
802.11b	7 Mbps
802.11g	36 Mbps
802.11a + 802.11b	49 Mbps
802.11a + 802.11g	78 Mbps

NOTE   If you are using a Cisco Catalyst 4000 Series switch as the main router in the network, ensure that it contains, at a minimum, either a Supervisor Engine 2+ (SUP2+) or Supervisor Engine 3 (SUP3) module. The SUP1 or SUP2 module can cause roaming delays, as can the Cisco Catalyst 2948G, 2980G, 2980G-A, 4912, and 2948G-GE-TX switches.

Quality of Service

Ensure that the VoWLAN architecture provides effective QoS. Because of the absence of dedicated bandwidth on wireless LANs, though, providing QoS is difficult. In fact, QoS is generally available only to downstream traffic from the access point. Completely regulating upstream traffic from a wireless client to the access point is not possible. Therefore, make sure that the VoWLAN solution has QoS that makes sense and statistically provides good quality service for specific numbers of concurrent phone calls.

For example, Cisco access points and 7920 Wireless IP phones use a technique similar to IEEE 802.11e called enhanced DCF (EDCF). It allows the radios to adjust their contention window values to all for greater access to the medium, which then allows the wireless IP phones and access points to have greater use of the medium (over data devices), which improves QoS. Also, Cisco access points using IOS Release 12.2(11)JA or later support up to eight queues for downstream QoS. The queues are configured by Layer 2 or Layer 3 access lists or VLAN number or through dynamic registration of the 7920 wireless IP phone. Cisco, however, recommends that you configure only two of the queues for optimum voice performance. Place the voice (RTP) and signaling (SCCP) traffic in the highest-priority queue. The data traffic should be placed in a best-effort queue. This, in combination with EDCF, provides the best statistical results for voice QoS.

In addition, the Cisco 7920 phone automatically announces its presence to the Cisco Aironet access point, and the access point in turn allocates a high-priority queue for the downstream traffic associated with the call for that particular phone. This process is done via Cisco Discovery Protocol (CDP).

Placement of Access Points

To satisfy requirements for coverage, number of users, and utilization, you must determine optimum installation locations. This involves first performing capacity analysis and then completing a thorough RF site survey.

Wireless Capacity Analysis

Before determining the placement of access points, you must consider the coverage area (radio cell size) that each access point will produce. Traditionally, for data-only applications, companies install the access points configured in a manner that produces the largest radio cell size. This method minimizes the number of access points needed and reduces costs for hardware. With relatively lightly loaded networks, which is generally the case with e-mail, web browsing, and wireless bar code scanners, this method results in plenty of capacity to provide good performance to users. The influx of heavy web video users, however, might begin to strain wireless networks deployed for maximum signal coverage.

<table>
<tr><td>NOTE</td><td>For the Cisco 7920 wireless IP phone, Cisco recommends that you have no more than 15 to 25 total 7920 devices per 802.11b access point. Of these devices, each 802.11b access point can support no more than eight G.729 or seven G.711 concurrent calls per access point.</td></tr>
</table>

A wireless LAN supporting voice applications usually requires greater capacity than one supporting typical data applications, such as e-mail and web browsing. As a result, you must take into account the maximum number of simultaneous voice devices that will need to operate on the network. This is necessary to determine the density of access points necessary to support all the voice (and data) traffic. In some cases, where few simultaneous calls are being made on the network, you can install access points with maximum radio cell sizes to minimize costs. In other cases, especially when there are many voice users, reducing the radio cell size of each access point might be necessary to increase the capacity of the wireless network. This method effectively results in having each access point service fewer users, which improves capacity and performance.

<table>
<tr><td>NOTE</td><td>The use of a larger voice sample size (such as 40 ms) configured in the phone could result in a larger number of simultaneous voice calls, but it will also increase the end-to-end delay of the VoIP calls. Thus, you should ensure that the sample size is 20 ms for best performance.</td></tr>
</table>

When analyzing capacity, refer to the requirements defined for the number and placement of voice users and their corresponding utilization. For example, a hospital may require a total of 100 users to be equipped with wireless IP phones. The challenge is to determine where these users will operate the phones and how many will be placing calls simultaneously from the same location. This information is difficult to determine because users are mobile, and where the users will roam and how many will be active at any given time may not be well understood. Make your best estimate, however, based on interviews with potential users. Also, consider planning for some additional capacity to support emergency situations. For a hospital, for example, you may want to support disasters that may require supporting a large triage operation outside the hospital.

To calculate access point density, determine how many simultaneous voice users will be within a given area. An area to use as the basis for this calculation is the typical coverage area (radio cell size) of the access points that you plan to deploy. For 802.11b, this area is approximately 10,000 to 15,000 square feet. You may find, for example, that the majority of the 100 hospital users will be distributed within the hospital. There it is likely that a maximum of three voice users will be simultaneously making calls in each of the 10,000-square-foot areas within the hospital. Based on this example, you could deploy the access points with maximum radio cell size. This method would result in having approximately three simultaneous voice users associated with each access point. As discussed in Chapter 3, the number of calls that an 802.11b access point can support is eight. Thus, the use of maximum-sized radio cells will provide good performance.

Now, assume that the hospital will also require the simultaneous use of 12 wireless IP phones from the corporate conference room, which is roughly 600 square feet in size. For this area, you need to deploy at least two 802.11 access points to support the users. Each access point will service up to eight users, so two will service up to 16. This capacity is plenty for that area and even gives some room for expansion. Both access points would be installed in the conference room and would be set to different RF channels. In addition, the radio cell size of each access point should be made smaller to just fit within the conference room to keep users from outside the conference room from connecting to the access points.

If requirements call for a great deal of simultaneous voice users, the radio cell size of all access points may need to be made smaller to increase the capacity to the required level. For example, a conference facility may predict that as many as 20 users could simultaneously place calls with their wireless IP phones within every 10,000 square feet of the conference facility. If you are deploying 802.11b, you will need three access points covering each of the 10,000-square-foot areas to produce enough capacity to support the calls. Each access point will service up to eight simultaneous calls, so the total supported will be 24. To make this arrangement work effectively, you need to reduce the radio cell size of each access point to cover approximately one-third of the 10,000-square-foot area.

RF Site Survey

With wireless systems, predicting the propagation of radio waves and detecting the presence of interfering signals without the use of test equipment is very difficult. Even if you are using omnidirectional antennas, radio waves do not really travel the same distance in all directions. Instead, walls, doors, elevator shafts, people, and other obstacles offer varying degrees of attenuation, which causes the RF radiation pattern to be irregular and unpredictable. As a result, performing an RF site survey is often necessary to fully understand the behavior of radio waves within a facility before installing wireless network access points.

The ultimate goal of an RF site survey is to supply enough information to determine the number and placement of access points that provides adequate coverage throughout the facility. An RF site survey also detects the presence of interference coming from other sources that could degrade the performance of the wireless LAN.

The need and complexity of an RF site survey varies depending on the facility. For example, a small three-room office might not require a site survey. This scenario can probably get by with a single access point (or more, depending on the number of users) located anywhere within the office and still maintain adequate coverage. If this access point encounters RF interference from another nearby wireless LAN, you can likely select a different channel and eliminate the problem.

A larger facility, such as an office complex, apartment building, hospital, or warehouse, generally requires a thorough RF site survey. Without a survey, users will probably end up with inadequate coverage and suffer from low performance in some areas. You certainly would not want to relocate and add access points to the facility after installing and interconnecting 20 access points or more.

When conducting an RF site survey, perform the following tasks:

- **Obtain a facility diagram**—Before getting too far with the site survey, locate a set of building blueprints. If none are available, prepare a floor plan drawing that depicts the location of walls, walkways, and so on.

- **Visually inspect the facility**—Be sure to walk through the facility before performing any tests to verify the accuracy of the facility diagram. This is a good time to note any potential barriers that may affect the propagation of RF signals. For example, a visual inspection can uncover obstacles to RF, such as metal racks and partitions, items that blueprints generally do not show. Also, look for possible mounting locations, and do some preplanning on potential installation points. If the facility has primarily a drop ceiling with removable ceiling tiles, you likely have many installation locations to select from. The access points can be installed just about anywhere above the ceiling tiles, assuming the mounting point is not directly adjacent to large metal obstacles, such as heating vents.

- **Identify user areas**—On the facility diagram, mark the areas of fixed and mobile users. In addition to illustrating where mobile users may roam, indicate where they will not go. You might get by with fewer access points if you can limit the roaming areas.

- **Determine preliminary access point locations**—By considering the location of wireless users and range estimations of the wireless LAN products you are using, approximate the locations of access points that will provide adequate coverage throughout the user areas. Plan for some propagation overlap among adjacent access points, but keep in mind that channel assignments for access points need to be far enough apart to avoid interaccess point interference. Be certain to consider mounting locations, which could be vertical posts or metal supports above ceiling tiles. Be sure to recognize suitable locations for installing the access point, antenna, data cable, and power line. Also think about different antenna types when deciding where to position access points. An access point mounted near an outside wall, for example, could be a good location if you use a patch antenna with relatively high gain oriented within the facility.

- **Gather tools**—You need at least one access point that you can use for testing purposes. Configure the access point with the same settings that you plan to deploy, especially the transmit power. You might want to do some testing to determine the best combination of transmit power and antenna types to produce the applicable radio cell size to support the required number and utilization of users. Keep in mind that it may be necessary to reduce the Effective Isotropic Radiated Power (EIRP) of the access point to produce smaller radio cells.

Note   Always use diversity antennas on the access points in indoor and outdoor environments to reduce impacts of multipath propagation. Diversity makes use of two antennas that help reduce the impacts of multipath propagation.

- **Coordinate access to the facility**—In most cases, you need permission to perform RF testing in a facility. A hospital, for example, has restrictions on where and when you can enter certain areas, such as the operating rooms and radiology department. Before starting the testing, check with the managers of each department and get approval to perform the testing. You might need to schedule visits with each department separately, depending on the organization. In some places, such as airports, you will probably need an escort working with you for security purposes. Whether or not an escort is required, you may need someone along who can unlock doors from time to time.

- **Verify access point locations**—This step is when the real testing begins. Many wireless LAN vendors, including Cisco, provide free RF site survey tools that identify the associated access point, data rate, signal strength, and signal quality. You can load this software on a laptop or PocketPC and test the coverage of each preliminary access point location. Alternatively, you could use a site survey tool available from several different companies, such as AirMagnet, Berkeley Varitronics, and Helium Networks.

- **Install an access point at each preliminary location, and monitor the site survey software readings (either signal level or SNR level) by walking varying distances away from the access point**—You should walk through the facility and find where the radio cell exists of the access point being tested. Be sure to perform the testing with the antenna of the access point near the location where it will be installed. There is no need to connect the access point to the distribution system; however, you do need AC power. So be sure to take along an extension cord (or use a battery with an AC power converter).

NOTE   When testing each access point location for voice applications, ensure that there is 11 Mbps of link speed and at least 25 dB SNR throughout the radio cell of each access point. Also, strive for 15 to 20 percent overlap between the radio cells of adjacent access points.

Keep in mind that the communication between the wireless client and the access point includes an uplink path from the client to the access point and a downlink path from the access point to the client. For example, when a user opens a web browser, the client device sends a URL (Uniform Resource Locator) page request through the uplink path to the access point. Then the web pages are sent through the access point to the client over the downlink path. Another example is when a person, such as Mary, is talking on a wireless IP phone to Bob. In this case, Mary's voice packets flow over the uplink path from her IP phone to the access point, and Bob's voice packets eventually travel over the downlink path from the access point to Mary's phone. At least this is what one hopes occurs; otherwise, none of these applications will work properly.

As mentioned in Chapter 4, "Wireless LAN Technologies," access points periodically send beacons, which travel over the downlink path from the access to the client devices. Most Wi-Fi site survey tools receive these beacons and display the signal strength and SNR (signal-to-noise ratio) associated with the beacon signals. A person performing an RF site survey determines the optimum installation location for access points by using the beacon signal strength to determine where adequate coverage is provided. For example, you might define the target range boundary to be 25 dB SNR (Cisco's recommendation for the 7920 Wireless IP phone). You then use a test tool to ensure that at least 25 dB or better SNR exists throughout the covered area. Keep in mind, however, that this value is only in relation to the downlink path. It does not take into consideration the uplink signals from the client devices.

Something to consider is that most access points have a significantly higher EIRP, which is the transmit power plus antenna gain, as compared to wireless clients. Access points, for example, are typically set to their highest transmit power, which may be 100 mW. This is done to seemingly maximize the signal propagation and coverage from each access point to minimize the number and costs of access points. Wireless clients, though, tend to have a much lower EIRP due to smaller, lower-gain antennas and the desire to conserve battery power. In this situation, the downlink signal is strength is relatively high, and the uplink signals are much weaker. This means that the effective range between the access point and the client device is governed by the uplink signal strength. As a result, the use of only access point beacons (that is, downlink signals) for determining coverage will lead to much better coverage than what will actually be available when the clients interact with the access point. The downlink communications will be fine, but weaker uplink signals will limit the effective range and likely disrupt communications when client devices move into areas where uplink signal strength is not good enough to support communications.

To avoid falling into this trap, consider the following tips:

- **Identify the client devices**—Start by determining which client device has the lowest EIRP. You can do this by looking at the specifications for the device. Be certain to take into consideration the transmit power that you will be setting in the device (turning the transmit power up higher than the default value may be possible, which will help matters) and the antenna gain. If the specifications do not define the EIRP values, you need to do some testing. Associate each client to an access point, and log in to the access point to view the association signal strength of each device. Do this test with the client devices located at the same distance from the access point. Identify the client device having the lowest association signal strength. Make sure that the client devices you plan to support will ensure two-way communications in all covered areas for the client device having the lowest EIRP or weakest uplink signal when associated with the access point.

- **Base range measurements on the weaker uplink signal**—The EIRP of the client device might be lower than the access point that you plan to use in the deployment. Or the signal strength of the client device at the access point (viewed by logging in to the access point) might be lower than the signal strength of the access point beacons at the client device. (This is measured by the client device or signal measurement tool located next to the client device.) In either of these cases, you need to take the uplink signal into consideration when performing signal coverage testing. Be sure to use the weaker wireless client if the network will support multiple client devices.

- **Perform signal testing by measuring the uplink signals**—To do this task, you measure a client's uplink signal strength as you walk with the device throughout the covered area. Of course, you need to log in to the access point, probably with a wireless laptop (through a web browser) to view the signal values. In addition, you need to periodically have the client device send something to the access point and refresh the access point display to see signal updates as you move the client device about the facility. In some cases, the weaker client device and the laptop are the same device. This test can be cumbersome to perform if you need to carry the client device and a laptop while interacting with the access point's management screen.

- **Perform signal testing by measuring the downlink beacon signals with a calibration applied to the measurements**—To use test tools made for only measuring the downlink signals while performing an RF survey, figure out a calibration factor before performing the survey. You can do this by finding the EIRP specs for the access point and weakest client device and subtracting the access point EIRP from the client device EIRP. The resulting value is the calibration factor. If the calibration factor is positive, add the calibration factor to the cutoff that you are using to define the range boundary. Doing so reduces the measured effective range sufficiently to compensate for the weaker uplink signal strengths. For example, if you find that the calibration factor is +10dB, and you are using 15dB SNR as the range boundary cutoff, the calibrated range boundary cutoff is 25 dB. As a result, you need to ensure that there is 25 dB SNR to have enough coverage to compensate for the weaker uplink signals of the client device. If you find a negative calibration factor, downlink beacon signal values are weaker than the uplink. With this condition, which is rare unless you purposely turn down the access point transmit power, you do not need a calibration factor. Because the downlink signals are weaker, range boundary measurements based solely on the downlink signals yield a network having sufficient coverage for the client devices.

- **Consider turning down the transmit power of the access points**—If you want to maximize performance, consider adjusting transmit power of the access point to balance the uplink and downlink signal strengths. You can do this by turning transmit power down by a value equivalent to the calibration factor. For example, if the calibration factor is +3 dB, turn down the transmit power of the access point by 3 dB. Doing so makes the downlink equal the uplink signal strength, which increases the density of access points and increases cost due to a larger number of access points required to cover an area. However, it may improve performance because of higher capacity. Fewer users will associate with each access point. If you pursue this approach, just measure the downlink signal strength of the access point beacons without any calibration factor.

No matter how you deploy a wireless LAN, just be sure to take into account the differences between the uplink and downlink signal strengths. By ignoring the weaker client device signals, you may end up with a network that does not provide required coverage, and users will not be happy! Keep in mind, though, that some wireless IP phones, such as the Cisco 7920, have site survey utilities that you can use to verify that you have the coverage necessary for the phone to operate effectively.

NOTE   For wireless IP phones, have the same transmit power on the access point and on the phones. This method helps balance the uplink and downlink signal strengths and minimizes dropped calls.

Take note of data rates and signal readings at different points as you move to the outer bounds of the access point coverage. In a multifloor facility, perform tests on the floor above and below the access point. Keep in mind that a poor signal quality reading likely indicates that RF interference is affecting the wireless LAN, which would warrant the use of a spectrum analyzer to characterize the interference, especially if there are no other indications of its source. Based on the results of the testing, you might need to reconsider the location of some access points and redo the tests.

After determining the installation location for access points, define the RF channels for each access point. With voice applications, do not use the option to search for the least-congested channel. This option forces roaming to occur too often, which can cause an excessive number of dropped calls. Always use channels that are a minimum of five radio channels apart so that they do not overlap, and set channels to avoid other RF signal sources. This includes channels 1, 6, and 11 in the United States. Take a look at the installation locations you identified for each access point, and assign a channel number to each access point. Do this in a manner that reduces channel overlap of channels.

Interaccess Point Interference Makes a Difference

In terms of throughput, not much of a problem exists with access points set to the same channel if the load on the network is light. The addition of beacons from multiple access points with common channel settings has insignificant impact. Nevertheless, keep in mind that if all the access points are set to the same channel, users may have trouble roaming from one access point to another. This situation makes it difficult for radio cards to distinguish the access points.

I have run tests that show significant decreases in throughput of a particular access point as you increase the load on an adjacent access point set to the same channel. For example, in one of my workshops, I had two 802.11g access points (A and B) both set to channel 6 and separated by about 150 feet. With AirMagnet Analyzer, I ran throughput tests against access point A, with access point B shut down. I then powered up access point B and ran a throughput test before and after introducing a load on access point B. For the load, all the students connected to access point B and continually pinged access point B with large (1500-byte) packets.

After powering up access point B with no load (the access point was only emitting beacons), I found that the throughput on access point A was only about 5 percent lower. While applying the load on access point B, however, the throughput on access point A took a sharp nosedive. The addition of the heavy user traffic on access point B caused 70 percent throughput degradation on access point A!

Just to be complete, I then set access point A to channel 1 and left access point B on channel 6 (the preferred configurations) and reran the tests. As expected, I found no drop in throughput on access point A. As a result, it is certainly well worth configuring adjacent access points to nonoverlapping channels, especially when heavier loads are present.

Document Findings

When you are satisfied that the planned location of access points will provide adequate coverage, identify on the facility diagrams recommended mounting locations. Of course, the installers will need this information. Also, provide a log of signal readings and supported data rates near the outer propagation boundary of each access point as a basis for future redesign efforts.

The site survey documentation should include the following:

- **Test scope**—This explains the location of the facility, date and time that testing was performed, and type of technologies included in the testing, such as 802.11b/g and 802.11a.

- **Test team**—Identify the names and affiliations of each person involved with the testing.

- **Requirements**—Describe each requirement that impacted the RF survey, such as required coverage areas, number and utilization of users, required technologies and configuration of access points, and any other design specifications, such as radio cell size.

- **Methodology**—Explain how each step of the survey was conducted.

- **Test tools**—Identify all tools used in the survey, such as access points, RF signal measuring devices, and so on.

- **Test results**—Describe all results, especially the recommended installation points for all access points, radio cell coverage area of each access point location, and anything else that will impact the installation of the access points. Take photos of recommended installation locations to aid preinstallation planning.

Dueling with Microwave Ovens

RF interference causes wireless clients and access points to hold off transmitting, which causes delay and lower throughput. This resulting decrease in performance can make browsing websites sluggish and cause voice conversations to have poor quality. In cases where interfering signals are strong enough, the wireless clients may not be able to access the LAN at all for an indefinite period of time. This is rare, but possible.

I ran some tests to see how much impact a typical microwave oven has on wireless LAN operation. I did this within offices inside the building of my company, Wireless-Nets, Ltd., a three-story facility with typical wood-and-drywall construction for inside walls. A single access point does not have any problems covering the entire facility.

The access point was a Cisco Aironet 350 Series, which was initially set to its maximum transmit power of 100 mW. As a wireless client, I used a laptop with AirMagnet monitoring software. AirMagnet can continually transmit packets of a specified size for a period of time while measuring signal strength, noise levels, packet retransmission rates, and throughput.

The microwave included in the testing is made by GoldStar and resides in a break room. The label on the back of the microwave indicates that it consumes 1200 watts of power and operates at 2450 MHz, which is close to 802.11b channel 9.

Before turning on the microwave, I set the access point to channel 9 (a worst-case situation) and took some measurements within the break room to use as a baseline. The access point signal level resulting from the beacons within the break room was –63 dBm, sufficient for solid 11-Mbps associations. Throughput tests indicated 667 packets per second (pps) while sending 1532-byte frames.

While holding the wireless client within one foot of the microwave, we recorded some measurements with AirMagnet while the microwave was set to high and heating up a large bowl of water. The throughput fell to 90 pps, a drop of more than 85 percent.

This is a substantial reduction in performance, but it is the worst-case situation. The access point was set to the same frequency as the microwave, and it is unlikely that someone would use a wireless client so close to the microwave.

A more realistic distance from the microwave is from one of the break tables, which is about eight feet away from the microwave. At this range, I reran the throughput tests, resulting in 178 pps. This still equates to about a 75 percent decrease, something that would likely make users unhappy.

To see what a 75 percent decrease in throughput feels like, I tried surfing to a website that had a few graphics. With the microwave running, the pictures came in painfully slowly. I also surfed around a bit to other web pages, and sometimes the pages would freeze.

After turning off the microwave, I cleared the browser cache and found no problems surfing the same web pages. The pages loaded lightning fast.

I also repeated the tests down the hall about 20 feet away with the microwave running and still experienced fairly sluggish responses. In fact, throughput from there was still only 260 pps. Obviously, the microwave was making the wireless LAN crawl at surprisingly great distances from the microwave.

Something to consider is that these tests were run with only one active wireless client. The results would have been much worse if there were more users on the network.

Curious to know what channels the microwave would affect the most, I ran the throughput tests again with the access point set to different channels. On channels 1, 2, 3, 4, 5, 6, 7, 8, 9, 10, and 11, the throughput was 660 pps, 658 pps, 655 pps, 651 pps, 643 pps, 574 pps, 434 pps, 258 pps, 178 pps, 191 pps, and 210 pps, respectively. Based on these numbers, the microwave was most critically impacting channels 8, 9, 10, and 11.

I also found that the impact is more severe near edges of the range boundary of the access point where signal levels are lower. To test this, I lowered the transmit power of the access point to 1 mW, which caused the signal power to decrease to –77 dBm. This level is close to the range boundary of the wireless LAN.

As one would expect, the hit on throughput was even more with the weaker signals. The resulting throughput was about 10 percent lower than the case where the signal levels from the access point were higher at –63 dBm.

What do you do about interference from microwave ovens? Consider the following countermeasures:

- Change access point channels. The microwave in use with this testing did not severely degrade channels 1 through 6. Therefore, avoid the use of these channels in areas of the building where microwave ovens operate. In fact, web browsing was very fast with the microwave running and the access point set to channel 1 and channel 6. Keep in mind, however, that your microwave ovens may operate at different frequencies within the 2.4 GHz band. Check the label on the back of the microwave, which should provide the center operating frequency.

- Avoid using the wireless LAN near microwave ovens. Keep at least 10 feet away from operating microwaves while actively using wireless LAN applications. This eliminates working from most company break rooms when the microwave is in use. The actual impacts would only be intermittent, though, when someone runs the microwave for a few minutes while heating up a burrito or cup of soup.

Chapter Summary

The design of a wireless LAN, which describes how the system will satisfy requirements, is more rigorous for voice applications as compared to data-only applications. You start by specifying the overall system architecture, which includes determining which deployment model best satisfies requirements. The single-site model includes the call processing at the same site where users are located. This approach is suited for smaller deployments having a single location. For larger deployments, the multisite WAN model with centralized call processing may be necessary if the system spans multiple office locations. The centralization of the call processing, however, means that a disruption in the WAN decreases the system's reliability and availability. With this model, though, you can implement backup mechanisms, such as redundant WAN links in the branch router, SRST, or a combination of SRST and the ISDN. The most flexible approach for larger voice implementations is the multisite WAN model with distributed call processing. In this case, the system's availability and reliability are enhanced because of less reliance on the WAN. Before installing the wireless LAN, you must perform capacity analysis and determine the appropriate radio cell size for the access points that will support call requirements. In addition, the performance of an RF site survey will determine the optimum installation location for each access point. You conduct this testing with an active access point and document the findings in a way that tells installers where to install each access point.

Chapter Review Questions

1 Which VoWLAN deployment model is best for supporting multiple sites where the WAN may have limited reliability?

2 The single-site deployment model provides outgoing calls through a PSTN. True or false?

3 Survivable Remote Site Telephony (SRST) supports reliable backup for both data and voice traffic. True or false?

4 Why is it advantageous to define a single VLAN for all voice traffic on a wireless LAN?

5 What issue may result if multicasting is used on a wireless LAN supporting voice applications?

6 What mechanisms do Cisco 7920 wireless IP phones and access points use to improve QoS?

7 How many simultaneous voice users can a typical 802.11b access point handle?

8 When is it necessary to use smaller radio cell sizes for each access point?

9 With voice applications, you should always set the access points to automatically configure the RF channel. True or false?

10 Why must you take into consideration both the uplink and downlink signal strengths when performing an RF site survey?

Objectives

Upon completing this chapter, you will be able to

- Install and configure access points for supporting voice applications.
- Understand the steps involved with installing and configuring Cisco CallManager and wireless IP phones.
- Verify the operation of a VoWLAN system.

CHAPTER 8

Installing, Configuring, and Testing a VoWLAN System

This chapter defines the installation and configuration steps for VoWLAN systems and provides real-world tips that minimize risks when installing the system. When deploying a VoWLAN system, you need to install and configure access points, Cisco CallManager software, wireless Internet Protocol (IP) phones, and possibly switches and routers. The chapter also describes details on the various types of tests that should be run to verify that the system is meeting requirements and needs of the users.

Installing Access Points

With voice systems, you must carefully install and configure the access points to ensure adequate signal coverage and performance for supporting voice communications. This process is often different from and more critical than installing access points for supporting data-only applications. The spacing of the access points for voice must ensure good-quality communications throughout the facility, especially when roaming.

Getting Started

Before getting too far with the installation process, be certain that you have completed a detailed RF site survey, as described in Chapter 7, "Designing a VoWLAN Solution." The RF survey identifies the optimum installation location for access points that will best serve voice applications. Be certain to install access points as identified in the survey.

Familiarize yourself with the access point hardware. For example, Figure 8-1 shows the connectors found on a 2.4-GHz access point. Two antenna connectors make use of diversity antennas, which helps counteract impacts of multipath propagation and improve range.

Do some planning and be prepared to complete the following steps:

Step 1   Mount the access points.

Step 2   Align antennas.

Step 3   Establish electrical power.

Figure 8-1 *Access Point Layout and Connectors*

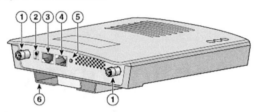

1	2.4-GHz antenna connectors	4	Console port (RJ-45)
2	48-VDC power port	5	Mode button
3	Ethernet port (RJ-45)	6	Status LEDs

You should refer to the hardware installation manuals for the access points that you are installing. Doing so provides valuable details on the most effective way to mount the access point. The following sections give you an idea of the common methods.

Mounting Practices

Most access points ship with mounting brackets. Cisco, for example, generally provides a mounting bracket similar to the one shown in Figure 8-2. Use the bracket to mark the positions for mounting holes, install the bracket, and then attach the access point to the bracket. Be certain to install the mounting bracket and access point at the location indicated by the RF site survey. (See Chapter 7 for more details on completing an RF site survey.)

Figure 8-2 *Typical Mounting Bracket*

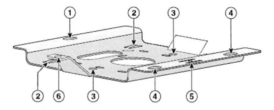

1	Access point mount	4	Access point mounts
2	Cable tie points	5	Locking detent
3	Ceiling mount holes	6	Wall cable access

If mounting the access point on a vertical or horizontal flat surface, such as a wall or solid ceiling, install the bracket screws into studs to ensure that the access point will be securely fastened to the surface. If studs are not available, use wall anchors specially made to reinforce the surface for mounting hardware.

NOTE	Do not mount access points within 3 feet (91.4 cm) of metal obstructions, such as heating and air conditioning shafts, plumbing pipes, and large light fixtures.

Many facilities have suspended ceilings; you can mount the access point either above or below the ceiling tiles. Generally, installing the access points above the ceiling tiles is best, mainly because it keeps the access point out of view of people inside the building. This procedure provides greater security because it is more difficult for hackers and vandals to find an access point, and it is more aesthetically pleasing. In fact, some companies may require that access points be placed out of view.

Be certain, though, that the access points you are using are suitable for operation above ceiling tiles (in the building's environmental air space). Generally, the access point must have a metal enclosure and have adequate fire resistance and low smoke-producing characteristics for operation in a building's environmental air space. Section 300-22(c) of the National Electric Code (NEC) covers this requirement.

Figure 8-3 shows an example of mounting a Cisco access point above the ceiling tiles. The Cisco access point mounting bracket integrates into the T-bar grid above the ceiling tiles. The T-bar box hanger and bracket mounting clip enable you to orient the access point antenna just above the top surface of the ceiling tile. You do not need to extend the antenna through the ceiling tile for it to operate correctly.

Figure 8-3   *Mounting Above Removable Ceiling Tiles*

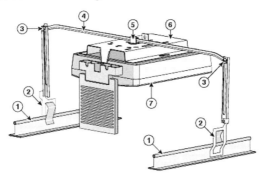

1	Suspended ceiling T-rail	5	Bracket mounting clip
2	T-rail clip	6	Access point mounting bracket
3	Height adjustment screw	7	Access point
4	T-bar box hanger		

If you find that you need to mount the access points below removable ceiling tiles, which could be the case if not enough room exists above the tiles, you can generally do so using special mounting clips. Figure 8-4 illustrates mounting hardware for installing Cisco access points below removable ceiling tiles. An advantage of mounting below ceiling tiles is that finding and assessing the status of the access point is much easier for an administrator.

Figure 8-4 *Mounting Below Removable Ceiling Tiles*

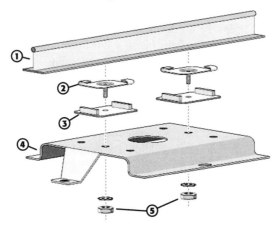

1	Suspended ceiling T-rail	4	Mounting bracket
2	T-rail clips	5	Keps nut (contains an attached loack washer)
3	Plastic spacer		

After mounting the access point, you can install a means for using a padlock provided by some vendors to lock the access point to the mounting bracket to provide added physical security. Also, you can make use of special communications boxes for securing the access points in case you are concerned about theft or vandalism.

If you need signal coverage outside, try to install the access points inside a facility that protects the access point from rain and snow. You can install the access point just inside the building, for example, and run a cable to an external antenna mounted outside. Just be sure to use low loss antenna cable to avoid significant cable losses. If you must install the access point outside, place it inside a weatherproof enclosure.

WARNING The following are warnings related to the installation of wireless access points:

- Do not install access points near unshielded blasting caps or in an explosive environment. RF signals from the access point (or radio clients) may cause explosives to ignite.

- Based on FCC radio frequency exposure limits, keep access point antennas at least 7.9 inches (20 cm) or more from the body of all persons.

Antenna Alignment

After connecting the antennas to the access point, ensure that they are vertical to the ground. For example, when mounting the access point near the ceiling, point the antenna down. Doing so maximizes the signal propagation horizontal to the ground, which improves range. If the RF site survey was done with the antennas aligned vertically to the ground, and you align them horizontally during the installation, the signal coverage will likely be spotty. Users will not be able to communicate from some of the places within the facility, and roaming likely will not work properly.

Electrical Power Distribution

Most access points receive electrical power through the Ethernet cable that interfaces the access point to the infrastructure switch. Figure 8-5 identifies four options for powering the access point. Options 1 through 3 are power-over-Ethernet (PoE) configurations. In these cases, electrical power flows along with data on the same Ethernet cabling. This eases installation because there is no need to distribute separate electrical wires to each access point.

Figure 8-5   *Power Options for Access Points*

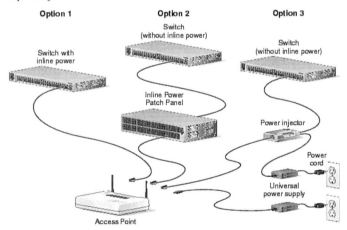

The following list describes each of the electrical power distribution options:

- **Option 1: Integrated inline PoE**—This is the preferred method for providing power to the access points because it requires only a switch with integrated inline power. For example, the Cisco Catalyst 3500XL, 3550-24 PWR, 4000, and 6500 switches provide this type of configuration. The switch port can supply the electrical power to the access point. The switches you already have deployed may not have inline power, though, making this option not feasible.

- **Option 2: Inline PoE via Patch Panel**—This option makes use of an inline power patch panel in conjunction with your existing switches that do not have integrated inline power. The Cisco Catalyst Inline Power Patch Panel supports this configuration.

The patch panel injects electrical power into the Ethernet cabling. If you have wiring closets and available room in racks, consider using this approach.

- **Option 3: PoE Power Injector**—If your network infrastructure does not make use of rack-mounted equipment, consider using this approach. The Cisco Aironet Power Injector (AIR-PWRINJ-FIB or AIR-PWRINJ3) is an example of this approach. You need a separate power injector plugged into an electrical outlet for each access point, which is mainly practical for smaller installations.

- **Option 4: electrical outlet power (not shown on figure)**—In this case, you simply use a power supply separate from the Ethernet cabling to supply power to the access point. This method is not recommended for most installations because you need to provide electrical outlets near each access point, which is not practical for larger installations.

Configuring Access Points

After the access points are installed at locations that will provide optimum signal coverage, as determined by the RF site survey, you need to configure the access point settings. The following sections provide the common settings that you should consider when configuring access points that support voice applications.

Configuration Setting Access

In some situations, a wireless switch may automatically configure each access point based on global settings. If you plan to configure each access point manually, you must connect to the access point by connecting a laptop to the access point via serial cable and running terminal emulation software on the laptop, or interface with the access point's administration over the network using a web browser. In either case, you should configure the security before connecting the access point to the network containing corporate resources. This ensures that the network is fully secure before becoming operational.

Keep in mind that some access points, such as the Cisco Aironet 1242, ship with no IP address configured. In this situation, you must initially configure the IP address through a terminal connection or plug the access point into the network and have the access point obtain an IP address using Dynamic Host Configuration Protocol (DHCP), which is normally enabled by default. After DHCP assigns the IP address, you can check the DHCP logs on the network and find the IP address assigned to the access point, which is generally based on the Media Access Control (MAC) address of the access point.

Firmware

The access points that you receive may have been manufactured a while ago, and updated firmware may be available. If this is the case, upgrade the access point firmware before configuring and using the access point. Be certain to check vendor recommendations on which firmware release to use for voice applications. The recommended release may not be the most current version. Figure 8-6 shows where to find the firmware version number on a Cisco-Aironet 1240 access point.

Figure 8-6   *Access Point Firmware Version*

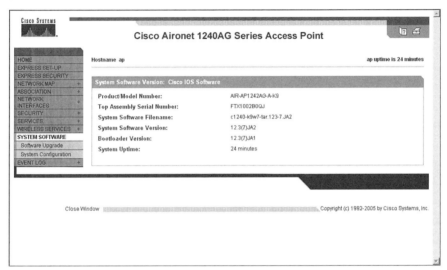

VLANs

If possible, establish a separate virtual local-area network (VLAN) for the voice traffic. This method allows much better performance and ease of management of the voice applications when data applications are sharing the same access points. With voice traffic on a separate VLAN, special quality of service (QoS) mechanisms especially tailored for voice applications can be deployed on the voice VLAN. Be sure, however, to enable applicable QoS mechanisms for the voice VLAN. If you have a choice, give data traffic a lower priority. Doing so helps maximize the performance of the voice solution.

SSID

Assign a Service Set Identifier (SSID) to the access points that will distinguish the voice network (VLAN) from other networks. Select a name that is recognizable to ease configuration of the wireless IP phones, but consider not naming it something that gives away the application. For example, an SSID of "WiFiVOIP-LAN" is an example of an SSID that you should avoid. This SSID would give a hacker some good information on which types of tools to use to exploit the application.

You have the option to broadcast or not broadcast the SSID for the voice network. The nonbroadcasting of SSIDs does not add much more security to the network because packet sniffers easily detect SSIDs from 802.11 frames other than beacons. So, going ahead and broadcasting the SSID of the voice system to make installation much easier is probably best. However, some VoWLAN system solution providers may require that the SSID not be broadcast.

NOTE   Most access points have Address Resolution Protocol (ARP) caching disabled, which can cause performance problems with wireless IP phones. Caching ARP requests to avoid time delays associated with ARP lookups is better. Be certain to enable ARP caching on all access points.

Transmit Power

Be sure to adjust the transmit power of the access point to the value used when the RF site survey was conducted. Doing so is critical to ensuring that the signal coverage is optimum. In some cases, you need to set the transmit power of the access point lower than the maximum level to compensate for weaker radio devices in the wireless IP phones. Ideally, the radios in the access points and clients should be set to the same transmit power to avoid one-way voice conversations. Some wireless IP phones have automatic power control to ensure that the power levels remain the same. Figure 8-7 shows an example of a transmit power setting on a Cisco-Aironet 1242 access point. The Complementary Code Keying (CCK) Transmitter Power (which is 14 dBm in this example) corresponds to the transmit power of the 2.4-GHz 802.11b radio. This configuration is part of the network settings page for the 2.4-GHz radio.

Figure 8-7   *Transmit Power Settings*

CCK Transmitter Power (dBm):	◯-1 ◯2 ◯5 ◯8 ◯11 ◉14 ◯17 ◯20 ◯Max
OFDM Transmitter Power (dBm):	◯-1 ◯2 ◯5 ◯8 ◯11 ◯14 ◯17 ◉Max
Limit Client Power (dBm):	◯-1 ◯2 ◯5 ◯8 ◯11 ◯14 ◯17 ◯20 ◉Max

RF Channel

Avoid using auto RF channel settings. For example, Cisco access points allow you to search for the least-congested channel. Figure 8-8 part A shows this setting. This configuration is part of the network settings page for the 2.4-GHz radio. If you enable this setting, the access point periodically searches for better channels on the selected channels, which are channels 1, 6, and 11 in this example. If another channel has less congestion, the access point changes channels. Even though this feature might offer a higher throughput because of operation over a channel with less congestion, the changing of channels forces the wireless IP phones to roam, which can cause dropped calls. When deploying VoWLAN systems, assign the RF channels manually, as shown in Figure 8-8 part B. In this example, the access point uses only channel 1. Use nonoverlapping channels, such as channels 1, 6, and 11, as discussed in Chapter 7.

Figure 8-8   *RF Channel Settings*

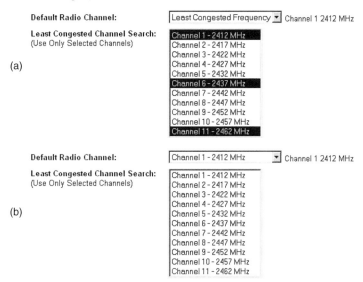

Data Rates

In most cases, set the data rate of the access point to the highest value, and do not allow auto rate shifting. Also, disable all lower data rates to ensure that the wireless IP phones will have the higher-performance connections with the access point. Just be sure that the RF site survey was conducted with data rates set the same way. For example, Cisco recommends that the access points be set to allow only 11-Mbps data rates for its 802.11b-based 7920 Wireless IP Phone. Figure 8-9 shows the Cisco-Aironet 1242 access point configuration page for setting ideal data rates for voice applications. This configuration is part of the network settings page for the 2.4-GHz radio. In this example, the access point operates at only 11 Mbps.

NOTE   On the voice VLAN, configure security based on the design. See Chapter 7 for more details on security options.

Figure 8-9 *Data Rate Settings*

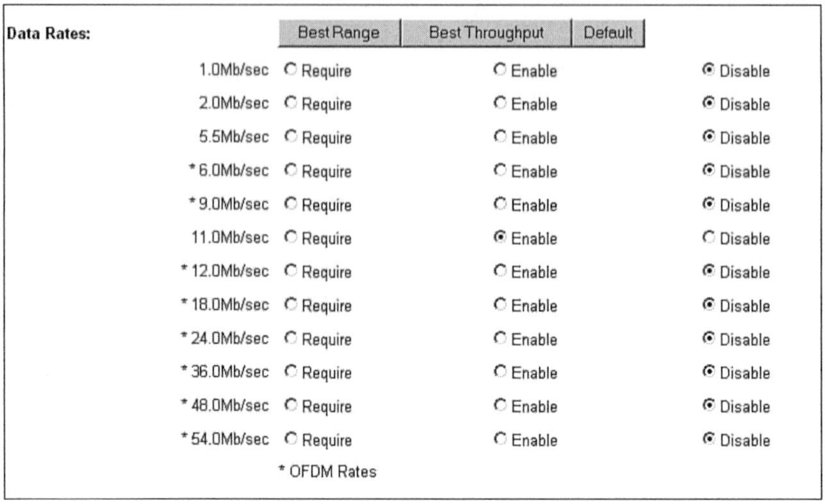

Data Rates:	Best Range	Best Throughput	Default
1.0Mb/sec	○ Require	○ Enable	◉ Disable
2.0Mb/sec	○ Require	○ Enable	◉ Disable
5.5Mb/sec	○ Require	○ Enable	◉ Disable
* 6.0Mb/sec	○ Require	○ Enable	◉ Disable
* 9.0Mb/sec	○ Require	○ Enable	◉ Disable
11.0Mb/sec	○ Require	◉ Enable	○ Disable
* 12.0Mb/sec	○ Require	○ Enable	◉ Disable
* 18.0Mb/sec	○ Require	○ Enable	◉ Disable
* 24.0Mb/sec	○ Require	○ Enable	◉ Disable
* 36.0Mb/sec	○ Require	○ Enable	◉ Disable
* 48.0Mb/sec	○ Require	○ Enable	◉ Disable
* 54.0Mb/sec	○ Require	○ Enable	◉ Disable
* OFDM Rates			

Filtering

Filtering nonessential wired network traffic is best to ensure that it does not flow over the wireless LAN. This minimizes unnecessary traffic over the wireless LAN, which can erode capacity. To improve performance of the access points, attempt to filter this traffic on Layer 3 switches. For example, 3270 terminal emulation applications may be running over the wired network infrastructure. In this case, consider blocking the associated Systems Network Architecture (SNA) traffic from getting onto the wireless LAN.

NOTE   As part of your VoWLAN solution, consider installing Cisco PIX Firewalls and Cisco IDS.

Protection Mechanisms

If you plan to have 802.11g wireless devices associating with the access points of the voice system, enable protection mechanisms, such as CTS-to-self, on the access points if you are using 802.11b-based wireless IP phones. Doing so significantly reduces the number of retransmissions due to collisions between the 802.11b and 802.11g radios. The result is better voice quality. Some access points enable these protection mechanisms automatically when any single 802.11b radio associates with the access point.

Installing and Configuring Cisco CallManager Software

When installing and configuring Cisco CallManager software, which is required to make even a basic VoWLAN operational, be certain to review all related documentation before getting started. You need to carefully follow the installation details provided by the vendor to set up the system properly. To give you an idea of the types of tasks you will likely encounter, the following sections provide an overview of the installation and configuration steps. The actual system you will install may include some, all, or different features than what the following sections explain.

Cisco CallManager Software Installation

One of the first items to consider when installing Cisco CallManager software is that the server hardware has the minimum requirements for running the software. Server sizing depends on the features you plan to use, so consult with vendor-specific installation details to verify server hardware.

After installing the software on the server, which will likely be Microsoft Windows or Linux, you need to interface with the Cisco CallManager administration screens to perform configuration tasks. In most cases, you do so via a web browser from a separate computer connected to the same network as the Cisco CallManager server. Cisco CallManager installations do not allow you to use the Web browser on the server platform.

You begin the configuration process by activating the Cisco CallManager service. For example, with Cisco CallManager, you enter the configuration screens and select "Service Activation" under "Tools." You then activate associated services, such as Cisco Database Layer Monitor, Cisco CallManager, Cisco Realtime Information Server (RIS) Data Collector, and Cisco Telephony Dispatcher. These types of actions prepare the software for call processing. At this point, you can probably add monitoring and alarm support, which make it possible for the administrator to learn about problems before they become issues. If more than one Cisco CallManager server exists, you can also configure calling groups, which allow load balancing and failover capabilities.

NOTE	Because the Cisco CallManager software platforms initially supported wired Voice over Internet Protocol (VoIP) phones, verify that the version of Cisco CallManager software is what Cisco recommends for supporting wireless voice deployments. For example, the minimum version of CallManager that Cisco recommends is 3.3(3) SR1 for the Cisco 7920 phone.

System Parameters

You need to configure many system parameters after starting the CallManager services. This defines the structure of the telephony system. The following sections give you an idea of the types of system parameters you need to set up.

Device Pools

A device pool defines common characteristics for the wireless IP phones. For example, a device pool may be set up to represent a particular branch of the company or a specific area or location of the company. Thus, the device pools should be based on the company's organizational structure and the location of users. If there are multiple sites, consider setting up a separate device pool for each site. Or, if the system will have both wired and wireless IP phones, you can set up one device pool for the wired phones and one for the wireless phones. This technique makes managing the wireless IP phones much easier.

Partitions

Partitions provide security and call routing by dividing the route plan into logical subsections. They further break down the users within the device pools into subsections. The subsections can be based on locations and class of service. This could be the case, for example, where security personnel at an airport would be given a higher class of service than others.

Calling Search Space

The calling search space includes a list of partitions that users can access. You can use this method to provide added security. For example, managers may be given access to all partitions, whereas employees may be able to access only specific partitions.

Regions and Locations

In a Cisco CallManager system, a region generally specifies which codecs specific users will use. The locations provide call admission control (CAC) for regulating voice quality through limitation of bandwidth.

Route Groups

A route group defines a list of gateways and ports for outgoing trunk selection in priority order. You can establish various route groups and assign users to them. When setting up route groups, consider the pros and cons of the service providers and cost of trunks.

System Schedules

The system schedules is a feature for differentiating weekends, holidays, after hours, workdays, and so on. The definition of different system schedules will allow you to handle calls differently depending on the day of the week and time of day.

Languages

Cisco CallManager software supports different languages. You can set up specific languages to be used for prompting subscribers and callers.

Subscriber Setup

When all system parameters are defined, you are ready to establish the subscribers, who are users who will use the wireless IP phones. Define variables that will apply to groups of (or all) subscribers, such as account policy, classes of service (CoS), enhanced phone security, public distribution lists, and subscriber templates. When you create a subscriber, the system sets up an account for the subscriber that includes a mailbox where the system stores voice messages.

NOTE	Before creating too many subscribers, verify that the system is working properly. Establish at least one subscriber, and check that calls are handled the way that you intend.

Be sure to assign subscribers for receiving messages that are not associated with a specific recipient. For example, a caller may leave a voice message in the general mailbox. Just be sure that you assign one or more subscribers to receive these messages.

Generally, the system will establish a subscriber account with many default settings. You might want to change some of these before having the subscribers use the system.

Device Mobility Issues

Because of the mobile nature of wireless IP phones, the following issues can occur when deploying Cisco CallManager solutions:

- **Inappropriate codec and PSTN gateway selection**—Often no dynamic method exists for updating a phone's region and device pool for determining the type of codec to use. This can result in using the wrong codec. In addition, no way exists to update the dial plan to specify the appropriate local Public Switched Telephone Network (PSTN) gateway, which may cause a phone to use a remote PSTN gateway. The problem with this is that a phone being used to make an emergency 911 call through the remote PSTN gateway will result in emergency services being sent to the location of the remote PSTN gateway and not to the location of the wireless IP phone that initiated the call.

- **Inaccurate bandwidth accounting**—Sometimes, as with Cisco CallManager, the bandwidth allocation of each phone is based on the phone's assigned "home" location. Mechanisms are not available that update the phone's location to change bandwidth allocation. As a result, bandwidth for that phone may be subtracted from locations where the phone is not even operating. Also, the bandwidth is not taken into consideration at the location where the phone is roaming. This may cause oversubscription of the wide-area network (WAN) bandwidth.

To avoid these issues, you need to manually reconfigure the CAC location, device pool and region, and calling search space when a phone moves from one physical location to another. Keep in mind that this will likely raise emergency 911 issues.

Configuring Wireless IP Phones

After installing the access points and setting up the Cisco CallManager system, you need to configure the wireless IP phones to enable operation on the network. Be certain to review and follow all configuration documentation provided by the phone vendor. The following sections give you an idea of the types of configurations that you will be making to the phone.

NOTE You can generally configure a wireless IP phone via the keypad on the phone or through the use of a configuration utility running on a laptop and connected to the phone. For example, with Cisco 7920 Wireless IP Phones, you can use the Cisco 7920 Configuration Utility to configure the phones from a graphical user interface (GUI) on a laptop or PC.

Firmware

As with access points, the wireless IP phones may have been manufactured a while ago, so verify that the firmware is up to date. If not, update the firmware to the newest version. You can generally find the firmware version through the menu options on the phone. For example, you can view the firmware version on a Cisco 7920 via the following menu sequence: **Phone Settings > Phone Status > Firmware Info > Firmware Version**. Then check the vendor's website for new a newer version.

Most wireless IP phones have mechanisms to prevent firmware from being corrupted. For example, all Cisco 7920 firmware versions after 1.0(6) have this feature. On the 7920, you can upgrade firmware via Trivial File Transfer Protocol (TFTP) from Cisco CallManager or via Universal Serial Bus (USB) through the Cisco 7920 Configuration Utility. If power loss on the phone occurs during the upgrade, you must use the Configuration Utility to recover the phone.

Network Settings

As with any other client device, set the phone to use either DHCP or static IP addresses, depending on the system's design. In most cases, DHCP is the best option because it is flexible and very easy to administer. It is not as tedious to configure. In some cases, especially if using static IP addresses, you need to set the primary gateway and Domain Name Service (DNS) to the correct values. On most phones, such as the Cisco 7920 Wireless IP Phone, you can power-cycle the phone to release and renew the phone's IP address if DHCP is enabled. In addition, the loss of signal coverage alone does not generally release the phone's IP address.

RF Settings

You need to configure the RF settings on the phone based on the system's design. Figure 8-10 shows the RF network options available for the Cisco 7920 Wireless IP Phone using the Cisco 7920 Configuration Utility. These are commonly found on other wireless IP phones as well.

Figure 8-10 *Cisco 7920 Phone RF Network Settings*

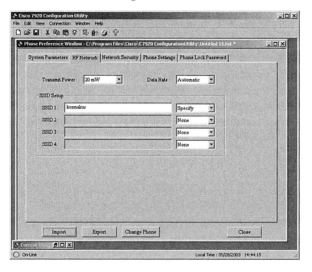

Transmit Power

Set the transmit power to match the access point transmit power. As discussed earlier, a lower transmit power setting on either the phone or access point causes one-way communications to occur, especially when the phone gets farther away from any of the access points. Be certain that the transmit power setting in the phone and access point are the same as configured when performing the RF site survey. If not, limited signal coverage may prevail.

Data Rate

The data rate should be set to either automatic or the static data rate chosen for the access point. To ensure that the phone uses the proper data rate, set the phone's data rate to a static value, such as 11 Mbps. As with transmit power, be certain that the data rate settings are the same as those configured when performing the RF site survey.

SSID Settings

The SSID set on the phone must match the SSID configured in the access points. This setting allows the phone to associate with the voice network and make use of the security and quality of service available on the VLAN associated with that SSID. If the SSIDs do not match, the phone will not associate with the access point, and it will not be able to make or receive any calls.

Security Settings

The security settings on the phone must be set as specified in the design. For an example of setting security on a wireless IP phone, see Figure 8-11, which shows the security screen for the Cisco 7920 Wireless IP Phone using the Cisco 7920 Configuration Utility. In this example, open authentication and a key for 128-bit Wired Equivalent Privacy (WEP) is configured in the phone. The WEP key in this case is entered as 26 hexadecimal characters (1–9, A–F). Of course, this must match what is configured in the access points. As an alternative, you could use Lightweight Extensible Application Protocol (LEAP) for authentication. With this particular system, you can assign up to four WEP keys, making it easier to change the phones to different WEP keys in the future. However, you need to configure only one WEP key.

Figure 8-11 *Cisco 7920 Phone Security Settings*

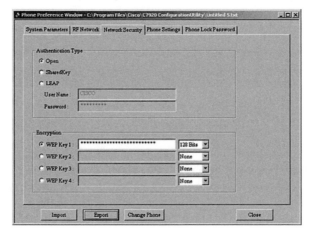

Phone Settings

Figure 8-12 shows, using the Cisco 7920 Configuration Utility, the phone settings available for the Cisco 7920 Wireless IP Phone. In this example, you can identify the greeting and welcome messages based on names given to these messages. Also, you can set ring tones on this screen. If you are not happy with the ring tones available in the phone, check the vendor's website for ring tone downloads. Cisco, for example, makes a louder ring tone available. For Cisco implementations, the Cisco Discovery Protocol (CDP) is enabled with time-to-live (TTL) and time interval set to the values shown in the figure. In addition, you can use this screen to update the phone's firmware. You first need to download the new firmware to a laptop or PC and then transfer the firmware to the phone over a cable connection. Some VoWLAN systems allow firmware updates to be made over the wireless network from the Cisco CallManager software. In addition, some wireless IP phones have built-in HTTP servers that allow you to configure the phone over the network from a web browser on a PC.

Figure 8-12 *Cisco 7920 Phone Settings*

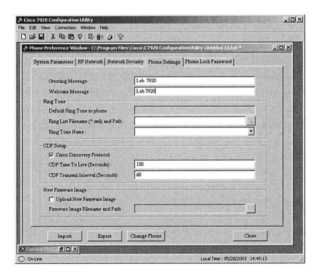

Verifying System Operation

The final step in installing and configuring a VoWLAN system is to verify that everything works properly. You may have done some verification tests when setting up Cisco CallManager, but do not overlook the need to run some overall system tests. The following sections describe tests that you should perform.

Association Tests

Make sure that each wireless IP phone will associate with at least one or more access points that are part of the installed system. This is an initial test just to see whether the phone can establish a wireless connection. Confirm this connection before moving on with other testing.

The phone should have an indicator that confirms that association has been made. Power up the phone and check whether the phone indicates an association. If the phone will not associate with an access point, recheck the phone configuration, especially the SSID, authentication type, and WEP password. These parameters must match those configured on the access point for association to be successful. Also, ensure that you are operating the phone in an area where signal coverage exists. You can generally do this by observing the signal status on the phone.

Authentication Tests

From at least one or more access points that are part of the installed system, be sure that each phone properly authenticates with the system. If only WEP security is in use, the phone will not authenticate with the access point if the WEP on the phone does not match the WEP key configured in the access point. In this case, the phone will not even associate with the access point. When using LEAP, the phone may associate with the access point but not authenticate with the LEAP authentication server. Thus, verify that the phone is actually authenticating with the authentication server. To do this, you probably need to access the server's authentication logs. If the phone is not authenticating, check that the LEAP username and password entered in the phone are the same as those configured in the authentication server.

Registration Tests

Make sure that each phone properly registers with the Cisco CallManager software and receives the applicable phone number. If the phone does not register properly, which is usually identified as an indicator on the phone, recheck that the phone is actually configured in the Cisco CallManager software. If the phone is configured in Cisco CallManager, recheck that the phone has the proper IP address, subnet mask, primary gateway, and DNS settings. Keep in mind that the phone may associate with an access point but not be able to obtain an IP address. The IP address should correspond with the address plan for the location where it is connecting to the network.

Phone Call Tests

After you have verified that the phone is successfully connecting to the system and is a legitimate subscriber, you are ready to see whether you can actually place calls. The goal is to determine whether the phone can make a connection with another phone and that voice quality is acceptable. This testing ensures that the wireless network and supporting wired infrastructure are supporting the phone calls adequately.

Start by placing a call on each phone from a stationary location. Place a call, preferably to someone on a wired phone, and talk for at least a minute while assessing voice quality. If you find that the quality is poor, check the signal coverage at that location. For example, you should only observe from the phone's location a single access point on a particular nonoverlapping channel (1, 6, or 11) with a signal level that is at least 15 dB higher than other access points set to the same nonoverlapping channel. The presence of more than one access point set to the same RF channel and having similar signal levels may cause significant interference that reduces voice quality. In addition to checking the wireless network, you might also recheck the quality of service settings on the Cisco CallManager software to be sure that it is set properly.

After you have the stationary calls working satisfactorily, place a call and walk through the facility while talking to someone on a wired phone. As you walk, monitor the voice quality. If everything is working okay, you should hear consistent quality as you traverse the facility and the phone roams from one access point to another. If you detect poor sound quality at any point, check the signal strength indicator on the phone. A reduction in sound quality may occur when the signal strength is low. To make roaming phone call tests easier to perform, wear an earpiece for listening to the voice quality and monitoring the signal strength indicator on the phone at the same time.

When performing the roaming tests, ensure that the phone can "see" at least two access points (each on nonoverlapping channels) from anywhere within the covered area. This can often be done by observing the phone's wireless connection utility. If you cannot see two or more access points on nonoverlapping channels, a phone roaming from one access point to another may not be smooth enough to maintain good voice quality. To make voice quality consistent, you might need to re-engineer the wireless network by moving or adding access points.

If the phone is connected to a particular access point and does not roam even if located directly under another access point, there may be more than one access point having relatively high signal strengths on overlapping RF channels. In this case, you may be able to fix the problem by adjusting the transmit power of one of the access points. Or, you might need to re-engineer the wireless LAN. Another reason that the phone may not be roaming in this scenario is that the nearby access point is not operating. So, check the status of the access point.

Another problem with roaming is that the phone may roam from one access point to the other too slowly. In this case, check the phone wireless utility to ensure that there is indeed another acceptable access point to roam to. The problem could be that no other access points have enough signal strength for the phone to roam. If the phone appears to roam promptly to the next access point, there may still be excessive delay problems on the wired network infrastructure.

Sometimes the phone may roam okay in regards to the network, but the phone loses connection with Cisco CallManager. In this case, check to be certain that the phone is not traversing different IP subnets, which can cause a Layer 3 connection loss and disconnection from Cisco CallManager. In addition, if using Cisco LEAP, make certain that some of the access points are not blocking Transmission Control Protocol (TCP) ports associated with LEAP.

NOTE   If you find that moving with the phone throughout the facility causes phone calls to drop or act erratically when the phone is roaming from one access point to another (and the wireless network is installed optimally), the wired infrastructure may not provide acceptable roaming delays. For example, the Cisco Catalyst 2948G, 2980G, 2980G-A, 4912, and 2948G-GE-TX switches are known to introduce substantial roaming delays. Cisco does not recommend using these switches in a wireless voice network. Also, if a Cisco Catalyst 4000 Series switch is used as the main Layer 3 switch in the network, ensure that it contains, at a minimum, either a Supervisor Engine 2+ (SUP2+) or Supervisor Engine 3 (SUP3) module. The SUP1 or SUP2 module can cause roaming delays.

Load Tests

As final testing for the VoWLAN system, make use of multiple wireless IP phones throughout the facility. Ideally, you should distribute and use the phones in a similar manner as they will actually be used when operational. Find some volunteers or actual users to help you with these tests. You can give them each a phone, instruct them on how to use it, and have them initiate calls with others. To simplify testing, you can start by having the group of callers place calls from the same location, and then have them separate uniformly throughout the facility while continuing voice conversations and monitoring voice quality. If the requirements specify that parts of the facility need greater capacity, have an appropriate number of test users use the phones from that area. Again, you should strive to test the system as users will use it.

Follow-up Tests

Because the RF conditions within a facility will change over time, retesting a VoWLAN system periodically is important. As a general rule, perform follow-up tests every 6 to 12 months. Of course, user complaints of voice quality will prompt you to perform follow-up testing earlier.

For follow-up testing, unless user complaints otherwise dictate, you can probably get by with performing only the load tests. Also, focus on testing the areas of the facility users may have identified as having poor voice quality or an inability to place calls. This is likely because the signal coverage in those areas is not good enough, but some testing will provide a basis for resolving the problem more effectively.

NOTE	Sometimes users may complain that the wireless IP phones, such as the Cisco 7920, may get warm. Because of frequent transmissions, a wireless phone heats up more when placing calls, especially for extended periods of time. You can turn down the transmit power on the phone to reduce the heating, but keep in mind that this will likely change the signal coverage area. If it is much different than planned, coverage holes may appear. If a phone is constantly scanning for access points, which may be the case when the placement of access points is not optimum, the phone will generate heat similar to what it does when placing an active call. If this is the case, you need to re-engineer the wireless network to provide better coverage. In most cases, the phone's increased heat dissipation is normal and does not exceed manufacturer's specifications. However, it can be annoying to users.

Battery Life Issues

Most wireless IP phones have active and standby modes. For example, the Cisco 7920 Wireless IP Phone enters active mode when there is an active call, key activity, roaming, or loss of network connectivity. The 7920 enters standby mode to maximize battery life and talk time after a minute of idle time in a stable RF environment. In addition, the 7920 enters standby mode 2 seconds after every active scan. When operating in an area where signal coverage is spotty or weak, the 7920 remains in active mode while continually scanning for access points. Thus, the phone's operating environment impacts battery life.

Under general operating environments, a wireless IP phone battery provides approximately 4 hours of talk time and 20 hours of standby time. As a result, battery life will be considerably less if the user talks more on the phone. Also, poor signal coverage will cause batteries to last for less time because the phone's radio is in active mode, scanning for access points more often.

NOTE	To conserve battery life, instruct users to turn off their wireless IP phone when leaving the coverage area. Also consider not using vibrate mode and the background light on the phones to reduce draw on the battery.

Chapter Summary

The effective installation and configuration of access points for voice applications is critical for providing a good experience for users. If configuration parameters, such as RF transmit power and data rate, are not set right on the wireless IP phones or access points, poor voice quality and possibly dropped calls will run rampant throughout the facility. Installing access points at optimum positions and using the same configurations that were used when performing the RF site survey are crucial.

The installation of Cisco CallManager software requires you to pay close attention to the installation manuals provided by the vendor. You will be installing the software on a dedicated server and then configuring the system and subscribers. Much of the Cisco CallManager software will be configured in a manner that depends on the organization structure of the company.

After you have the access points and Cisco CallManager software installed and configured, you are ready to configure the wireless IP phones. Ensuring that the transmit power and the data rate settings on the phone match the access point configurations is crucial. If not, users will likely experience problems.

Before handing the phones over to users, complete verification tests to ensure that everything is working okay. You should start with verifying association, authentication, and registration for each phone. Then place calls from stationary locations and while walking through the facility. After you troubleshoot and fix any problems, do some load testing with multiple users.

Chapter Review Questions

1 When installing access points for voice applications, you orient the antennas on the access points horizontal to the ground. True or false?

2 What are advantages of mounting access points above ceiling tiles?

3 What are some warnings that must be taken into account when installing access points?

4 What are the three options for distributing electrical power to access points over the data cable?

5 Which access point configuration parameters must be set to the same values used when performing the RF site survey?

6 The transmit power of the access point should always be set to the highest value to maximize range of the access point. True or false?

7 If a wireless IP phone will not associate with an access point, what may be the problem(s)?

8 Why should the wireless IP phones be configured with an SSID that corresponds with a special VLAN for voice applications?

9 If a wireless IP phone associates and authenticates successfully but cannot register with Cisco CallManager and place calls, what might be the problem(s)?

10 How can you maximize battery life on a wireless IP phone?

Objectives

Upon completing this chapter, you will be able to

- Understand the elements needed to effectively support a VoWLAN system.
- Understand configuration management elements to monitor and control.
- Identify the important aspects of monitoring the network.
- Explain the process of conducting a security assessment of the VoWLAN system.
- Understand the elements needed to effectively maintain the network and provide engineering and help desk support.

CHAPTER 9

Supporting a VoWLAN System

Operational support can contribute to nearly 50 percent of the total life cycle costs of a VoWLAN system. As a result, be sure to fully plan related operational support. Support elements for wireless local-area networks (LAN) are similar to those for typical wired networks; however, wireless support must take into account the uniqueness of radio wave propagation. Also, the effective operation of a voice application depends a great deal on the preciseness of the configuration of the wireless LAN. VoWLAN systems require unique support elements and tools. This chapter discusses these elements and provides examples of tools that are effective at supporting a VoWLAN system.

Configuration Management

Configuration management consists of controlling changes made to the wireless LAN after installation. Changes may involve installing or moving access points; altering access point configurations, such as radio frequency (RF) channel; or updating firmware. In larger systems, configuration management may also be necessary to keep requirements for additions to the system from expanding endlessly without good reason.

Network managers need to review any changes that may impact the performance or security of the wireless. The review ensures that relevant impacts are taken into account that involve additional costs and use of resources necessary to support the request. In some cases, changes may merely involve supporting a larger number of users, who may or may not require modifications to the network. Other instances could include a need for wider RF coverage and additional access points.

A company should use a change request form as an input into the configuration management process. The purpose of this form is to summarize the requested change in a manner that makes it fairly simple to determine the level of review needed to accept or reject the proposed change. For example, the addition of a new application would likely require review by security and engineering functions to determine whether mechanisms are in place to safeguard the application and provide adequate levels of performance. Change requests should be archived in a database, with reviews of request status done at least quarterly.

A key aspect of configuration management includes the development and management of a baseline architectural design and support plan. When someone proposes or requests the deployment of a new wireless LAN or a change that prompts modification to an existing wireless LAN, the company should use this baseline as the basis for validating and verifying the design and assessing the impacts. This process includes determining the impact of the proposed change on the overall wireless LAN and peripheral systems.

The implementation of an effective configuration management process also includes the establishment and use of a configuration management database, which includes a listing of all installed components, configuration settings, media access control (MAC) addresses, and applicable diagrams that document the current state of the wireless LAN. This database should include a listing of all hardware and software, such as wireless Internet Protocol (IP) phones, access points, and call managers (including configurations) that are part of the VoWLAN system. As the company accepts changes to the wireless LAN configuration, it would then update the database to reflect the new state of the system. As network management staff move on to jobs elsewhere, this updated database keeps the knowledge of the wireless LAN composition from leaving the company, too.

Anyone, including users, should be able to request a modification to the wireless LAN. The following sections offer some examples of typical configuration management items that may require attention.

RF Channel Changes

The maintenance staff could request adjusting the RF channel on a specific access point, possibly because they have evidence that the access point is interfering with another one. Before authorizing this change, be sure to think about effects of the new channel setting on all access points. To maximize the capacity and performance of the wireless LAN, access points within range of each other should be set to noninterfering channels.

Transmit Power Changes

In some cases, a request may come about because of the need to either increase or decrease the range of a particular access point. For example, an access point may need to be set to a lower value to enable the installation of additional access points for the purpose of reducing cell size and the number of users associated with each access point. This change could allow more voice users to operate within a particular area. Also, the overall effect of this change could be to increase the throughput available for each user. When making this type of change, ensure that it will result in adequate coverage in all user areas. If making a change that increases transmit power, be certain that interaccess point interference is kept to a minimum and that each of the affected access points can support the density of voice users operating the applicable area.

New Applications

A user or manager may request a new application, such as video conferencing, that will traverse the wireless LAN. As a result, carefully size up the network to ensure that there will be enough capacity to support the application along with existing data and voice applications. Other cases may include setting up public wireless Internet access to an existing wireless LAN that currently services only company applications. In this case, some engineering will likely be necessary to keep public and company traffic separate and secure.

Signal Coverage

If users complain that holes exist in the coverage throughout some parts of the facility, likely from voice calls that have poor quality or are disrupted from time to time, an alteration is necessary to improve signal coverage. This alteration will likely entail the repositioning of existing access points or installation of additional access points, but try moving the access points or making other configuration changes, such as transmit power, before spending money on new hardware. In addition, check whether firmware updates are available, and read the release notes to determine whether any applicable updates will fix the coverage issues.

Firmware Version

A company should periodically update the firmware of the access points and possibly wireless IP phones to take advantage of performance, security, and interoperability enhancements that the manufacturers offer. Before actually updating the firmware, though, perform enough testing with the new firmware on access points and wireless IP phones in a lab environment to ensure that the firmware will support all applications in use on the wireless LAN. Also, refer to any notes that have been posted on the manufacturer's website and associated forums about troubles that anyone has had with the new firmware. Sometimes new firmware introduces serious problems. Experiencing these potential problems in the lab setting before subjecting dozens or hundreds of users to the problems would be best. If problems with the new firmware are severe enough, wait for the manufacturer to fix the problems in a future firmware release before updating the firmware. Also, keep an eye on vendor websites for any security alerts about the vendor's products that you are using on the network. This information is often communicated via press releases and security e-mail lists.

Security Improvement

A company may discover that its existing wireless LAN does not have security mechanisms that fully protect company assets. This situation could result from the company's having completed a security audit that uncovers weaknesses in the wireless applications and associated networks. In this case, the addition of access controllers or enhancements to access points may be necessary. Of course, these types of changes should be made only after defining security requirements and analyzing potential solutions.

Network Monitoring

Network monitoring continuously measures attributes of the wireless LAN. This monitoring plays a key role in proactively managing the network in a way that enables smooth upsizing to support a growth of users and the ability to solve issues before they hamper performance and security.

Incorporate alerts that inform maintenance staff when an access point is not operating properly or not operating at all. An access point can be down for days, weeks, or months without anyone knowing. Keep a close eye on access points and take corrective actions when necessary, hopefully before partial coverage affects users too badly.

Also consider installing an intrusion detection system (IDS), which monitors for any unauthorized wireless device connecting to the network. For example, someone from outside the facility may connect to an access point, and the IDS will alert the system administrator or security manager that an unauthorized person may be attempting to access resources on the network. Actions can be taken to disable access from this unauthorized device.

The following sections offer elements you should consider monitoring when planning operational support for a wireless LAN.

Performance Monitoring

Continually measure the usage of access points and voice managers to provide valuable information necessary to properly scale the VoWLAN system as user traffic changes. The use of access points acts as a gauge to indicate when additional access points and wide-area network (WAN) bandwidth are necessary. In addition, network monitoring should keep an eye on sources of RF interference and raise flags when the interference is high enough to cause significant degradation in throughput.

Coverage Monitoring

Alterations made to a facility, such as the addition of office partitions and an influx of additional employees, cause attenuation and make radio waves propagate differently. These alterations cause coverage of the wireless LAN to change, often limiting wireless user access to the network. In extreme situations, an access point may become inoperative due to a broken antenna or firmware fault, which requires maintenance or rebooting before users can associate with the access point.

Because most companies deploy wireless LANs having access point range boundaries that radically overlap, however, total loss of connectivity may not occur. Instead, users experience lower performance in certain parts of the facility. In this case, users tend to not complain too strongly to the IT group about the problem, making it tricky for network administrators to determine whether an access point is down. Network monitoring is certainly a remedy to this problem. In addition, consider running throughput tests at different parts of the facility to ensure performance is adequate.

Configuration Monitoring

When installing access points, several configuration parameters, such as Service Set Identifier (SSID), RF channel, and transmit power, are set. Monitoring these configuration settings over time is important. Network managers should be aware of the configuration of all access points to facilitate effective updates to the network. Documentation of the access point configurations can be easily lost. Monitoring of the configurations enables accurate, centralized records of the setting values.

In addition, a hacker may attempt to reconfigure an access point to a default configuration that is insecure and compromises the security of the network. Tools should continuously monitor all the access points in the network and alert the IT staff if anything strange is going on, such as an unauthorized person attempting to log in to an access point. The IT staff can set the performance and security thresholds at any value they want and change them at any time. Some software packages also have auto-repair features, which automatically return the access points to their proper settings if someone tampers with the settings or a maintenance person reboots the access point due to a malfunction.

Security Policy Management

In general, the security element of operational support VoWLAN systems—or any system, for that matter—involves managing the network to ensure no issues persist that can hinder the network. Good security policy requires foolproof encryption and authentication, as well as solid policies that the company enforces regarding configuration of the VoWLAN system.

As discussed in Chapter 7, "Designing a VoWLAN Solution," it's very important that the system implement effective encryption and authentication. When defining security policy for VoWLAN systems, be sure to specify encryption of packets for at least over the airwaves. As mentioned in Chapter 5, "VoWLAN Security Solutions," Wireless Encryption

Protocol (WEP) is the native 802.11 encryption mechanism and has its faults, but it's better than nothing. You should, however, strive for using better techniques, such as Wi-Fi Protected Access (WPA) and 802.11i if they are available for the wireless IP phones you are using. You could also implement a virtual private network (VPN).

The following are some additional policies that you should consider when planning operational support for a VoWLAN system:

- **Installation control policies**—Enterprises should have policies in place that require anyone installing wireless access points and base stations to first have approval from a designated IT group. The company should strictly forbid the connection of unauthorized wireless access points to the corporate network. In fact, all access points should satisfy specific configuration policies. The reason for this policy is to keep anyone from attaching an access point to the corporate network that does not have adequate security configurations, which would enable a hacker to easily access corporate resources.

- **Monitoring policies**—Continually monitoring for the presence of rogue access points to ensure there are no open, unprotected entry points into the corporate information system is important. You can perform this monitoring by placing monitoring pods throughout the facility to detect unauthorized access points, or (ideally) you can do monitoring over the Ethernet side of the network. If possible, a company should integrate the network monitoring function into tools in use for monitoring the existing Ethernet corporate network. Most access points offer Simple Network Management Protocol (SNMP), which provides an interface to existing wired network monitoring tools. In addition, consider monitoring for the presence of access points from other organizations and companies that are not part of your network. Doing so provides a basis for reengineering your wireless network.

- **Action plans**—If network monitoring discovers a breach of security occurring at a specific access point, temporarily disabling that access point is a good idea. As a result, strive to use access points that enable you to remotely shut off the radio or disable the power through Power-over-Ethernet (PoE).

- **Security education and training**—Be certain to adequately train everyone involved with the network on security risks and countermeasures. For example, help desk personnel should understand that an unauthorized person may call them asking for the WEP key to access the network. In this case, methods should be in place to verify the identity of the person requesting the WEP key, thus ensuring that he or she is authorized to have the key.

- **Periodic testing policies**—Access points should be subject to periodic penetration tests and audits to ensure compliance with configuration policies. Without this testing, there is no way of telling whether the wireless LAN actually conforms in a way that satisfies security requirements. A combination of effective network monitoring and configuration management can replace the need for some of this testing, but be sure to conduct periodic testing to ensure that you do not miss anything.

Security Assessment Steps

After deploying a VoWLAN, you should implement a security assessment, which ensures that the VoWLAN complies with effective security policies. For most situations, this assessment is necessary whether or not the network implements effective security mechanisms. Do not put too much trust in the design of a system. It's best to run tests to be certain that the network is hardened enough to guard against unauthorized persons attacking company resources.

In fact, companies should conduct regular, periodic security reviews to ensure that changes to the wireless LAN do not make the system vulnerable to hackers. This review is best done via an outside audit consisting of independent testers who perform penetration testing. A review once a year may suffice for low-risk networks, but a review each quarter or more often may be necessary (and is recommended) if the network supports high-risk information, such as financial data, mail routing, and manufacturing control functions.

When performing a wireless LAN security assessment, consider completing the following steps:

- Review existing security policies
- Review the system architecture
- Review operational support tools and procedures
- Interview users
- Verify configurations of wireless devices
- Investigate physical installations of access points
- Identify rogue access points
- Perform penetration tests
- Analyze security gaps
- Recommend improvements

Review Existing Security Policies

Before going too far with the security assessment, become familiar with the policies that the company has for wireless LAN security. Doing so provides a benchmark for determining whether a company is complying with its own policies. In addition, you will be able to make an assessment and corresponding recommendations for policy modifications.

Determine whether the policy leaves any room for a hacker (for example, a disgruntled employee) to access or harm company resources.

For example, the policy should describe adequate encryption and authentication mechanisms. Also, the policy should mandate that all employees coordinate with the company's information systems organization before purchasing or installing access points. It is very important that all access points have configuration settings that comply with the policies and provide the proper level of security. In addition, you need to ensure that methods are in place to disseminate security policies to employees in an effective manner.

Review the System Architecture

Meet with information systems personnel and read through related documentation to gain an understanding of the system's architecture and configurations of access points. You need this information to determine whether any design flaws exist that cause weaknesses that could allow a hacker inside the system.

For example, if static WEP is in use, a hacker could use tools such as AirSnort to break through the encryption process. In addition, the dependence on 802.11 authentication alone will verify only the radio Network Interface Card (NIC) and not the user, which could enable an unauthorized person to steal someone's wireless-equipped laptop (or just the radio card) and access the corporate network.

Review Operational Support Tools and Procedures

Some security weaknesses materialize when a company supports a wireless LAN. As a result, learn as much as possible about existing support tools and procedures to spot potential issues. Most companies, for example, configure the access points over the wired Ethernet backbone through the use of Hypertext Transfer Protocol (HTTP) or Telnet. With this process, the passwords sent to open a connection with particular access points are sent in the clear (that is, unencrypted) over the wired network. As a result, a hacker with monitoring equipment hooked to the Ethernet network can likely capture the passwords and reconfigure the access point.

Interview Users

Be sure to talk with a sample of employees to determine whether they are aware of the security policies, at least to a level of security that they can control. For example, do the users know that they must coordinate the purchase and installation of wireless LAN components with the appropriate organization? Even though the policy states this fact, do not count on everyone having knowledge of the policy. A new employee or someone who has not seen the policy may purchase an access point from a local office supply store and install it on the corporate network (without any security settings enabled) to provide wireless connectivity within his or her office. Verifying that people are using personal firewalls and antivirus software (or that they know they should) is also a good idea.

Verify Configurations of Wireless Devices

A portion of the security policy should define appropriate access point configurations that will offer an applicable level of security. As part of the assessment, walk through the facilities having access points and use tools, such as AirMagnet or AiroPeek, to identify the access point configurations. These tools are packet sniffers, but they still obtain a great deal of information on the access point configuration from the packets sent over the wireless network. If the company has centralized support software (such as AirWave or CiscoWorks) in place, you should be able to view the configuration settings from a single console attached to the wired side of the network. This is to determine which security mechanisms are actually in use and whether they comply with effective policies.

For example, the policies may state that access points must disable the physical console port, but while testing you determine that most access points have the ports enabled. Of course, this situation would indicate noncompliance with the policies, and it would enable a hacker to possibly reset the access point to factory default settings with no security enabled. In addition, look at the firmware version of each access point to see whether it is up to date. Older firmware versions might not implement the more recent patches that fix encryption and other vulnerabilities.

Investigate Physical Installations of Access Points

As you walk through the facilities, investigate the installation of access points by noting their physical accessibility, antenna type and orientation, and radio wave propagation into portions of the facility that do not have physical security controls. The access points should be mounted in a position that would make it difficult for someone to go unnoticed and physically handle the access point. An access point placed on top of a bookshelf, for example, would be easy for a hacker to swap with an open one that doesn't have any security enabled. Or the hacker could attach a laptop to the console port to reset the access point. If the access points are all mounted above the ceiling tiles and out of view, however, someone would need to use a ladder and would probably be noticed by an employee or security guard.

Identify Rogue Access Points

A problem that is difficult to enforce and significantly undercuts the security of the wireless LAN is when an employee installs a "personal" access point in his or her office. Most of the time, these installations do not comply with security policies and result in an open, nonsecure entry port to the corporate network. In fact, hackers can use sniffing tools to alert them when such an opportunity exists. Therefore, scan for these unauthorized access points as part of the assessment. Most companies will be surprised to learn how many they will find. The most effective method for detecting rogue access points is to walk through the facilities with sniffing tools, such as AirMagnet or AiroPeek. In addition, the company should periodically scan the network for potential rogue access points from the wired side of the network.

Perform Penetration Tests

In addition to hunting for rogue access points, try going a step further and attempt to access corporate resources using common tools available to hackers. For example, are default passwords in use that allow easy access to the access point configuration screens? Can you use AirSnort to crack through WEP? Is it possible to associate with an access point from outside the company's controlled perimeter? Of course, if WEP is turned off, your job will be easy. If strong encryption and authentication techniques are in use, you will likely not find a way in.

Before performing penetration testing, develop a test plan that clearly explains how the testing will be done, and get permission from the network manager. Keep in mind that active scanning and probing of the network may cause significant degradation in performance of the network while the tests are being run. These actions may also bring down the network. Therefore, consider doing penetration testing after hours.

Analyze Security Gaps

The information you gather during the assessment provides a basis for understanding the security posture of a company or organization. After collecting information in the preceding steps, spend some time thinking about potential gaps in security. This includes issues with policy, network architecture, operational support, and other items that weaken security, such as the presence of unauthorized access points and abilities to penetrate the network. This process requires you to think like a hacker and uncover any and all methods that make penetrating and accessing (or controlling) company resources through the wireless LAN easier for someone.

Recommend Improvements

As you spot weaknesses in the security of the wireless LAN, research and describe methods that will counter the issues. Start by recommending improvements to the policies, which dictate what the company requires in terms of security for the wireless LANs. These improvements provide a basis for defining technical and procedural solutions that will strengthen the security of the system to a level that protects the company's interests.

Maintenance Functions

When deploying a wireless LAN, be certain to have a plan for fixing problems as they arise. Try to proactively find trouble spots and mend them before they affect users. Doing so reduces downtime, which certainly makes users much happier. These types of efforts fall into what most companies call the maintenance function. Effective maintenance staffs include hands-on people who are capable of troubleshooting problems and applying appropriate fixes.

The maintenance staff should be ready to repair the following types of wireless LAN problems:

- Inoperative access points
- Poor performance
- Poor signal coverage
- Broken hardware

In addition, the maintenance staff should regularly perform the following tasks:

- Keep firmware up to date
- Monitor performance
- Verify coverage
- Inspect access points

The following sections discuss these problems and tasks in greater detail.

Inoperative Access Points

Firmware bugs sometimes cause access points to fail in a manner that keeps wireless IP phones from associating with the access point. Often, a solution to getting things back to normal is just to reboot the access point. This generally puts the access point back on the air. With the access point in this "holding pattern," determine whether updates to the firmware are available, and report the problem to the vendor. Update the firmware if yours is currently out of date. In some cases, you might need to replace the access point, especially if an electrical surge has caused the problem.

Poor Performance

Wireless LANs are difficult to design and install in a way that provides good performance at all times, especially in cases with lots of users or high-performance applications, such as voice traffic phone calls. The shared medium access protocols of the 802.11 standard make throughput vary widely as conditions on the network change. As a result, maintenance staff needs to be ready to respond to users complaining about sluggish performance. Possible remedies to this problem include ensuring that adequate coverage exists, implementing bandwidth control mechanisms, possibly upgrading to 802.11g or 802.11a, or using a wireless LAN switch architecture.

Poor Signal Coverage

As discussed in Chapter 7, you should always perform an RF site survey to properly position the access points and determine whether any harmful interference sources are present that will disturb performance. Often, however, companies either do not perform a survey or alterations made within the facility change the propagation and coverage of the wireless LAN. Thus, users may eventually complain about having poor coverage in certain parts of the building. Maintenance staff then need to evaluate the areas having poor coverage and reorient the access points in a way that satisfies required coverage.

Broken Hardware

The two primary components of an access point that physically break are antennas and cable connectors. If a telephone technician rewiring phones accidentally clips off an antenna from an access point, poor coverage will result. The access point will probably continue to operate, but the range will be lessened without the antenna. A broken data cable, however, completely disables the access point, especially when using 802.3af power-over-Ethernet to supply electricity. These mishaps will happen sooner or later, so have adequate numbers of spare antennas and cables on hand. Having a spare access point or two is also a good idea.

The staffing of a maintenance crew that can fix problems associated with wireless LANs is one step toward having successful maintenance. Being proactive is far more important. The remaining sections offer some suggestions on preventive maintenance tasks that you should perform with wireless LANs to minimize downtime.

Keep Firmware Up to Date

Instead of waiting for an access point to fail, update the firmware when new releases become available, as mentioned earlier in this chapter. Doing so ensures that the access point operates with the latest features and freedom from defects to maximize performance and security of the network. Before moving access points to a new release of firmware, however, be sure to adequately review and test the new firmware. New releases have been known to cause more problems than the previous versions.

Monitor Performance

Be sure to review actual utilization of the access points, and track the average and peak values. The trends provide valuable information that you can use to determine whether you should begin implementing methods to increase throughput available for each user.

Verify Coverage

Do not wait until users complain about spotty coverage. The maintenance group should periodically perform tests to ensure that the access points are properly covering the building at applicable levels of performance. If discrepancies are found, reposition access points or add new ones.

Inspect Access Points

Walking around and visually inspecting the access points at least monthly is also important. For preventive maintenance purposes, check for any existing or potential damage. For example, you may walk through a large medical center and find several access points dangling by their data cables over some beams. A construction company came in to replace ceiling tiles and left the access points in these vulnerable positions for several days. Ideally, the access points should be neatly tucked away above the ceiling or securely mounted to beams or walls. Keeping the access points out of easy reach to avoid security problems is also best.

Engineering Functions

A company having a VoWLAN system should establish a reengineering function that assesses needs for changes and defines corresponding solutions. Engineering, of course, is a critical task when initially designing a VoWLAN system, but it is also very important to have available on an ongoing basis. Engineering and maintenance interact in a way that lengthens the life of the system.

The staff for engineering tasks may consist of "gurus" working directly for the company, most likely within the IT group. Especially after having a wireless LAN for a number of months or years, employees of the company can become experts in understanding the applicable technical aspects. In most cases, however, the engineering function will likely be an initial outsourcing venture.

When planning the operational support for a wireless LAN, ensure that an engineering capability exists to perform the following tasks:

- Advanced problem resolution
- Coverage expansion

- Capacity increases
- Firmware review
- Technology upgrade
- Design review

Advanced Problem Resolution

Because of the nature of wireless LANs, difficult-to-solve problems will likely arise. Users may have periodic loss of connectivity that causes applications to malfunction, or interference may inflict significant loss of throughput. In these cases, engineers may be necessary to analyze the problems and recommend how to proceed with a solution. For example, users may complain that the batteries in wireless IP phones do not last very long. An engineer may diagnose the problem and find that the radios in the phones are continually scanning for access points because the access points are not installed in locations where signal strength is sufficient throughout the facility. This would lead the engineer to redetermine the proper placement of access points.

Coverage Expansion

Companies occasionally expand the reach of the wireless LAN to cover new areas. This expansion generally requires engineering input to determine the effective placement and channel settings for access points. A hospital, for example, may begin by having only voice applications in the emergency department. After better understanding the advantages of voice telephony, the hospital may decide to expand the voice system to include other departments. This change will require designing the existing network to handle the greater amount of voice traffic and the addition of greater signal coverage.

Capacity Increases

In the early days of the life of a VoWLAN system, the number of users is normally much lower than the total available capacity. As time goes on, however, the company will probably deploy additional applications that increase the utilization of the wireless LAN. It is important to have network monitoring in place to watch throughput levels and engineer upgrades to the network when needed to handle ongoing needs to support a greater number of users.

Firmware Review

Within the maintenance function of operational support, technicians may find that upgrading the firmware of access points is necessary. Before making the upgrades, though, engineering should test and evaluate the new firmware. Doing so certifies that the changes being made will not adversely affect the network. Also, document any firmware updates in the master configuration database.

Technology Upgrade

Continually monitor the evolution of wireless LAN technologies and products to ensure effective migration in a manner that meets growing network utilization. For example, the engineering function should proactively review the potential upgrade from 802.11b to 802.11a, 802.11g, or 802.11n. A change in technology should occur, though, only after careful deliberation.

Design Review

The engineering function should also be involved in reviewing and verifying compliance of new designs with the common architectural design of the VoWLAN system. This review avoids haphazard expansion of the network that might have led to a network consisting of noninteroperable parts, such as the deployment of 802.11a-only access points with some users who just have 802.11b radio cards. A design review involves examining requirements and making certain that the requested changes fully satisfy requirements. In fact, reassessing requirements as the company moves forward might be necessary from time to time.

Help Desk Planning

A help desk provides first-level support for users. It is the first stop for users having difficulties with the network. Thus, when a problem arises, a user should know how to reach the help desk. The mission of the help desk is to solve relatively simple problems that users may be having and act as a conduit to the rest of the support operations. Help desk staff should mitigate problems by helping the users rather than making changes to the network.

When planning the operational support for a wireless LAN, establish a help desk that can respond to the following:

- Connection problems
- Poor signal coverage
- Poor performance
- System status
- Additional considerations

Connection Problems

Users commonly call the help desk when having connection problems. People at the help desk should be capable of solving simple connectivity issues, such as assisting users with configuring their radio card and operating system to comply with the proper SSID, IP address, and WEP key.

Poor Signal Coverage

Poor signal coverage sometimes occurs because of improper site surveys or changes made to the facility. If coverage is the complaint, the help desk staff could ask the user to temporarily operate from a different area if possible. Meanwhile, they should introduce a repair ticket for the maintenance group to fix the problem. An access point may have a broken antenna or require rebooting due to a software bug.

Poor Performance

Occasionally, a user may mention that applications are running too slow. In this case, the help desk will probably need to defer the problem to engineering to find the source of the problem. Possibly, network monitoring may indicate a high occurrence of broadcast packets on the network, which is introducing delays to users. Or, maybe too many users are active on the network. Major configuration changes or upgrades to new technology may be necessary.

System Status

The help desk should have up-to-date status on the well-being of the VoWLAN system. In addition to telling users that the network is down for a particular reason, more importantly users want to know when the network will be fully operational again. The job of the help desk is to help users, so be sure that status information is available. If a user calls in with a problem, be certain to let him or her know when it has been fixed.

Additional Considerations

Most enterprises should integrate the wireless LAN help desk functions into the existing corporate help desk. The company should, however, provide applicable training to the help desk staff to ensure they are ready to support wireless LAN-specific issues. Radio wave propagation leads to impairments, such as RF interference, which is beyond the knowledge of most IT staff.

If the help desk cannot solve the problem by working directly with the user, procedures should be in place to escalate the problems to advanced support functions. As a result, help desk staff should have a communications interface with maintenance and engineering to solve more complex problems that arise. In fact, often the help desk alerts maintenance when problems occur, primarily because users first contact the help desk when they have trouble using the network.

CiscoWorks Wireless LAN Solution Engine

The CiscoWorks Wireless LAN Solution Engineer (WLSE) is a centralized network management system for Cisco Aironet solutions. The following sections discuss the various WLSE features.

Automatic Access Point Configuration

WLSE automatically discovers and configures Cisco Aironet access points based on access point type, subnet, and software version. This feature eliminates the need to manually configure each access point separately. WLSE enables the administrator to update any of the access point configurations, such as WPA security settings, SSID, and RF channel. WLSE can also perform mass upgrades of older Cisco access points running VxWorks to newer Cisco IOS Software versions. WLSE stores the last four configuration versions for each access point so that an administrator can easily undo changes through a rollback procedure.

Assisted Site Surveys

WLSE's assisted site survey tool automatically identifies optimal RF channels and transmit power and periodically assesses performance with respect to baseline site-survey settings. These surveys ease wireless LAN installation by reducing the effort needed to perform RF testing in the facility before installing the network. WLSE generates notifications to the administrator when applicable configuration updates are necessary as the facility's RF dynamics change over time.

Centralized Firmware Updates

WLSE allows administrators to update firmware on access points and bridges on an individual or group basis. Timely firmware updates are critical for ensuring optimum performance, reliability, and security of the network.

Dynamic Grouping

Administrators can place access points that span different subnets into different groups to enable more intuitive network management. For example, one group of access points may be named "public," and another group may be named "engineering," regardless of where the access points physically reside on the network. This concept is similar to that of multiple virtual local-area networks (VLAN) at Layer 2.

VLAN Configuration

WLSE allows administrators to centrally configure and monitor VLANs on access points. This feature enables the administrator to separate traffic among different groups of users associating with the same access point. For example, one VLAN may be assigned to public users, and a different VLAN may be provided for staff members.

Multiple SSID Support

WLSE allows the configuration of up to eight broadcast SSIDs per access point radio. Each SSID can be assigned to a particular VLAN, facilitating the use of VLANs for separating user traffic. The SSID "public," for example, may tie to the VLAN connecting to the Internet from outside the demilitarized zone (DMZ) of the company network.

Customizable Thresholds

Administrators can define a variety of faults and performance thresholds, such as network load, RF usage, errors, and client associations, and specify actions and fault priorities. If data traffic through a particular access point reaches capacity, for example, WLSE can send an alert to the administrator via SNMP.

Fault Status

WLSE displays a view of all access points and device groups, with color coding and group icons that indicate fault status. Fault notifications are done via Syslog messages, SNMP traps, and e-mail. This notification is especially important with wireless LANs because a faulty access point, possibly due to a broken antenna, could go unnoticed for weeks or months if no monitoring functions are available. Users in this situation tend to adapt to the resulting coverage hole by moving to a different part of the facility to maintain connectivity. Careful monitoring of the fault status of access points eliminates this problem.

Intrusion Detection System

WLSE detects unauthorized access points and tracks wireless clients participating in the wireless LAN. For example, WLSE detects clients spoofing authorized Media Access Control (MAC) addresses, excessive probe requests, and unusual deauthentication frames that indicate potential man-in-the-middle or denial of service (DoS) attacks.

Security Policy Monitoring

WLSE monitors the network via SNMP and ensures that all access points are configured to ensure adherence to security policies. If an improper configuration is found, WLSE issues alerts via e-mail, Syslog, or SNMP trap notifications. This precludes someone from making use of a rogue access point attaching to the corporate network. WLSE detects improper configuration of the rogue device and promptly alerts the administrator.

Secure User Interface

WLSE includes a secure, role-based, Hypertext Markup Language (HTML) user interface to facilitate remote access to the management functions. As a result, an administrator can make use of WLSE functions while sitting in an office, when traveling, or from home. All communications between the administrator and the WLSE are done via Secure Socket Layer (SSL).

Air/RF Scanning and Monitoring

Cisco Aironet access points have integrated RF scanning and measurement features that collect information about the RF environment, which may include rogue access points and users. WLSE analyzes this data and provides reports and alerts when rogue devices are found or when RF coverage is not optimum. WLSE also helps determine the source of RF interference. These features reduce the need for installing dedicated sensing devices to monitor for rogue access points.

Self-healing Functions

If an access point fails, WLSE can automatically increase the power and corresponding coverage of surrounding access points to compensate for the coverage hole. This feature quickly fixes coverage hole problems while the administrator replaces the failed access point. WLSE also has a backup mechanism that automatically takes over and notifies the administrator if the primary WLSE fails.

Reporting, Trending, Planning, and Troubleshooting

WLSE tracks actions taken by clients to aid in troubleshooting network access problems. For example, a user may be having trouble associating with an access point. The administrator or help desk can view recent transactions with the applicable access point and determine the source of the problem.

NOTE   For more information on Cisco WLSE, refer to the following link: http://www.cisco.com/en/US/products/sw/cscowork/ps3915/index.html.

Chapter Summary

The operational support of a VoWLAN system is significant. If you do not effectively manage the configuration; monitor the network; periodically review security; and perform maintenance, help desk, and engineering functions, users will likely experience poor performance. Through configuration management, you need to keep track of elements such as RF channels, transmit power, and new applications to ensure that the system continues to provide good service. Network monitoring can spot issues with the network before they cause problems for users, and periodic security assessments will shield the system from hackers and better protect company assets. The maintenance staff should be in place to troubleshoot and fix problems, such as access points that need to be rebooted, and engineers should be on hand to tackle more in-depth issues that may require redesign of the network. The combination of all of these support elements will keep the system supporting intended requirements.

Chapter Review Questions

1 What types of changes to a VoWLAN system should operational support managers be concerned with?

2 Why is it important to continually monitor the status of access points?

3 What is the reason for having a policy for requiring anyone installing wireless access points to first have approval from the IT group?

4 When conducting a security assessment, what questions should you ask users?

5 When inspecting access points during a security assessment, what constitutes a good mounting location for access points?

6 If you learn that new firmware is available for the access points installed within your facility, how should you proceed?

7 What are common problems that help desk personnel will encounter from users?

8 What element of the wireless LAN will you likely need to consider as voice traffic increases?

9 What are two primary components of an access point that may physically break?

10 What function can you employ in operational support to determine that a hacker may be tampering with the network?

Answers to Chapter Review Questions

Chapter 1

1 What types of user devices can VoWLAN systems replace?

Answer: Wired telephones, cellular telephones, and two-way radios

2 VoWLANs are an extension to a wired VoIP system. True or false?

Answer: True

3 Which wireless LAN technologies can adequately support voice traffic?

Answer: 802.11a, 802.11b, and 802.11b

4 What are two quantitative benefits of VoWLAN solutions?

Answer: Improved communications among employees and lower long-distance telephone charges

5 Improved safety is not a benefit of VoWLAN solutions. True or false?

Answer: False

6 What are examples of operational costs of a VoWLAN solution?

Answer: Planning, installation, and testing services

7 The initial financial study must include all technical details of the requirements, design, installation, and support. True or false?

Answer: False

8 What are the primary elements that comprise the capital costs of a VoWLAN system?

Answer: VoWLAN handsets, voice gateways, and wireless access points

9 What is the purpose of conducting initial analysis for a VoWLAN system?

Answer: To determine enough details to define benefits and costs of the system

Chapter 2

1 What are the primary components of a VoWLAN solution?

Answer: Wireless IP phones, call manager, voice gateways, and wireless LAN infrastructure

2 What are the two main Cisco wireless IP phone approaches?

Answer: 7920 Wireless IP Phone (hardware) and Cisco IP Softphone (Windows-based software)

3 What functions does a call manager have on a VoWLAN system?

Answer: It processes calls on the network, registers IP phones, and administers dial and route plans.

4 What is the purpose of a voice gateway?

Answer: It interfaces IP telephony to other types of networks and systems.

5 Why is a wireless switched network better for supporting voice applications?

Answer: It offers better performance, such as faster handoff between access points.

6 Why would an existing "thick" access point solution not be the optimum solution for supporting voice applications?

Answer: The system is costly to scale up to more users.

7 What are examples of Cisco's traditional "thick" access points?

Answer: Cisco Aironet 1300, 1230, 1200, 1130, 1100, and 350 Series access points

8 What Cisco access point is used with a wireless switch?

Answer: Cisco 1000 Series Lightweight Access Point

9 Why might a wireless mesh network not provide adequate performance for voice applications?

Answer: Delays between wireless access points may contribute to significant end-to-end delays that impair phone calls.

Chapter 3

1 What is the audible frequency range that VoIP systems support?

Answer: 300 Hz to 3,400 Hz

2 What is the function of a codec?

Answer: The codec converts analog voice and video signals into digital signals (and vice versa).

3 In what scenario does compression offer the greatest savings in capacity?

Answer: When the scene does not change very much, such as of a person sitting at a desk

4 What protocol provides the end-to-end network transport functions for real-time streaming of data?

Answer: Real-time transport protocol (RTP)

5 What are the biggest differences between VoIP and standard analog telephone systems?

Answer: For controlling the flow of calls, VoIP uses messages sent in packets, and analog telephones use audible tones sent over the telephone circuit. Analog phone systems establish a physical connection between phones, and VoIP establishes a virtual connection.

6 What is the purpose of a gateway in an H.323 system?

Answer: The gateway provides connections between terminals, such as wireless IP phones, and the standard PSTN.

7 What VoIP is used between Cisco VoIP phones and Cisco CallManager?

Answer: Skinny Client Control Protocol (SCCP)

8 What is the signal-to-noise ratio if the noise is –90 dBm and the signal is –65 dBm?

Answer: 25 dB

9 How much delay can most wireless IP phones tolerate to avoid dropping a call when roaming from one access point to another?

Answer: 100 ms

10 How can you design a wireless LAN to minimize the impact of microwave oven interference and neighboring wireless LANs?

Answer: Tune access points near the microwave oven to nonconflicting RF channels.

Chapter 4

1 How do 802.11 frames flow from one wireless IP phone to another wireless IP phone in an infrastructure wireless LAN?

Answer: The access point relays the frames from one wireless IP phone to another. The frames do not flow directly between the phones.

2 Explain at least two methods for increasing the capacity of a wireless LAN.

Answer: 1) Collocate multiple access points in the same area by setting them to non-conflicting RF channels, and implement a form of load balancing so that only part of the wireless IP phones connect to each access point.

2) Reduce the transmit power of each access point, which reduces the radio cell size, increases the density of access points, and reduces the number of wireless IP phones connecting to each access point.

3 Which IEEE 802.11 standard is being developed to standardize and improve roaming between access points?

Answer: 802.11r is developing a standard for roaming.

4 Which 802.11 physical layer theoretically has the greatest capacity for supporting voice calls?

Answer: 802.11a has the greatest capacity because it offers the largest number of nonconflicting RF channels in the same area.

5 Why is it an advantage to set the wireless IP phone and access point to operate at the highest fixed data rate?

Answer: Despite the fact that range will be less, a fixed operation at the higher data rates ensures that the phone will have good performance.

6 What are some disadvantages of using 802.11b/g wireless LANs for supporting voice communications?

Answer: 802.11b/g operate in the 2.4-GHz band, which includes significant RF interference sources, such as microwave ovens, cordless phones, and other wireless LANs. Also, 802.11b/g has less capacity compared to 802.11a.

7 Why is the disabling of SSID broadcasting not a foolproof security mechanism?

Answer: The disabling of SSID broadcasting eliminates the SSID from beacon frames, but the SSID can still easily be found in probe request frames sent by radio cards when scanning or when the radio card initially associates with the access point.

8 What are nonconflicting RF channels relevant to 802.11b/g?

Answer: 1, 6, and 11

9 What is a reason to implement RTS/CTS?

Answer: The use of RTS/CTS can reduce collision rates when wireless devices, such as wireless IP phones, are too far apart to hear each other, but they are connected to the same access point. This is referred to as the hidden node problem.

10 What is a problem that will occur when 802.11b clients associate with an 802.11g access point?

Answer: All 802.11b and 802.11g clients will use protection mechanisms, which reduce the performance of the wireless LAN.

Chapter 5

1 What are the primary security implications of a wireless LAN?

Answer: Passive monitoring, unauthorized access, and DoS

2 When WEP is implemented, all users of the wireless LAN must use the same encryption key. True or false?

Answer: True

3 What encryption type does TKIP use?

Answer: RC4, which is the same as WEP

4 What version of WPA implements AES encryption?

Answer: WPA2

5 What is the primary difference between WPA and 802.11i?

Answer: Products conforming to WPA require interoperability testing.

6 What part of the network do WEP, WPA, and AES protect?

Answer: Only between the wireless client device and the access point

7 Which two forms of authentication are part of the 802.11 standard and are not effective for protecting wireless LANs?

Answer: Open systems authentication and shared key authentication

8 The disabling of SSID broadcasting prevents a hacker from obtaining the SSID of the wireless LAN. True or false?

Answer: False

9 Why should you use strong SNMP community strings?

Answer: To keep a hacker from reconfiguring an access point into a mode that makes it insecure

10 What are methods that you can use to keep the radio signals inside the building?

Answer: Paint walls with metallic paint, turn down the transmit power of the access point, and use directional antennas.

Chapter 6

1 What are the steps of analyzing requirements?

Answer: Identify potential requirements, verify and validate requirements, and document requirements

2 Who should review and comment on the requirements?

Answer: All stakeholders, such as managers of the company

3 Why is defining requirements crucial?

Answer: To provide a foundation for the design

4 What are examples of requirements elements that you should define?

Answer: Number of users, applications, coverage, roaming, security, environment, analysis of expected future growth, and existing systems

5 What type of testing should you consider performing when analyzing the environment?

Answer: RF signal testing to determine the noise floor and presence of existing wireless LANs

6 What areas of the facility may be questionable to include as covered areas?

Answer: Elevators, stairwells, restrooms, and utility rooms

7 Why are stairwells difficult to cover?

Answer: In many cases, the stairwells are encased in concrete-reinforced steel and fireproofing material, which offer substantial attenuation to radio signals.

8 What are typical noise floor values for the 2.4–2.5-GHz band (802.11b/g)?

Answer: –95 dBm and –85 dBm

9 Why should you identify the location of equipment and wiring closets?

Answer: To determine whether access points can be installed within 100 meters (300 feet) of the termination points where switches will be installed. Also, the location of wiring closets will likely be where IT staff needs signal coverage.

10 What is a typical policy or preference that a company may have regarding requirements?

Answer: A company might have already deployed a wireless LAN compliant with 802.11b/g, and it will likely want the VoWLAN solution to operate over the existing network.

Chapter 7

1 Which VoWLAN deployment model is best for supporting multiple sites where the WAN may have limited reliability?

Answer: Multisite WAN with distributed call processing

2 The single-site deployment model provides outgoing calls through a PSTN. True or false?

Answer: True

3 Survivable Remote Site Telephony (SRST) supports reliable backup for both data and voice traffic. True or false?

Answer: False. SRST supports only voice.

4 Why is it advantageous to define a single VLAN for all voice traffic on a wireless LAN?

Answer: To keep Layer 3 roaming from occurring

5 What issue may result if multicasting is used on a wireless LAN supporting voice applications?

Answer: The quality of voice conversations may suffer because of delays in obtaining voice frames.

6 What mechanisms do Cisco 7920 wireless IP phones and access points use to improve QoS?

Answer: Enhanced DCF and multiple downstream queues

7 How many simultaneous voice users can a typical 802.11b access point handle?

Answer: Seven for G.711 or eight for G.729

8 When is it necessary to use smaller radio cell sizes for each access point?

Answer: To increase the capacity of the wireless LAN to support a larger number of simultaneous voice users

9 With voice applications, you should always set the access points to automatically configure the RF channel. True or false?

Answer: False

10 Why must you take into consideration both the uplink and downlink signal strengths when performing an RF site survey?

Answer: To compensate for the uplink signal strength likely being less than the downlink signal strength

Chapter 8

1 When installing access points for voice applications, you orient the antennas on the access points horizontal to the ground. True or false?

Answer: False

2 What are advantages of mounting access points above ceiling tiles?

Answer: It makes the installation more aesthetically pleasing and makes it difficult for someone to find and steal the access points.

3 What are some warnings that must be taken into account when installing access points?

Answer: Do not mount and operate them in areas where there are unshielded blasting caps, and keep access point antennas at least 7.9 inches (20 cm) away from the body of all persons.

4 What are the three options for distributing electrical power to access points over the data cable?

Answer: Switch with integrated inline power, inline power patch panel, and individual power injector

5 Which access point configuration parameters must be set to the same values used when performing the RF site survey?

Answer: Transmit power and data rate

6 The transmit power of the access point should always be set to the highest value to maximize range of the access point. True or false?

Answer: False

7 If a wireless IP phone will not associate with an access point, what may be the problem(s)?

Answer: The SSID in the phone and access point do not match; the access point is not operational; the phone is in an area where signal coverage does not exist

8 Why should the wireless IP phones be configured with an SSID that corresponds with a special VLAN for voice applications?

Answer: This generally allows voice QoS to be implemented for the voice traffic.

9 If a wireless IP phone associates and authenticates successfully but cannot register with Cisco CallManager and place calls, what might be the problem(s)?

Answer: The phone does not have the correct IP address; the phone has not been set up in Cisco CallManager software as a legitimate subscriber

10 How can you maximize battery life on a wireless IP phone?

Answer: Reduce active scanning by effectively designing, installing, and configuring the wireless LAN; instruct users to turn the phone off when outside the signal coverage area; avoid using vibrate mode and the background light on the phone

Chapter 9

1 What types of changes to a VoWLAN system should operational support managers be concerned with?

Answer: RF channel, transmit power, new applications, signal coverage, and firmware versions

2 Why is it important to continually monitor the status of access points?

Answer: An access point may fail due to firmware defects or other reasons, causing it to become inoperative and unable to accept associations from wireless IP phones.

3 What is the reason for having a policy for requiring anyone installing wireless access points to first have approval from the IT group?

Answer: The reason is to keep someone from attaching an access point to the corporate network that does not have adequate security configurations, which would allow a hacker to easily access corporate resources.

4 When conducting a security assessment, what questions should you ask users?

Answer: You need to be sure that the users understand the security policies regarding the VoWLAN system.

5 When inspecting access points during a security assessment, what constitutes a good mounting location for access points?

Answer: The access points should be mounted out of sight of users, preferably above the ceiling tiles.

6 If you learn that new firmware is available for the access points installed within your facility, how should you proceed?

Answer: Ensure that the new firmware does not have any reports of serious errors, and verify the operation of the firmware on an access point in a lab environment before deploying the firmware on all access points within the facility.

7 What are common problems that help desk personnel will encounter from users?

Answer: Connection problems and poor signal coverage

8 What element of the wireless LAN will you likely need to consider as voice traffic increases?

Answer: You need to consider the capacity of the access points. If the capacity is being reached on some of the access points, you might need to install additional access points.

9 What are two primary components of an access point that may physically break?

Answer: Antennas and cable connectors

10 What function can you employ in operational support to determine that a hacker may be tampering with the network?

Answer: You can monitor configuration changes made to access points. A hacker might try to change the configuration of an access point to make it less secure and enable him to access corporate assets.

GLOSSARY

802.3. A standard published by the Institute of Electrical and Electronic Engineers (IEEE) that defines the signal characteristics and operation of a wired local-area network (LAN). Defines the use of carrier sense multiple access (CSMA), which is similar to 802.11 wireless LANs.

802.11. A standard published by the IEEE that defines the radio characteristics and operation of a medium-range radio frequency local-area network. Specifies the use of CSMA as the primary method for sharing access to a common air medium.

802.16. A standard published by the IEEE that defines the radio characteristics and operation of wireless metropolitan-area networks (MAN).

A

access point. A type of base station that wireless LANs use to interface wireless users to a wired network and provide roaming throughout a facility.

active scanning. A roaming function for 802.11–based clients that sends probe request frames to search for other access points.

Ad Hoc mode. A configuration of a wireless network that allows communications directly from one user device to another, without the need to travel through a base station. Ad Hoc mode applies to both wireless personal-area networks (PAN) and wireless LANs.

analog signal. A signal whose amplitude varies continuously as time progresses. A radio wave is an example of an analog signal.

antenna. A physical device that converts electrical signals into radio or light waves (and vice versa) for propagation through the air medium. Antennas may be omnidirectional, distributing radio waves in all directions, or directional, focusing the radio waves more in one direction than others.

association. A process whereby an 802.11 station (computer device) becomes a part of the wireless LAN. After association, the user can use network services.

authentication. The process of proving the identity of a user or base station. The use of usernames and passwords is a common authentication method, but many other more sophisticated authentication mechanisms exist. For example, digital certificates can offer a means of authentication without user intervention.

B

base station. Hardware that interfaces wireless computing devices together and to a wired network. Access points and wireless routers are types of wireless LAN base stations.

Bluetooth. A specification published by the Bluetooth Special Interest Group that defines the radio characteristics and operation of a short-range, low-power radio frequency network. Many devices today support Bluetooth, and 802.15 has developed applicable standards.

bridge. A device that interconnects two networks at Layer 2. A bridge forwards data packets to another network based on the Media Access Control (MAC) address found in the packet header. Bridges play a key role in the deployment of wireless MANs.

C

carrier sense access. A process of sharing a common medium by first determining whether the medium is idle before transmitting data. This is part of the CSMA protocol.

carrier signal. The primary radio frequency (RF) signal that "carries" data through the air medium. Various modulation types vary the carrier signal frequency, phase, or amplitude to represent information.

CDMA (code division multiple access). A process whereby each user modulates his or her signals with a different, noninterfering code.

client device. Hardware having a user interface that enables the use of wireless network applications. Client device is another name for a computer device. A wireless client is a type of client device.

CompactFlash (CF). A very small network interface card (NIC) for personal digital assistants (PDA), cameras, and other small computer devices. Bluetooth and 802.11 CF NICs are readily available.

computer device. Any endpoint of a wireless network, such as a laptop, PDA, or robot. The computer device is often referred to as a client device.

CSMA (carrier sense multiple access). A process that allows multiple 802.11 stations to share a common air medium. Stations attempt to transmit data only when no other station is transmitting. Otherwise, collisions will occur, and the station must retransmit the data.

D

DCF (distributed coordination function). A part of the 802.11 standard that defines how stations will contend for access to the air medium. DCF makes use of CSMA to regulate traffic on the network.

DHCP (Dynamic Host Configuration Protocol). A protocol that automatically assigns unique Internet Protocol (IP) addresses within an assigned range to network devices. Most home and public wireless LANs implement DHCP, making it very easy for users to gain access to the network. DHCP automatically assigns a valid IP address to these users.

digital certificate. An electronic message that contains the credentials of a particular user. Digital certificates are used as a means for authenticating users or their computer devices.

digital signal. A signal that varies in amplitude steps as time advances. Digital signals represent data within a computer device. The digital signal must be converted to an analog form (known as modulation) before the data can be sent through the air medium.

direct sequence spread spectrum. A type of spread spectrum where a spreading code increases the signal rate of the data stream to spread the signal over a wider portion of the frequency band. An 802.11b wireless LAN makes use of direct sequence.

directional antenna. A type of antenna that focuses radio waves and range more in one direction than in others. Directional antennas are commonly found in wireless MAN and wireless WAN systems. The directivity of the antenna increases range in one direction and decreases range in other directions.

distribution system. A wired system that physically interconnects access points in a wireless LAN. A common distribution system for wireless LANs, for example, is Ethernet.

E–F

encryption. The scrambling of data bits according to a key before sending the data over a network. Wired Equivalent Privacy (WEP) and Wi-Fi Protected Access (WPA) are examples of protocols that implement encryption that wireless LANs use.

Ethernet. A name that describes 802.3 wired LANs. Ethernet is a common type of network that companies use to interconnect PCs and servers. Ethernet provides the distribution system of most wireless LANs.

FDMA (frequency division multiple access). A process that divides a relatively wide frequency band into smaller sub-bands, where each user transmits voice and data over his or her assigned sub-band.

frequency. The number of times per second that a signal repeats itself. Often measured in Hertz (Hz), which is the number of cycles occurring each second. Frequencies of wireless LANs, for example, are within the 2.4-GHz and 5-GHz bands.

frequency hopping spread spectrum. A type of spread spectrum where the transceiver hops from one frequency to another according to a known hopping pattern to spread the signal over a wider portion of the frequency band. Older 802.11 wireless LANs use frequency hopping.

FSK (frequency shift keying). A modulation process that makes slight changes to the frequency of the carrier signal to represent information in a way that is suitable for propagation through the air.

G

gatekeeper. Provides most of the call control actions, such as access control, bandwidth management, translation between telephone number and IP address, and call transfer for H.323 systems.

gateway. Provides connections between voice terminals and the standard Public Switched Telephone Network (PSTN).

GPS (global positioning system). A system that enables people having a GPS client device to easily determine their geographic position. GPS offers the basis of an excellent navigation system, as well as location-based services over wireless networks.

H

H.323. An umbrella specification defined by the International Telecommunication Union–Telecommunication Standardization Sector that includes a group of protocols for sending voice and video over IP-based networks.

hacker. A person who has the ability to steal information that resides on a network. Hackers often try breaking into corporate systems for fun and exploit the vulnerabilities of wireless networks. Not all hackers, however, are criminals.

hotspot. The location of a public wireless LAN. Hotspots are found in areas where people congregate with computer devices, such as at airports, hotels, convention centers, and coffee shops.

I–J–K

interference. Unwanted signals that disrupt the operation of a wireless network. The presence of interference decreases the performance of a wireless network.

interoperability. A condition whereby computer devices can successfully interface with a wireless network.

IP (Internet Protocol). A protocol that routes packets between computer devices attached to a network. IP places a header field in front of each packet that contains the packet's source and destination IP address.

IP address. A number that represents the address corresponding to a connection of a network device to the network. For example, every wireless network interface card (NIC) has an IP address. Each NIC must have an IP address associated with it if the user will be making use of Transmission Control Protocol/Internet Protocol (TCP/IP) applications, such as sending and receiving e-mail, browsing the web, or interfacing with a corporate application server.

IPsec (IP Security). A protocol that supports secure exchange of packets at the network layer of a network. IPsec is commonly implemented in virtual private networks (VPN) and encrypts data packets across the entire network (often referred to as end-to-end encryption).

L

LAN (local-area network). A type of network that spans the area of a building or campus. A LAN uses wired cabling (Ethernet) or wireless connections (IEEE 802.11) to interface client devices to resources, such as application software and databases, on the network.

LEAP. A Cisco-proprietary authentication mechanism for securing wireless networks.

location-based services. The ability to track the location of users and deliver information to them that relates to position within a particular area.

M

MAC (Media Access Control) layer. A part of a network architecture that manages and maintains communications on a shared medium. The MAC layer is the brains of a NIC or base station and enforces the rules all devices must follow.

MAN (metropolitan-area network). A type of network that spans the size of a city or metropolitan area. A municipal network, which may use mesh network technology and point-to-point links, is a type of MAN.

medium. The space in which communications signals, such as radio waves, propagate. With wireless networks, the medium is air.

medium access. A process whereby multiple computer devices share a common medium. The most common medium access method for wireless networks is CSMA.

modulation. Creates a radio or light signal from the network data so that it is suitable for propagation through the air medium. Examples of modulation types are FSK, PSK, and QAM.

N

NAT (Network Address Translation). A standard that maps official IP addresses to private addresses that may be in use on their internal networks. For example, a broadband Internet service provider may offer a home only one official IP address. NAT, along with DHCP, enables the home owner to have multiple PCs and laptops sharing the single official IP address.

NIC (network interface card). A hardware device that interfaces a computer device to a network. Also known as a radio card and client card.

noise floor. The amplitude of electromagnetic signals in a particular area while the wireless network is not operating.

O

OFDM (orthogonal frequency division multiplexing). A process that divides a modulated signal into multiple subcarriers before transmission through the air medium to improve performance. The 802.11a and 802.11g wireless LANs and some proprietary wireless MANs use OFDM.

optical fiber. A long piece of glass having a very small-diameter covering that carries light signals from one end to the other. An optical fiber cable has a protective coating, making it difficult to distinguish from copper-based cables.

P

PBX (private branch exchange). The hardware and software necessary to process phone calls for a company over the standard Public Switched Telephone Network (PSTN).

PC card. A credit card–sized device (also called a NIC) that provides extended memory, modems, connectivity to external devices, and, of course, wireless network capabilities to small computer devices, such as laptops and PDAs. Many PC cards are available that implement Bluetooth and 802.11 technologies.

PDA (personal digital assistant). A small device that people can use to store contact information, schedules, and to-do lists. Some PDAs run software programs, such as e-mail clients and web browsers.

point-to-multipoint system. A system whereby communication is directly from one user to several others.

point-to-point system. A system whereby communication is directly from one user to another.

power-save mode. An 802.11 function that (when enabled) allows wireless client radios to enter a sleep mode that draws less current and extends battery life.

PSK (phase shift keying). A modulation process that makes slight changes to the phase of the carrier signal to represent information in a way that is suitable for propagation through the air.

Public Switched Telephone Network (PSTN). The standard circuit-switched telephone system that supports phone calls between most homes and businesses.

public wireless LAN. A type of wireless LAN, often referred to as a hotspot, that anyone having a properly configured computer device can access.

Q–R

QAM (quadrature amplitude modulation). A modulation process that makes slight changes to the amplitude and phase of the carrier signal to represent information in a way that is suitable for propagation through the air.

radio NIC. A type of NIC that transmits and receives RF signals.

RADIUS (Remote Authentication Dial-In User Service). An authentication and accounting system that many wireless Internet service providers (WISP) and high-usage enterprises use to handle access control and billing on wireless networks.

repeater. A device that receives and retransmits signals for the sole purpose of extending range.

RF signal. A radio frequency signal that is designed to propagate through the air medium.

rogue access point. An access point that is unauthorized and has configuration settings that may enable someone to gain access to network resources.

router. A type of base station that routes packets from one location to another based on a destination IP address. A router implements special networking protocols, such as DHCP and NAT, that enable users to use TCP/IP applications.

RTP (Real-time Transport Protocol). A protocol that provides end-to-end functions suitable for applications transmitting real-time voice and video over IP-based networks.

S

Session Initiation Protocol (SIP). Developed by Internet Engineering Task Force (IETF) RFC 2543. Defines a protocol based on Internet specifications, such as Hypertext Markup Language (HTML) and Simple Mail Transfer Protocol (SMTP), for sending voice and video over IP-based networks.

signal-to-noise ratio (SNR). A value measured in dB that is the signal power (in dBm) minus the noise power (in dBm).

Skinny Client Control Protocol (SCCP). A lightweight alternative to the full-blown H.323 standard implemented in Cisco wireless and desktop IP phones.

snooper. Someone who casually and usually inadvertently interfaces with a wireless network. A war driver, who drives around to find active wireless LANs, is a type of snooper.

spread spectrum. The spreading of the carrier signal over a wider part of the frequency spectrum. Direct sequence and frequency hopping are two types of spread spectrum.

SSID (Service Set Identifier). A name given to a particular wireless LAN in which the SSID assigned to a wireless client must match the SSID configured in the access point.

T

TCP (Transmission Control Protocol). A protocol that establishes and maintains connections between computer devices attached to a network. TCP operates at the transport layer and is used in conjunction with IP, which is commonly referred to as TCP/IP.

TDMA (time division multiple access). A process that allows only one user to transmit in any given time slot. Each user has use of the entire bandwidth during its assigned time slot.

terminal. An endpoint of a Voice over Wireless LAN (VoWLAN) system, such as a wireless IP phone.

terminal emulation. A mechanism for users to interface over a network to applications running on a centralized computer. VT-220, 3270, and 5250 are types of terminal emulation.

TKIP (Temporal Key Integrity Protocol). Enables each wireless station to use a different encryption key that changes often, which fixes the key distribution problem of WEP.

transceiver. A device that both transmits and receives information. The transceiver resides in a radio NIC.

U–V

UDP (User Datagram Protocol). A connectionless protocol that runs at the transport layer and is similar to TCP, except UDP offers very few error recovery services.

VLAN (virtual LAN). A logical collection of network devices that communicate with each other over the same physical network. Network devices on one VLAN cannot communicate with network devices on a another VLAN (unless provisions are made to connect the different VLANs).

VoIP (Voice over IP). A technology for sending voice signals over an IP-based network.

VoIP endpoint. A hardware device, such as a wireless IP phone, at both ends of a voice conversation using VoIP technology.

VoWLAN (Voice over Wireless LAN). A wireless LAN that supports the transmission of voice information, generally through the use of VoIP protocols.

VPN (virtual private network). The use of special software on the client device that controls access to remote applications and secures the connection from end to end using encryption.

W–Z

WAN (wide-area network). A type of network that spans a continent or country. Enterprises often use a WAN to interconnect their facilities located in different areas.

WEP (Wired Equivalent Privacy). A part of the 802.11 standard that defines encryption between devices connected to a wireless LAN.

Wi-Fi. A brand name given to wireless LANs that comply with standards as defined and published by the Wi-Fi Alliance. Wi-Fi standards are based on the 802.11 standard.

Wi-Fi Protected Access (WPA). A security protocol defined by the Wi-Fi Alliance that enables computer devices to periodically obtain a new encryption key. WPA version 1 implements TKIP and WEP, whereas WPA version 2 implements the full 802.11i standard, which includes AES.

wireless IP phone. A mobile phone specially designed to send and receive phone calls over an IP-based network, such as a wireless LAN.

wireless LAN. A network that satisfies wireless networking needs within the area of a building or college campus. 802.11 and Wi-Fi are popular standards defining wireless LANs.

wireless MAN. A network that satisfies wireless networking needs within the area of a city. Wireless MANs make use of 802.16 and proprietary standards.

wireless WAN. A network that satisfies wireless networking needs over a large geographical area, such as a country or the entire world. Satellites offer a means of extending radio signals over a wireless WAN.

WISP (wireless Internet service provider). A company that offers wireless connection services to the Internet for homes and offices. WISPs often provide wireless access in public wireless LAN hotspots.

Yagi antenna. A specialized directional antenna that uses multiple signal reflecting elements attached to a boom.

INDEX

A

AC (alternating current), 95
access
    access points. *See* access points
    unauthorized, 102
    VPNs, 106
    wireless medium, 85
        DCF, 85–86
        PCF, 86
    WPA, 104–106
Access Control Server (ACS), 151
access points
    automatic configuration, 207
    BSS, 77
    Cisco 7920 Wireless IP Phone, 30
    configuring, 172
        data rates, 175
        filtering, 176
        firmware, 172
        protection mechanisms, 176
        RF channels, 174
        SSIDs, 173
        transmit power, 174
        VLANs, 173
    density, calculating, 154
    inspecting, 203
    installing, 115, 157, 167–168
        antenna alignment, 171
        electrical power distribution, 171–172
    inter-access point interference, 161
    locations, determining, 156
    mounting, 130, 168–170
    passive monitoring, 101–102
    physical installations of, 199
    placement of, 153
        documentation, 161–164
        RF site surveys, 155–161
        wireless capacity analysis, 153–155
    RF signals, 58
        characteristics, 58–59
        FCC rules, 62
        gain, 59
        modulation, 58

        OFDM, 61
        SNR, 60
        spread spectrum, 60–61
    rogue, 115–118, 199
    self-healing functions, 209
    switches, 152
    transmit power, 160
    troubleshooting, 201
    verifying, 157
    wireless networks, 36–38
accounting, bandwidth, 180
ACK (acknowledgement) frames, 83
ACS (Access Control Server), 151
action plans, 196
active scanning, 82
Ad Hoc mode, 84–85
Adaptive Wireless Path Protocol, 43
addresses, assigning IP, 29
Admission Request (ARQ), 52
AES (Advanced Encryption Standard), 8, 43, 104–105
agents, call processing, 147
AID (association identifier), 82
AirMagnet Analyzer, 132
Alerting message (H.323), 52
algorithms, video, 49
aligning antennas, 171
alternating current (AC), 95
analysis
    calling patterns, 142
    ROI, 16–24
    security gaps, 200
    VoWLAN requirements, 123
        applications, 124–125
        budgets, 136
        client devices, 133–134
        coverage areas, 127–129
        documenting, 138
        environments, 130–132
        existing systems, 134–135
        identifying, 124
        policies/preferences, 135–136
        roaming, 129–130
        schedules, 137
        security, 132–133

T